"Carter and Sokol delve into the characteristics that make men and women say, 'I'm scared, so go away.' [A] valuable contribution." —*Booklist*

COULD UNRESOLVED COMMITMENT CONFLICTS BE CLOUDING *YOUR* PROSPECTS FOR FUTURE HAPPINESS? TAKE THIS QUIZ AND FIND OUT.

- *Does your partner feel that your married friends lead boring lives?* People with commitment issues never "settle." They hold out for the "perfect" mate: that superhuman someone who may not even exist.

- *Have you met your lover's friends and family?* If not, your partner is building distance into your relationship—and keeping you an arm's length from intimacy.

- *Is your partner most intensely interested in you when you seem to be pulling away?* For commitmentphobes, love is not frightening until it is returned. They pursue avidly—then withdraw.

- *Is your partner drawn to unavailable lovers?* If his last paramour was married, if her ex was a long-distance liaison, then your proximity may be too close for your partner's comfort.

"Advice and sympathetic hand-holding for those whose anxieties about commitment are messing up their love lives."
—*Kirkus Reviews*

Also by Steven Carter and Julia Sokol

WHAT SMART WOMEN KNOW

MEN WHO CAN'T LOVE

WHAT REALLY HAPPENS IN BED

MEN LIKE WOMEN WHO LIKE THEMSELVES

HE'S SCARED, SHE'S SCARED

Understanding the Hidden Fears
That Sabotage Your Relationships

Steven Carter
and
Julia Sokol

A Dell Trade Paperback

A DELL TRADE PAPERBACK

Published by
Dell Publishing
a division of
Bantam Doubleday Dell Publishing Group, Inc.
1540 Broadway
New York, New York 10036

The trademark Dell® is registered in the U.S. Patent and
Trademark Office.

ISBN: 0-440-50625-5

Reprinted by arrangement with Delacorte Press

Printed in the United States of America

Published simultaneously in Canada

February 1995

20 19 18 17

BVG

For Max, with love.

To Our Readers:

We are writers, not therapists. Our insights come primarily from our own experiences and from the experiences of countless men and women who struggle with many variations of the conflicts described in this book.

Therefore we want to make it clear that this book is not meant to be a substitute for professional psychological help. It is not our intention to diminish our information and experience, or to diminish the information shared by those we have interviewed. But we do need to emphasize its limitations. Every person's struggle is unique and deserving of individual attention and examination. This book is intended to provide a starting point in that process.

Acknowledgments

A book of this size and scope could not be completed without a great deal of help and support. We would like to take this opportunity to thank everyone who contributed in some way to the realization of this work.

First, our most special thanks to the many men and women who so generously donated their time to be interviewed for this project. Their stories give this book a richness that is immeasurable.

We also wish to thank our agent, Barbara Lowenstein, for believing in us and our work.

It is very important for us to acknowledge certain people for their invaluable creative contributions: Peter Coopersmith, Frederick Friedel, Eric Weiss, Nancy Weiss, Donna Miller, Dr. Irene Harwood, and M. J. Kelly. Thank you all so much.

Very special thanks must go to all of the following people, each of whom was a source of tremendous help and support: Ken Starr, Michael Frankfurt, Helen Sokol, Marilyn and John Whitney, Sonja Eisenberg, Lloyd Sheldon Johnson, Rhonda Rudner, Michael Petruzillo, Cheryl Pelavin, Cheryl Barnes Cabasso, Matt Stolper, Norman Haggie, Paul Trudeau, Stacey Cahn, Randy Levine Miller, Sheila Starr, Joshua Levine, Alfred and Sydelle Carter, Jane Brinker, Bob Tabian, Sloan Harris, Al Secunda, Leonard Post, Charles Bernstein, Chip Kaplan, Neil Anderson, and Rita Williams.

A very special thank you to Don Schimelfenig for understanding all those hours spent on the phone and at the computer.

Finally, our thanks to the beasts and the children—Paddington, Carla, Maggie, Tom, and Huck—for the love they always give without any fear of commitment.

Contents

Part Two: Understanding Your Fears and Facing Your Conflict

Appendix: Managing Your Conflicts and Changing Your Relationships —A Guide for You and Your Partner

Introduction

There are people who go through an entire lifetime without once experiencing—or encountering—any anxiety about commitment. Many others, however, find the issue of commitment a recurring and controlling theme in most, if not all, of their personal involvements.

Some of you may have no difficulty pinpointing the ways in which commitment conflicts affect your personal relationships. For example:

- If you are deeply involved with a partner who is actively running away from you and the love you offer, then you have been forced to deal with someone else's commitment conflicts.
- If your need to maintain "space" has been an issue in all of your relationships, then you can't help but be aware of your struggles with commitment.
- If you been unable to sustain a committed relationship, no matter how hard, or often, you try, then you are probably painfully aware of your difficulty with commitment.
- If you have an intense need to maintain independence and a single life-style, if you fear marriage means someone will try to "clip your wings," then you may be fully conscious of your desire to avoid a committed relationship.

But for some of us, commitment issues are not always out in the open. Instead they are hidden and subtle, clothed in an assortment of disguises. For example:

- If you find that you prefer idealized fantasies to flawed human partners, then you may not realize how commitment fears are affecting your life.
- If you consistently commit yourself to inappropriate or unavailable partners, you may not always see how your conflicts are contributing to a destructive pattern.
- If you are very "picky" or have a pattern of faultfinding, then you may fail to take into account how much of this is caused by commitment issues.
- If you are unable to recover from a failed love relationship, then you may be unable to recognize how your own fears are contributing to your paralysis.
- If something about your attitude and life-style discourages potential partners, then you may not be aware of the barriers you have constructed against commitment.

In this book we plan to take a long and careful look at the issues and anxieties that surround commitment and explore how these issues may be implicated when men and women have difficulty finding and keeping the love they deserve. We believe that many of us have failed to address the ways in which we are made anxious by commitment, the complicated ways in which we avoid commitment, and the ways in which commitment conflicts may be creating chaos in our personal lives.

We often hear from men and women who are expending tremendous amounts of time and energy trying to cement a relationship with decidedly reluctant partners. We know that it is extremely difficult for people such as this to believe that *they* have a problem with commitment. Often they feel *too* committed. If you fall into this category, we understand the way you feel, and we only ask that you bear with us as we try to illustrate how your own conflicts can catapult you into these painful roles.

Many women are initially brought face-to-face with commitment conflict through their involvement with a reluctant partner. For that reason we're going to try to present the various fears and anxieties from both points of view—male and female—so that you can get a sense of how these anxieties play out in relationships.

We realize that when we talk about the fear of commitment, we have to be very careful not to lump everyone together into one category. There are a multitude of reasons why someone might have commitment conflicts. Some women legitimately worry about getting stuck in traditional marriages that leave them little room for growth. Men may worry that they will be expected to take on the major financial responsibility for a family. Some people are frightened of repeating a dysfunctional family system; others hesitate at fidelity or the notion of sustaining love over a lifetime. Some people have realistic and logical reasons; others can't explain why the idea of one love/one relationship leaves them with a gnawing fear in the pit of their stomach. In fact there are probably as many reasons why we worry about commitment as there are people who worry.

There are also different degrees of conflict, and men and women often experience their conflict in completely different ways. For some people the idea of commitment triggers only mild discomfort or nervousness; others have a more intense reaction; still others experience the overwhelming fear we call commitmentphobia. Some people are made anxious just by the mention of marriage; others have no idea that they have any anxiety whatsoever until after the ceremony has actually taken place.

We will talk about some of the reasons why we might be afraid as well as examine the different levels and kinds of commitment fear and the conditions under which they occur. And in that context we will try to give some insight into what we refer to as commitmentphobic relationships—relationships that can be characterized by one partner wanting "more" while the other wants "space." We will provide an in-depth look at what happens when these relationships become obsessive.

We realize that each of us has his or her own definition of what commitment means. For some people it's marriage—pure and simple—and nothing less will do; for others it means a willingness to work on an exclusive relationship; for others it represents intimacy. For still others it's a jumble.

We see commitment simply as a promise to participate in a *well-intentioned, monogamous, open-ended, responsible,* and *realistic* relationship. We like to think of our definition as a broad and reasonable one. We believe it's a mistake to view commitment exclusively in the context of marriage. As we will discuss later, we also think it's a mistake to think that marriage per se is the acid test for commitmentphobia.

Our point of view is that a set of good *intentions* is the most important thing to bring to a relationship; it is infinitely more important than a marriage license because it means that you have a willingness to make the relationship work and keep working. Being well-intentioned does not mean that you should put up with abuse, of any kind, for the sake of keeping the relationship together, and it does not mean that you should stay in a miserable or unfulfilling situation with a partner who refuses to put in his or her best efforts. However, it does mean that you bring honesty, effort, and openness to the relationship. It means that you are not intentionally concealing any negative agendas, and it means that your hopes for the future of the relationship are serious and sincere.

Monogamy is a necessary ingredient in any committed relationship. We know there are those who disagree with this and who feel that it is too conservative or traditional a value. We know that there are couples who maintain that they are committed even though they have agreements that allow for sexual activity with other people. Nonetheless we firmly believe that monogamy is part and parcel of commitment.

By open-ended we mean *open to the possibility of continuing the relationship indefinitely*. An open-ended relationship allows for growth and change, while it protects the emotional investment of both partners. To us, being open-ended means more than just staying together as long as the relationship is working, to us it also implies the desire to make it work. Being open-ended means being able to look to the future with possibility and not with terror.

You can't have true commitment without *responsibility*—responsibility to the relationship, to one's partner, and to oneself. Responsibility means many things. It means not promising more than you can emotionally deliver and it also means not holding back emotions you are capable of giving. Being responsible is a promise to stay sensitive to your partner's feelings, and it is an implicit agreement not to run away just because you get scared.

Finally a *realistic* attitude is essential to commitment. To be committed to someone means being able to dispense with fantasy and see and accept your partner's faults, foibles, weaknesses, and imperfections.

Well-intentioned, monogamous, open-ended, responsible, and realistic—these are the qualities that reflect a willingness to stay in the relationship and keep working at it even at those times when it would be so much easier to quit. That to us is commitment.

SOME REASONS FOR READING THIS BOOK

Typically it is the people who care about us who point out our problems with commitment. In fact some of you may be reading this book at the request of friends who believe that you are running away from an important relationship. Perhaps you are responding to other friends who tell you that you are always too "picky" to form any relationships. If that is the case, please understand that we don't mean to sound judgmental. If you're afraid, naturally you feel conflicted. This does not make you a horrible person or an anomaly or a psychological misfit. You are simply someone who struggles with this fear. We hope that looking closely at the ways this fear operates in your life will illuminate for you some aspects of your conflict and your behavior in relationships.

Some of you may be reading this book because you care deeply about a partner who is running away from love. We know how distressing that can be, and we will try to help you find new ways of dealing with your situation constructively. Years of conducting interviews have convinced us that people with commitment problems gravitate toward each other. Therefore we ask you to read this book with an open mind, allowing for the possibility that your own conflicts may be contributing to your unfortunate romantic choices. We sincerely hope that recognizing how commitment anxiety is affecting your life will help you make the necessary changes to get the love you want.

OUR MISTAKE: NOT GIVING ENOUGH WEIGHT TO WOMEN'S CONFLICTS

In 1987 we outlined the "commitmentphobic syndrome" for the first time in our book *Men Who Can't Love*. We are extremely proud of that book because we feel it has helped a lot of people. But we now realize that it was a mistake not to talk more about women's fears. Sure, we *mentioned* that women can put up barriers against commitment, but after giving this point brief lip service, we then turned our attention to what we considered to be a more glaring issue.

Although the interviewees for *Men Who Can't Love* were chosen at random, few women—if any—told us that they experienced commitment anxiety. Instead they had story after story about men who had walked away from love. Men, on the other hand, although they had ample opportunity to discuss women who had avoided commitment, failed to do so. Instead they were most articulate when discussing their own anxieties.

This has changed. A far more skeptical generation has come of age. They have seen and heard enough about divorce and the fragmented family structure to be much more sensitized to the issues surrounding commitment. In the last eight years, since we first started interviewing people about commitment conflicts, we have noticed a marked and profound change in attitude. Women now have a stronger sense of independence and of their own power, and more of them are questioning the merits and weighing the downside of traditional relationships. As they do so, they become more aware of their own anxieties and how these anxieties may have propelled them to act out in relationships. The man who can't commit has met his match in the woman who isn't so sure herself.

If there is one thing that has become exquisitely clear to us over the past several years, both from the mail we receive and the people we've interviewed, it's that men do not have the copyright on commitment anxiety. This syndrome transcends gender. Sure, tons of men have it. But plenty of women have it too, and their ranks are growing every day.

Initially it was easy to blame men for more of the world's relationship struggles. Their destructive behavior was all too obvious.

Today we know more and we know different. Today we are much clearer about the ways women's commitment conflicts are played out in their choices, their beliefs, their feelings, their fantasies, and their behavior. The women we know are insisting upon assuming responsibility for their lives and their relationships. They resist being cast as victims and instead want to come to terms with the ways in which they participate in the dynamics of their relationships.

This doesn't mean that we're letting men off the hook, and it doesn't mean that we're forgiving men for all their destructive behaviors. We recognize that there are still far too many situations and relationships in which men hold an unfair advantage, and it's important to continue to be aware of this.

But the years since the publication of *Men Who Can't Love* have shown us that there is another side to the commitmentphobic dynamic, and that other side is a woman who, for reasons we will examine in this book, is participating. She may be actively participating or she may be passively participating. But she is participating.

We think it's important to note here that there are a growing number of women who are realizing that they have put too much pressure on themselves to get married. Many of these women complain that they are tired of feeling guilty because they have not fulfilled parental or societal expectations. We don't want them to feel more pressured by us. From where we sit, this book is not about staying single or getting married. It's about understanding your patterns, making good choices, and avoiding destructive relationships.

OUR OWN STRUGGLES WITH COMMITMENT

We came to writing about commitment issues the hard way. We both have long histories of dealing with our own conflicts: our own anxiety attacks, our own flights from commitment, and our own relationships with partners who were running away. Writing is as much a personal exploration as it is a professional investigation, and it's no secret that writers write about those matters that concern them. We are as affected by commitment issues as our readers. It is not our intention to separate ourselves or portray ourselves as being above the struggle. We are not therapists; we are writers. Our insights and our material represent eight years of interviewing men and women about their relationship experiences and their feelings about those experiences.

COMMITMENT IS A CHOICE

For all of us—male and female—commitment fears are part of the price we pay for having freedom and having choices. With freedom comes the threat of the loss of freedom, and it is this very threat that is so often at the core of the struggle with commitment. In and of itself, fear of commitment is not the problem. But if it's hurting you it's a problem, and if it's hurting someone else it's a problem.

It's important for everyone—male and female—to become aware of how their behavior can hurt others and learn to modify it accordingly. For that reason we've included sections with suggestions for ways in which both partners in a relationship can modify their behavior.

Though commitment conflicts may be more obvious today than ever before, that doesn't mean that everyone has given up on relationships. Many people want to know more about building and maintaining committed relationships, even in the face of their fear. They want to know how to push forward in spite of their anxieties. They want to know how to find the right partners, how to make themselves into the right partners, and how to work more constructively toward the goal of commitment.

Fear or no fear, people want relationships. And they want more meaningful, loving, and supportive relationships. We hope this book will help our readers achieve these goals.

PART ONE

When What You Want Is What You Fear

"Every time we get close to commitment, one of us does something to ruin it."

—JONATHAN, twenty-eight

"I panic at the idea of marriage and a family . . . I want love, but if I try to imagine what it would be like living in a house with an average husband and children, I feel nothing except terror."

—MARCIE, thirty-two

"Barbara is a wonderful girl, but I'm not prepared to get married . . . at least not now. I don't want to hurt her, but I'm afraid that's going to happen. Either I'll marry her and make her miserable or I won't and I'll break her heart."

—DANIEL, thirty-six

"He wants more than I'm ready to give. I don't want to lose him, but I wish he would stop badgering me about the future."

—ANGELA, thirty-three

"Every man I've really cared about has run away from the closeness. Is it me? Is it them? What's wrong?"

—NANCY, thirty-nine

"I've broken one engagement, left one marriage, and ended at least a half dozen serious relationships because I couldn't handle commitment. I've got a great track record. . . . At least I'm honest."

—ROBERT, forty-five

CHAPTER ONE

Whose Fear Is It, Anyway?

To one degree or another, all of us are torn between two fundamental urges. On the one hand, each of us has a profound desire to merge with another human being and become a part of something larger than self; on the other, we have an equally basic need to feel independent, free to make choices without constraint or compromise. Finding a way to balance the urge to merge with the desire to be free is what commitment is all about. Here's the problem: These two needs are diametrically opposed.

A commitment to another person, almost by definition, is going to necessitate compromise and limit your sense of freedom. This may engender powerful feelings of anger, anxiety, and resentment. Fail to commit and there are other possible emotional costs —loneliness, a sense of incompleteness, and alienation. It's a catch-22 that we must all face.

For years now we've all heard about the male struggle with commitment. "The reluctant groom" is a well-known figure in our society. But are there women who are equally scared? In one word: Yes.

Some women have no difficulty acknowledging both their conflicts and their fears. They say that they worry about getting stuck playing out a traditional role in a traditional household. They say that the little house with a picket fence is their *Nightmare on Elm Street.*

But what about the woman who says that's exactly what she

3

wants but she can't find it? She finds it difficult to believe that she could be running away from long-term love. Typically when she looks at her behavior in relationships, she is most conscious of the amount of love, care, and, yes, commitment that she has showered on the men in her life. Her attitude: Bring on the husbands who come home at the same time every night, bring on the babies, bring on the barbecues and the joint checking accounts.

You tell a woman like this that she is conflicted about commitment and she answers, No way, not me! She thinks we should talk to the men in her life. She thinks they are the ones with problems. We don't disagree with her, but we think she is also conflicted. We think the way her conflicts play out may be directly connected to why she isn't getting the loving relationship she wants. In order to protect herself, a woman such as this needs to understand more about her partner's behavior, but she also needs to understand more about herself.

It wasn't that long ago that both men and women made commitments for better or worse. It was a societal expectation, and most people conformed. The exceptions were considered oddities or oddballs, spinsters or misfits, mama's boys, or sad sacks. That was simply the way it was.

It was thought that men needed to get married in order to have regular sex, someone to cook their meals, wash their dishes, and care for their children. Women, on the other hand, needed fathers for their children, protection from the world, and breadwinners for the family unit. Of course both sexes wanted love and companionship, but the way things were set up, mates were essential in order to provide certain specific supports. No one believed any man could cook, care for a baby, or do the laundry adequately. And certainly no one believed that women could be genuinely effective in the marketplace.

Marriage involved more than a meeting of the hearts: it was a very practical solution to the problems of living. Then things started to change, and along with these changes came drastic shifts in the marital equation.

In the 1960s several things happened to spur the change in attitudes: The birth control pill went on the market and birth control became legal and available throughout the country. Then, in 1966, Masters and Johnson published *Human Sexual Response,* and the sexual revolution went into full swing.

As the sexual revolution progressed, there were immediate effects on the way people viewed commitment. Probably most significant was that one no longer had to be in a committed relationship to have regular sex. At first, perhaps, this message registered most profoundly with men, many of whom felt that they no longer had to say "I do" in order to convince women to share their beds. It wasn't long thereafter before women started complaining of boyfriends who had commitment "problems." It seemed suddenly as though there was an epidemic of men who were avoiding the old marital agreement. We all heard stories of men who needed time, needed space, weren't sure, hadn't dated enough, hadn't been with enough women, or had been with too many of the wrong women. In the meantime men were also learning to be a lot more domestically self-sufficient.

By the mid-1970s we were beginning to see the effects of the feminist movement. Women began to find their power in the workplace, and more and more young women could expect to be economically self-sufficient. Other attitudes have changed as well. Although single motherhood is often an economic hardship, it is no longer the social stigma it once was. For many women it has become a viable option. And let's not forget those women who are questioning whether or not motherhood will play any role at all in their lives. In short the rules have changed for women and men.

Today we are seeing the first generation of women who have grown up after the women's movement. And every day we are hearing more and more stories of women who are resisting traditional commitments—women who no longer feel that they need husbands in order to have meaningful lives.

Wasn't anyone afraid of commitment before the sexual revolution? Or earlier than that, back in grandma's day? Of course they were. The fear of commitment is a natural human response. However, when you weigh the anxiety of "getting stuck" in a marriage against what it meant to be single at that time—social stigma, celibacy or highly erratic sexuality, economic insecurity—it's quickly apparent that the fear of being single was frequently greater than the fear of getting stuck. Right now there are simply more choices, particularly for women, and fewer reasons why someone should be afraid of being single.

Obviously this is an oversimplification of our history. Everyone has unique circumstances and different economic realities. However, the bottom line is that, fear or no fear, the need to commit and stay committed has changed. And for most of us that spells conflict.

FOR THE WOMAN READER

Both men and women have conflicts. Women, however, have special and complex consequences and realities that are gender specific. This can't help but put them at a disadvantage.

Men who are anxious about commitment often reassure themselves with the thought that their anxieties will eventually go away, and that even if this doesn't happen until they are in their mid-forties or later, they can still get married and start a family. Women, forced to deal with the realities of their biological clocks, are rarely able to be so sanguine about future solutions. To complicate matters, few consider it entirely acceptable for women to pursue men with the kind of freedom that men enjoy when they are interested in finding romantic partners. If she wants a relationship, even the most liberated woman may find herself feeling that she has few options other than "waiting" patiently for Mr. Right.

Those women who receive parental pressure to hurry up, get married, and produce grandchildren are often caught in an even more complicated dilemma; the inability to "perform" adequately in this area may make them feel as though they have failed in their filial duty. For women particularly, the pressure to get married combined with the anxiety that such matters are not totally within their control—they still have to wait for a man to propose—is often overwhelming. It may cause them to bury their anxieties about commitment in a way that is particularly self-destructive.

What this means is that women who don't explore their own commitment issues are at a disadvantage: They are unaware of the ways in which hidden conflicts influence and determine their choices. Consequently they often find themselves in destructive relationships, passively acting out their anxieties by becoming involved with men who are inappropriate or emotionally unavailable.

ACTING OUT THE COMMITMENT DILEMMA

Everyone who has a conflict between freedom and commitment —and fails to understand how that conflict reveals itself in his or her life—runs the risk of sabotaging every single romantic relationship. If you don't understand what you feel or how those feelings are affecting your behavior, you will probably find yourself acting out your ambivalence.

This means that you will almost certainly find yourself in a series of relationships that never seem to work out, relationships in which either you or your partners are running away from love.

Committed relationships are hard. It's hard to find one and it takes a lot of work to keep one. It's even harder when you don't understand how your commitment issues may be causing you to choose partners and situations that are doomed to failure. Everywhere we go, we hear stories about unresolved commitment conflicts. Typically these stories are about men and women who say they want a committed relationship, but whose behavior patterns say something entirely different. Tom, a thirty-one-year-old sales rep, is one such person.

For years everyone has told Tom that he has a problem. His girlfriends, his parents, and his friends all say that he is afraid of commitment. Tom says he can understand why they come to this conclusion, but from his perspective that's not the way it feels. His history spells out his conflicts.

At twenty-four Tom was weeks away from announcing his engagement to Angelica, a woman he had been dating for two years. Smart, kind, loving, and crazy about him, she thought they were building a future together, but suddenly Tom started backing off, putting off the engagement, and talking about needing time.

Tom says Angelica tried very hard to understand what he was going through, but even *he* couldn't figure out what he was feeling. At his suggestion they took a month's vacation from each other. Within that month he met and fell head over heels in love with Reba, a thirty-two-year-old divorced mother. At first Reba was less enthusiastic; she was very attracted to Tom, but she thought he was too young, and too poor to help provide the security she wanted to create for herself and her two children.

Their relationship continued for three years, during which time Tom couldn't stop thinking, or talking, about Reba—her needs, her kids' needs, her demands. He especially delighted in playing house with her and acting as substitute father to her children. His efforts paid off. Convinced that the two of them could provide a good environment for the children, Reba started looking for a larger apartment in a neighborhood that was more convenient for Tom's work.

No sooner had she found one than Tom began having second thoughts. After all, by now Reba was thirty-five, her children were approaching adolescence, and she wanted to have another baby before it was too late. Suddenly for Tom everything paled. He looked at Reba and where once he had seen only ivory skin, he now saw varicose veins. Where once he had seen adorable children, he now saw the prospect of rebellious teenagers and college tuition. Where once he looked forward to the comforts of being with Reba—home-cooked meals, adult conversation, cozy intimacy—now he felt bored, constrained, and old before his time. "Do I really need this?" he asked his friends.

But Tom was very conflicted about what he wanted. He was attached to Reba, he was sexually bonded to Reba, and he was emotionally dependent on Reba. He couldn't leave overnight. It took close to two years before Tom and Reba finally split up permanently—two difficult, painful years. When Tom articulated his confusion, Reba felt betrayed, abandoned, and angry, not only for herself but also for her children, who had become very attached to Tom.

He, understandably, felt guilty and overwhelmed; he spent most of his time trying to figure out what he was feeling and why he was feeling it. For two years, while the relationship unraveled, Reba spent much of her time trying to figure out what she could do to get things back on an even keel. This setup caused a lot of backing-and-forthing. Tom and Reba split up, they reconciled, they split up, they reconciled. Finally the pain was too great. Reba said enough is enough, and this time when Tom felt the old surges of jealousy coming over him at the idea of her dating someone else, he restrained himself from calling.

After Reba, Tom was much more careful. He vowed he wasn't going to jump into anything. So he developed his male friend-ships, cultivated a few women friends, and, very carefully, started to date again. People introduced him to a great many women, but he didn't like any of them. When he had been with Reba, he would look at some of these very same women with complete lust, but now that he was no longer with her, they seemed flighty and immature, wrapped up in their careers and their shopping. They didn't seem real or sufficiently down to earth. Tom wanted to settle down with the right woman—if only he could meet the right woman; if only he could find someone like himself, someone who wanted what he wanted. Someone intelligent, who could under-stand his conflicts.

That's when Tom met Susan. At twenty-seven Susan's romantic résumé included one serious crush and two serious relationships. The crush happened when she was in college. It was directed toward an English instructor in the process of divorcing his wife. For the most part the relationship between Susan and her instruc-tor consisted of aborted meetings, furtive phone calls, and smol-dering looks during class. Although there was infrequent physical contact between them, she thought of little else. When the instruc-tor and his wife reconciled, it took her months to recover from her sense of rejection. The entire episode occupied nearly two years. While her friends were out dating, she was at home daydreaming about her married friend and reading all the books that he had ever mentioned.

Susan didn't date again until after graduation, when she met and got engaged to a successful young businessman. The match made both sets of parents ecstatic. It made Susan anxious. After the initial thrill of getting engaged wore off, she started having second thoughts. She didn't fancy leading the life of a young ma-tron. She wanted time to develop her own career, and she began to wonder whether she had dated enough. At one time she be-lieved she loved her fiancé, but as the wedding date neared, she got more and more depressed, and she started having nightmares that she knew were directly related to what she was feeling. She confided in her friends, but they all assured her that she would get over these "jitters," and that even if she didn't, she was so lucky to have met such a terrific guy.

One night, two weeks before the wedding, as she was sitting in a restaurant with her fiancé and both sets of parents, planning the final wedding details, her anxiety became so intense that she thought she was going crazy. She had a hard time breathing and she wanted to scream. She felt like someone in a film script, and she imagined herself running off with the waiter. At that moment every man in the room looked more attractive, more interesting, and more desirable than the one she was engaged to marry.

When they got home, she cried and told her mother. Her mother cried and told her father. Together they helped her tell her fiancé. It was a hideous experience. Afterward Susan felt that she should change direction, and she applied for and got a job in another city. That's where she met Ben.

Ben was everything her fiancé wasn't—poetic, interesting, spontaneous, and emotional. Like Susan he was looking for a place to live, and when he suggested that they find an apartment together, she jumped at the opportunity, even though she had known him a brief three weeks. She had never responded to anyone as strongly as she did to Ben. She quickly discovered that Ben's intensity included long periods when he was in moody retreat, times when he stopped talking, withdrawing from her in all ways, including sexually. By now she was so wrapped up in Ben that his withdrawals made him seem even more fascinating. She soon became an expert on Ben's psychology, his childhood, his fears, and his ambitions.

Because he was a musician, Ben spent many evenings away from home. Within six months hard evidence showed Susan that Ben wasn't always working. She saw that he could be unfaithful, unreliable, and untruthful. A pattern was established: He didn't come home, they fought, she cried, he retreated, she withdrew, they made up. Whenever he left the house, Susan suspected that he might be with another woman. Sometimes she was right, but even when she wasn't, she was overwhelmed with anxiety. She worried that he wouldn't return, she worried that something had happened to him, and she worried how she was going to break her dependency on him.

But then the relationship started improving; Ben became more stable, and Susan began to have hopes that things would work out. Then, on the morning of New Year's Eve, he approached Susan with a solemn face and told her that he was leaving. He had met somebody else and was considering marriage. Susan, who had made few friends in the city to which she had moved, went through a lonely depression that lasted for over a year. After Ben left, everything about him was infused with a rosy glow. Susan forgot the arguments and the painful nights alone and focused instead on the romantic beginning, the great sex, and on what could have been. In short, Susan was heartbroken, and her recovery from Ben took longer than the relationship had lasted. Eventually Susan's memories of Ben began to recede, the world began to look a little brighter, and she met Tom.

When Susan and Tom started their relationship, this is what they knew about each other:

- Susan and Tom both knew about the other's broken engagement, and each was sympathetic to the other's feelings about not wanting to get trapped into an early, traditional, "boring" marriage.
- Susan knew about Tom's relationship with Reba, and she admired him for wanting to take care of a woman and her children. She saw this as a sign of dependability. She sympathized with his withdrawal, because Reba was older and should have known that things couldn't work out.
- Tom knew about Ben and felt that Susan had been abandoned by a creep who didn't deserve her.

And so Susan and Tom started dating. At first Susan was available whenever Tom asked her out, and they saw each other three or four times a week. About three months into the relationship Susan started complaining that the relationship was too demanding—when Tom was with her, she didn't have enough time to do her own stuff. Tom said that he had many of the same feelings and, citing pressure at work, suggested that they limit their dating to weekends for a while. That's what they did for a month, but special events kept cropping up, and soon they were getting together mid-week as well. Once again Susan said the relationship was moving too quickly, and although they agreed to stay faithful, they decided to see each other less frequently.

For the next few weeks they spoke on the phone every night, they continued to meet once mid-week for a quick dinner, and they still saw each other every weekend. The big change was that they no longer automatically spent the night together. During this time Tom had to take a business trip to San Francisco; on the flight he met an extraordinarily nice and good-looking woman. Nothing happened, but they talked the whole trip, they had a drink together, and it seemed to Tom that the woman had romantic intentions.

Tom didn't want to be unfaithful to Susan, but he questioned what was going on between them. If he gave up other women and continued in a monogamous relationship with Susan, he felt the relationship should start moving forward. So he began to complain. He said Susan wasn't giving enough to the relationship; he wanted more. She said she understood his point of view, but she wanted time. Time and space.

In the meantime they met each other's parents; they met each other's friends. Tom's mother was thrilled. She decided that Susan was able to "handle" her son and that if she continued to give him enough rope, he would "hang himself" and propose. Susan's mother thought Tom was a nice guy, even though he didn't make as much money as Susan's ex-fiancé. She worried that her daughter never gave anyone a chance and that, unless she changed her ways, she would end up an "old maid."

As Susan and Tom tried to define their relationship, Tom continued to talk regularly to his airplane friend. He had already decided, however, that even if things didn't work out with Susan, he wasn't going to act on anything. This new woman had already indicated that she was anxious to meet someone, get married, and have a baby. Her baby agenda made him very nervous. Nonetheless she gave him the feeling that he was attractive to women, and this made him feel good about himself. Also Tom decided that it wasn't so terrible that he and Susan only spent one or two nights a week together; it left him with more time for work.

Tom and Susan marked their first anniversary together. A month later, on an impulse after a particularly romantic night, Tom began to talk about marriage. Susan felt certain she wanted to get married and she was absolutely certain she wanted children. And she knew she loved Tom. She just didn't feel one hundred percent certain that Tom was the one she should marry, so she said, "maybe . . . someday." This annoyed Tom, and he began pressuring for more of a commitment. Tom told Susan that he wanted to try to make this relationship work, and Susan said that if they could iron out more of their personality differences, she would consider marriage. But she is still concerned that they don't have enough money and that Tom spends every cent he makes. She also thinks, although she wouldn't tell Tom this, that he's not quite well read enough for her.

Tom says it seems to him as though every week Susan finds a new reason why they should wait a little longer before they set a logical goal for the relationship. Susan says this is because she needs more time before she settles down. She also worries that, despite his protestations to the contrary, Tom wants to be with someone who fits into a traditional wife-mother mold, and she doesn't think she'll ever be that kind of woman. When Tom is with her, sometimes she feels suffocated and burdened, much as she did with her ex-fiancé, but when she doesn't see Tom for a few days or when he seems to be ready to give up on the relationship, she becomes terrified of losing him.

Tom thinks that because of her past experiences with men, Susan is unable to trust him. He is torn between wanting to prove that he is trustworthy and wanting to forget the whole thing. Much as Tom says he loves Susan, he is growing annoyed with what he sees as Susan's withholding and he is thinking about seeing other women. He wonders, if he really loved Susan, would he be thinking about other women? And there is something else: when he thinks about the reality of marrying Susan, he begins to get a squeamish feeling in the pit of his stomach. Is it possible that what his friends say is true—that Tom is only interested in any woman so long as she is hard to get and that the minute it looks as though it could get real, he backs away? He says he doesn't think so. He says he wants to settle down, but he wants to retain his sense of freedom too. In the right relationship he is sure he can have both. Is it possible that Susan isn't the right woman for him either?

Does Tom have a problem with commitment? And what about

Susan's difficulties with commitment? *What is going wrong in this relationship?*

Here's what we think: When it comes to establishing a working relationship, we think both Tom and Susan are unable to confront the contradictory quality of their behavior. This is spelled out by the choices they have made, by the choices they have avoided, by their pattern in and out of relationships, and by the words they use to describe their feelings. Both Tom and Susan claim that they want nothing more than to find Ms. or Mr. Right and settle down in a committed relationship, but we think they are unable to recognize how they are undermining this possibility.

Tom, for example, acknowledges that he may be unclear about what he wants. Because two other women have been very hurt by his actions, he has a fair amount of guilt about some of his behavior. Nonetheless he thinks a large part of his romantic past falls into the unfortunate-accident category, and he is certain that once he is married to the right person, all of his conflicts will disappear.

If anything, Susan finds it even harder than Tom to believe that she has any commitment issues. For example, she doesn't think that her broken engagement proves anything except that her fiancé wasn't Mr. Right. She knows that at least two of the men in her life may have had issues with commitment, but she doesn't see what that has to do with her. She is sure she wants a family. She remembers how committed she felt when she was with Ben and even how committed she was during her college crush. If either of these men had suggested planning a life together, she would have done so in an instant.

THE MALE-FEMALE DIFFERENCE

Acting out commitment conflicts is just one more thing that men and women sometimes do differently. Tom and Susan's behavior patterns reflect some of those differences. They also point out how much easier it is for a woman to conceal her commitment issues from both herself and the rest of the world. There are two reasons for this: First, we have been conditioned to recognize the signs and attitudes of a man who is avoiding a committed relationship, but we have been so conditioned to believe that all "normal" women want marriage that we have not yet learned to recognize these same signs and attitudes in a woman. And in our society the man still does much of the initiating and choosing, and that makes it easier to see how his pattern is unfolding. We can look at the partners a man chooses and say, "See, she was all wrong. Bad decision." It's different for women. Since they are typically the responders, not the pursuers, it's easier for them to disguise their conflicts under a wide range of excuses, such as "there aren't enough men out there," or "the wrong men keep finding me," or "all of the good ones are taken."

It doesn't take a genius to say that "it takes two to dance," but the sentiment is true nonetheless. A woman may feel more like the victim of a man with commitment problems than a perpetrator, but if she is involved with him, she is still dancing, and she is still participating. Her willingness to do so can reveal a great deal about her own issues with commitment.

It's important to acknowledge that more and more frequently we hear of relationships in which it is the woman who is leading the dance away from commitment—or is, at the very least, an equal partner. Her behavior can be every bit as obvious as that of any man who has ever been accused of commitmentphobia or "cold feet."

For both sexes the courage to commit goes hand in hand with building a loving, long-term relationship. If you resist examining your emotional history and the ways in which commitment anxieties may subtly, or not so subtly, be affecting your personal life, you run the risk of establishing and repeating self-defeating patterns.

ACKNOWLEDGING YOUR DIFFICULTIES

Whether you are a man or a woman, unresolved commitment conflicts reveal themselves in a myriad of ways. They are written in our fantasies and in our expectations, in our dreams and in our nightmares; they show up in the relationships we start and the relationships we avoid, in the people we choose and in the people who choose us. Within a relationship commitment issues show up in the ways we handle everything from time and money to holidays and vacations.

Like Tom and Susan, many of us work long and hard to convince ourselves and everyone else in our lives that we don't have any problems making a commitment. We always have an explanation as to why our relationships don't work out, and typically that explanation has nothing to do with fear. We blame chemistry, we blame our culture, we blame the past loves who caused us pain, we blame circumstances, and most important we blame our partners' problems. We put forth these explanations because we haven't resolved *our own* conflicts.

LABELING THE COMMITMENT PROBLEM AND WHY THAT MAKES US UNCOMFORTABLE

As you read about the men and women in this book, you may find certain situations and patterns strikingly familiar, and yet you may resist wanting to see yourself as someone with "commitment problems." We feel a great deal of your resistance may be directly related to a monster that we helped create.

When we wrote *Men Who Can't Love*, we introduced the term *commitmentphobia* as a way of describing people who experience claustrophobic reactions to the notion of "forever after." We believe the word to be descriptive and accurate, but we appreciate the point of view of those who argue that it is not a "real" word. We also understand the annoyance of those who complain that it sometimes seems as though one cannot pick up a magazine or turn on a television talk show without hearing someone referred to as a commitmentphobic.

For each of us, relationship experiences are unique. They are so complex and so varied that it's hard to imagine that they fall under one label. To make them do so may feel unfair, judgmental, and almost insulting. None of us wants to think of ourselves as "types" of any kind, let alone commitmentphobic types. Nonetheless when external details are stripped away, human behavior tends to get reduced to a few basic dynamics. We believe very firmly that unresolved commitment conflict is one of these basic dynamics.

Your relationship history is not a mystery, and it is not an accident. It may feel like an accident, and it may look like an accident. But the choices you have made were made for a reason. Maybe not a very good reason, but a reason.

What does this mean? Well, for one thing it means that if you become uncomfortable when things get close, it's not simply because you need a larger apartment. If you've fallen in love with too many inappropriate people, it's not only because you have a big heart. If you've never been able to sustain a relationship for more than a year, it's not because of fluctuating biorhythms or transiting planets. If all of your partners had serious commitment problems of their own, it's not just an unfortunate coincidence. If you always choose people who are emotionally unavailable, it's not because socialization cuts us off from our feelings. If the love of your life is married to someone else, it's not just your bad luck. If everyone you meet is geographically unavailable, it's not an inevitable consequence of the jet age. If many of the people you get involved with have problems with addictions, it's not only because of the breakdown of the family system. If you can't find anyone who is "marriage material," it's not because there is a shortage of people who are. If everyone you cared about had a tragic flaw, it's not because everyone is tragically flawed.

The reasons why so many of your relationships have failed aren't out there somewhere in the ether; they are *right* here—within you. And chances are, unresolved commitment conflicts have a great deal to do with it.

MAKING SENSE OUT OF YOUR PAST

Your romantic history provides the evidence you need to determine whether you or your partner have commitment conflicts. Often we fictionalize our past experiences; we turn our reality into fantasy. We polish it up or paint it all black. We forget the bad, forget the good, or forget the whole thing. But true insight only comes from evaluating the true experience.

When we look at what has gone on in our relationships, we all have a tendency to focus on what was wrong with the *other* person. But by focusing exclusively on the failings of your partners, you escape looking at the more significant issue: Why were *you* with them? Just because *they* all had problems doesn't mean that *you* don't. We're not trying to condone hurtful behavior. But you need to start considering what keeps *you* from being in a more fulfilling relationship. And that means starting to think a little bit more about your own stuff. In other words, if difficult relationships seem to be part of your life, it's time to examine your own contributions to these difficulties.

DO YOU HAVE UNRESOLVED COMMITMENT CONFLICTS?

Here is a fact: To one degree or another the vast majority of us protect our freedom and are nervous about long-term commitment. The question to ask yourself is how great are your commitment conflicts? Are they merely affecting your relationships or are they destroying your relationships? Are your conflicts affecting your life, or are they controlling your life? Do you approach the possibility of commitment with a healthy sense of caution, or are you downright phobic? The first step in joining those who are able to form interpersonal unions that work is understanding how commitment conflicts reveal themselves.

Your romantic history is the single most telling factor in determining whether you have unresolved commitment conflicts. If you are conflicted, the following characteristics typically apply to your relationships:

1. *You have a history of relationships in which one partner wants more while the other wants less.*

Anyone with commitment conflicts will almost certainly experience the kind of relationship that is played out along the more-less theme. That "more" can be reflected by a partner wanting more time, more emotional closeness, or more actual commitment. Take a moment to review your romantic history.

Within your relationships are you usually the partner who wants less? If so:

- Your partners have typically complained that you are pulling back, withholding, or constructing obstacles and boundaries to avoid closeness or commitment.
- You may be conscious of wanting less and may methodically limit how much you give as a means of avoiding the expectation of commitment.
- You resent realistic expectations, such as intimacy, shared time, or fidelity.
- You are very skillful at avoiding commitment and have a complex repertoire of built-in behavior patterns, such as infidelity; these help you maintain distance.
- You are conscious of having disappointed and hurt your partners.

Within your relationships are you usually the partner who wants more? If so:

- You have often been anxious because you believe your partner is not giving you the sense of emotional security you need.
- You are conscious of always trying to get your partner to do or say something concrete that will cement the relationship.
- Your partners have frequently failed to fulfill your expectations.
- You spend an inordinate amount of time and energy trying to ease or push your partner into more of a commitment.
- Your partners have often hurt and disappointed you.

The more-less theme brings up an important point: When people with commitment issues get together, they rarely move forward together, side by side, at the same pace. Instead they are out of synch. One moves closer, the other moves away; one moves away, the other moves closer. And it isn't always the same person who is trying to propel the relationship forward. Partners can change places and go backward or forward many times depending upon circumstances. This is an exhausting and painful process.

2. *One or more important relationships in your history has ended because you or your partner got scared.*

Have you ever panicked and felt as though you wanted to run away from the person you were involved with? Have you ever been in love with someone who behaved this way? Outright panic is the trademark of a relationship in which one or both partners' problems with commitment have gotten out of control.

This level of commitment anxiety typically emerges when the situation becomes overwhelmingly "real." That's when panicked partners, having decided they will be stuck forever unless they "get out now," are most likely to act out their anxieties by becoming rejective and running away.

We have all heard of individuals unexpectedly leaving a relationship, a person, or a situation. Because the circumstances under which someone may run are so different, it's not always easy to see commitment anxiety as the unifying theme. Keep in mind: *Everyone has a different perception of what constitutes a permanent commitment.* For example, fear of "forever after" can take place:

- After a particularly good first date
- As an overreaction to the first night of sexual intimacy
- After a year of so of dating, just when the relationship has progressed to a level where a deeper commitment seems appropriate
- Right before the wedding, when one partner realizes that he or she is in deep water
- After marriage, when one partner wakes up and considers the enormity of the commitment that has been made
- As a reaction to the birth of a child
- As a reaction to the completion of a family (birth of the last child)
- As a reaction to a major joint purchase such as a house
- After many years of a solid marriage as a reaction to the aging process

3. *You have been involved in more than one relationship in which awkward limitations have been placed on intimacy.*

Intimacy is supposed to be a primary motivation in establishing a romantic relationship. But men and women with commitment issues often are unable to allow intimacy to develop in an easy way. Instead they inhibit closeness by setting up unreasonable boundaries or barriers that restrict the relationship and keep it from growing.

Boundaries are good. Boundaries are healthy. Many people work for years in therapy to learn to define and protect their own boundaries. But often people with commitment issues are not merely self-protective, they're downright exclusionary. They have lives so compartmentalized that no other person will ever know what is going on.

Establishing boundaries is a very effective way of staying in complete control of when, if, and how a romantic relationship develops and how close another person ever gets. Boundaries are also a way of informing others not to have any expectations. Here are some of the ways in which a determined man or woman can maintain distance and keep a relationship from growing:

- By setting up limits in terms of time and availability
- By denying access to parts of his or her world (not inviting a partner to family or work-related functions, not introducing a partner to friends)
- By refusing to participate fully in a partner's world (turning down invitations to special events, avoiding a partner's family and friends)
- By not sharing holidays, birthdays, and special occasions
- By not sharing special interests
- By placing peculiar restrictions on exchanges of money or gifts so that there will be no expectations
- By placing unreasonable restrictions on sexuality
- By establishing a life-style that clearly says, "I want to be alone"
- By making it clear that you perceive all expectations such as intimacy and/or exclusivity as unwelcome demands

4. *You have a history of becoming involved with inappropriate partners.*

In this day and age it seems peculiar to think of anyone as being inappropriate, and yet sometimes two people are so specifically not meant for each other that it is practically impossible for the relationship to survive. There may be insurmountable age differences, religious differences, cultural differences, political differences, or life-style differences. These are present from the very first date, and they are not going away. Often we initially overlook these built-in conflicts. Then as the relationship continues, we realize that there are things that are really important to us and that this relationship will never provide them.

If you're going to establish a meaningful relationship with an appropriate partner, you first need to face the many ways you have been selecting inappropriate partners. Sometimes it's obvious, but often it isn't. The person you're involved with may be wonderful and kind and nurturing and generous and great-looking and brilliant and deep; he or she may be all kinds of things. But there are so many insurmountable conflicts that the relationship can never grow. On some level, be it conscious or unconscious, you know it, and you're drawn to it.

Of course not all relationships have to progress to commitment. Two adults can certainly determine conjointly that they will be together for only a limited period of time because the differences between them are too great. For example, he is a conservative Republican, she is a liberal Democrat, but they decide they will have a pleasant but limited relationship—limited because if they ever discuss politics, it will get ugly. These are personal decisions made by two people, and that's okay.

But what about starting a relationship with someone you know you will ultimately reject for being too old, too young, too poor, too rich, too white, too black, too Hispanic, too Asian, too ethnic, too Waspy, too Catholic, too Jewish, too Protestant, and so on. Often it feels very liberating to run toward someone who is different from you, but if you know in your heart of hearts that you will never have the courage or the commitment to stay with the relationship, it's only fair to make sure that your partner is *completely* aware of your inner feelings.

And before you utter a word about how committed you have been to your inappropriate relationships, before you rush to the defense of every inappropriate partner with whom you have become involved, stop for a moment, and think. Could you be running toward people you eventually "discover" are inappropriate because you are running away from commitment?

5. *In all your important relationships either you or your partner have done something to create or maintain distance.*

Men and women with unresolved commitment conflicts crave distance. Yes, they want relationships. Yes, they want closeness. But they just can't be too close for too long. It's too threatening. So there are two choices: Either find a relationship with built-in distance—such as with an inappropriate partner—or manufacture or create distance in an existing relationship.

There are a wide variety of ways in which someone can create distance. Infidelity, for example, can be a way of finding distance. Getting lost in work or at the gym or behind a newspaper are other common ways. Any activity or behavior that is used to keep another person from getting too close is a way of maintaining distance and avoiding real commitment.

6. *Your most intense romantic feelings have been directed toward partners when they appear to be pulling away from a commitment to you.*

When a relationship is progressing smoothly, both partners' feelings for each other are evolving more or less on an even keel. When people with commitment issues get together, this is never the case. In fact it may very obviously be quite the opposite.

There can be something tremendously liberating about being in love with a person who is subtly, or not so subtly, pulling away. It allows you to pursue your love with the most tender or terrible passion. Love doesn't become frightening until it is returned in kind and threatens to become entrapment.

7. *You have a history of becoming involved with, or obsessed by, partners who are emotionally, circumstantially, or geographically unavailable.*

If you choose unavailable partners, then you are choosing relationships that already have a built-in sense of distance. And if you have a clear-cut pattern of falling in love with people who are, to all intents and purposes, unavailable, then, much as you may deny it, it is questionable whether you yourself are truly available for commitment.

Remember, an unavailable partner will never make you deliver on the commitment you say you want. He or she will never hold you accountable for all of the feelings and desires you are holding in your heart. He or she will never require the commitment you say you're prepared to give. Why? Because unavailable means unavailable.

Unavailable partners include those who are:

Geographically unavailable. It's the classic scenario. You live in New York, your beloved lives in L.A. You have great weekends together six times a year. Your phone bill is outrageous. Is this a relationship? It may be romantic, but there is too much fantasy and not enough reality. Of course you don't have to live in separate states to have a long-distance relationship. The same purpose can be served by becoming involved with someone who travels all the time or someone who is never there long enough for it to feel settled and real.

Emotionally unavailable. Usually those who are emotionally unavailable give you plenty of warning up front. They may actually tell you that they can't handle commitment. They may be emotionally elusive. They may tell you that others have found it difficult to relate to them. They may simply be unable to give that much, and this becomes apparent very quickly. They may be too elusive, a little too hard to reach, too hard to find, too hard to pin down, too hard to keep around. In short too distant, too controlled, too unavailable. A man or woman who behaves this way is warning you that he or she is afraid of intimacy. Why would you keep trying unless you're afraid of intimacy too?

Circumstantially unavailable. Okay, he's married, and she's involved with another man. So why are men and women in these situations so appealing, so desirable—so perfect? Even if someone sees you five days a week and calls five times a day, if he or she is involved with other partners, that special someone is unavailable for commitment.

It may seem like a cheap shot, but we have to ask the question. What easier way to disguise your reluctance to commit than to choose partners who are unavailable?

8. *Within a relationship your responses tend to be highly unrealistic and extreme—overly romantic, overly critical, overly involved, overly detached.*

Real commitment requires real compromise, real wishes, real hopes, real desires, and real people. One of the most effective ways of avoiding commitment is to avoid reality. Occasionally you may imbue a real-life partner with all the characteristics you ascribe to your fantasy mate, but that happy state rarely lasts very long.

That means that at all stages of a relationship, you're not authentically responding to your partner's reality. You are either overwhelmingly romantic, or you go the other way and become incredibly picky and critical out of all proportion to what is happening.

Real commitment takes place in a real world, and an unrealistic attitude toward your relationships and your partners is symptomatic of unresolved commitment conflicts.

9. *You have a history of becoming involved with people who have more difficulties with commitment than you do.*

You think that all you want is a commitment, but your partner is unable to commit. This scenario is the single most effective way of concealing your own commitment issues.

Entering a relationship with a man or woman with severe commitment anxiety means getting involved with pain and disappointment. It means devoting a large portion of your life to trying to force an unwilling partner to come closer. It means that you are always the person wanting more from the relationship. It means that you are always with somebody who is erecting boundaries and obstacles faster than you can tear them down. And it means that your whole attitude in relationships is one of trying to understand and change another human being.

If you are in love with someone with serious commitment conflicts, then you already know how exhausting and painful it can be. You probably can't believe that your own commitment issues could have had anything to do with selecting such a person. After all, why would anyone deliberately choose such pain? And, in truth, you probably didn't choose the pain. But people who have serious problems with commitment, any kind of commitment, typically telegraph this information in a myriad of ways. Sometimes they actually tell you straight out. Sometimes they simply give you the sense of distance that you may find desirable. Often they are highly seductive and, by words or deeds, they initially provide you with a highly unrealistic romantic scenario that fulfills your finest fantasy.

All of this provides an environment in which you rarely have to examine your own fears. If you spend all your time trying to analyze another person's problems, you rarely have time to think about your own. But when you are being totally honest with yourself, don't you have to admit that you saw their conflicts from the very beginning?

10. *You look at friends who have solid commitments and think that they have compromised in a way that you wouldn't.*

For those with unresolved commitment conflicts there is frequently something about a real, down-to-earth, settled relationship that looks downright boring. You look at friends who have become part of a settled couple, and while you envy them the *idea* of being part of a twosome, you don't really envy their lives. You feel that they have compromised in some way. Perhaps their spouses aren't good-looking enough, or exciting enough, or rich enough, or glamorous enough, or smart enough. And what do they talk about? Children, schools, dinner menus, petty household conflicts. Who wants that?

People with commitment issues tend to be certain that if they ever do settle down with another human being, along with comfort and coziness they will also experience a greater sense of freedom and a much, much more exciting day-to-day life than the average person.

11. *You believe that any difficulties you have with commitment will be resolved once you meet the "right" person.*

If you have commitment issues, the myth of the right person is the backbone of your denial system. Unable to compromise with mere mortals, you keep looking for that special someone. If you are unable to find such a person, you are obviously unable to have the right relationship. Consider the following example:

Dennis, a thirty-four-year-old executive, has absolute faith that all commitment requires is the right person. In the course of his life he meets a great many beautiful, intelligent, lovely women who are attracted to him. But none of them is quite right; either they are too dependent, too bossy, too passive, too aggressive, too career oriented, too baby oriented, too something. Once every two years or so Dennis meets someone he thinks could be the right person. But inevitably she lacks the ability to maintain a relationship. Perhaps she is just about to move to another state or even another country. Perhaps she is already involved with somebody else. Perhaps she has extremely unreasonable boundaries or rules about space. Or perhaps she simply doesn't want a relationship, at least not one with him. Whatever the reason, there is no way that his perfect woman is going to be making a commitment to him.

Dennis's attitude reveals another pattern that goes hand in hand with a life devoted to searching for the mythological perfect person: Men and women hooked on this myth can and do fall in love with people who fall far short of their ideal—provided that these partners are inappropriate or unavailable.

12. *The time intervals between your important relationships are often extreme.*

Most of us have read books or articles explaining how an individual handles the loss of a love, even when that loss is brought about through one's own actions—as in the case of a relationship that one has chosen to end. We know we need time to grieve, time to reevaluate, time to work through our feelings and understand what happened. And then we're ready to move on and love again.

Men and women with commitment issues rarely go through this process in a "normal" fashion. Instead once again they go to extremes. Some jump right into another "important" relationship, allowing too little time to sift through feelings. Others experience a depression that goes deeper and lasts far longer than the circumstances seem to call for. Traditionally this type of behavior had been associated with women.

We look at someone who runs from relationship to relationship and we realize that he or she can't possibly fall in or out of love that quickly; we watch someone pining over a lost love and we realize that he or she is holding on to a self-defeating illusion.

Both the jumpers and the mourners reflect the kind of unrealistic attitude toward romance that is so often symptomatic of unresolved commitment conflicts.

13. *You have difficulty reaching any decision that limits your future options.*

Choosing from a restaurant menu, deciding on a purchase (a computer, a VCR, a home, a car), making appointments in advance—all of these require a commitment. That's because commitment isn't just about romance. It's about life, and in life there are umpteen moments when you are going to have to make decisions, large and small.

People who struggle with commitment have a tough time deciding on anything permanent. Whether it's a residence or a job, they don't want to do anything they can't undo, and they don't want to get into anything they can't get out of. Wary of making the wrong choice, worried about getting trapped or stuck, nervous about losing their freedom and their choices, they can never comfortably close off any options. And no sooner do they make a choice—be it a new living-room sofa or a potential life partner—than they begin to question or find fault with the choice.

This quality frequently extends to "committing" to plans. We once interviewed a man who was unable to use a pen to write down dates in his calendar. Because he had to leave himself a way out, he always used pencil so that he could erase anything he had put down. Although few people are this extreme, men and women who are conflicted about commitment frequently resist planning too far ahead.

Commitment anxiety can surface anytime a decision has to be made. That's because there is no such thing as the perfect choice. Once we have made a choice, we must not only learn to live with what we have chosen but also with the knowledge of what we have given up.

Sometimes it's easier to recognize your commitment conflicts when they emerge in nonromantic areas. If you struggle with commitment, there are likely to be many such places in your life where your struggle is evident. That means that there is something going on in your psyche that transcends interpersonal chemistry, transcends cultural input, and transcends what happened to you at the high school prom.

14. *You become acutely uncomfortable when you feel someone is closing in on you or invading your space.*

Think about the expression "I need more space." Think about how it is used in relationships. Now for a moment forget about your love relationships. Let's just think about how it makes you feel when someone comes to visit and "invades" your space. How easily do you adjust? Do you find yourself "climbing the walls" when others take up your territory? How about when someone stands too close to you in the office or when someone moves an object on your desk. How anxious does it make you feel? How angry?

Remember that men and women with commitment conflicts need distance. They don't like feeling as though someone is closing in on them and limiting them in any way. That's why space and territory are always such major issues.

15. *In your head you always maintain psychological space and a possible way out of every situation.*

If you have unresolved commitment conflicts, you almost always maintain a secret little spot in your head in which you are free and alone. Here's how this works:

You're married, but in your head you have a built-in escape plan that you can put into operation on short notice. You're in a relationship, but in your head you know exactly how you can get out should you choose. You've held the same job for eight years, but in your head you might leave tomorrow, and just in case, you continue to read the employment ads. You own a house, but you have never fully decorated it because in your head you might sell it someday soon. If you have unresolved commitment issues, even if you never, ever take a single step toward leaving, psychologically you're always one step out the door in every situation. You're there, but you're not there. You're committed, but you're not committed. You haven't run away, but you know you can. And it's knowing you *can* that keeps you from fleeing. That's what gives you your sense of freedom.

If someone tries to remove that sense of freedom, you may well experience a sense of distress that is akin to what claustrophobics feel when someone is limiting their space. This response can include all of the classic phobic responses including intense anxiety and a need to break out, get away, run, and hide.

16. *You gravitate toward professions or employment conditions that allow you flexibility in terms of time and space.*

Because employment involves many of the same conditions as romantic partnerships, people with commitment issues often have very distinctive ways of handling their work lives. If you have a tough time committing yourself to anything that limits your freedom, you may try to avoid work that insists on rigid rules in terms of time and place. When forced to maintain nine-to-five routines, those with commitment conflicts may job hop, numb their discomfort with drugs or alcohol, or set up a peculiar system that allows them to dissociate from what they are doing.

For example, Paul is a schoolteacher. That means he has a definite set schedule. But as Paul explains it, he is able to tolerate his job because he is home every day by three-thirty and has long vacations and many holidays. Also, he has never stayed with any one school district for more than two years.

Brittany is an art director for a large company. The conditions of her job are such that, despite her long hours, she has no set arrival time, is free to arrange her own schedule, and is able to leave the office for long stretches in order to work with clients. Even so she resents it when she is expected to be a part of general scheduled meetings at the agency where she works.

You can see that what is most appealing to people like Paul and Brittany is self-employment, or work situations that allow a great deal of flexibility.

If you are conflicted about commitment—any kind of commitment—you're not alone. Here is a fact: The vast majority of us, to one degree or another, are afraid of commitment. *We all feel some conflict about it.* Despite this, some people are able to deal with their fears and forge lasting, meaningful, and loving relationships. But many others find themselves repeating self-destructive and unsatisfying patterns of relating, and they don't know why.

CHAPTER TWO

Commitment Fears and Commitment Fantasies

A COMMITMENTPHOBIC RESPONSE

> *"Just the idea of agreeing to be with another human being for the rest of my life makes my heart pound. Sometimes when I'm with my girlfriend, I feel as though somebody is about to cut off my air supply and that my survival depends on my getting away."*
>
> —Scott

Obviously Scott is not in any real physical danger from his long-time girlfriend, but he has anxieties and fears that he doesn't understand. He is unable to be realistic about his relationships, he is unable to take things one day at a time, and he is unable to make reasonable and carefully thought-out decisions about his personal life. He hates living alone, but whenever he gets close to being fully committed, he focuses on "forever"; this triggers physical and/or emotional reactions that seem uncontrollable. We call this response commitmentphobia.

Commitmentphobia is a claustrophobic response to intimate relationships. The dictionary defines *claustrophobia* as a fear of enclosed or narrow spaces. To a commitmentphobic that's what a relationship symbolizes—an enclosed space in which he or she may get stuck. Commitmentphobia comes with all the classic phobic symptoms:

31

- Headaches
- Gastrointestinal disturbances
- Nausea
- Nervousness
- Excessive sweating
- Chills
- Intense anxiety
- Palpitations
- Hyperventilation
- Labored breathing
- Suffocating sensations
- A general sense of dread

As most of us know, these are all "fight or flight" responses—the body's way of mobilizing itself against a threat. And it is how people with severe and active commitment conflicts respond when they feel they are involved in a romantic situation that bears the trappings of permanency. The brain sends a message to the body: "I'm terrified." And the body sends a message back: "Danger! Get OUT! NOW!"

You don't have to be in any real physical danger for the body to mobilize its defenses. If you perceive something as a threat, then the body reacts as though there is indeed a very real threat. "Give me liberty or give me death!" it cries. "Fifty-four forty or fight!" "Not another nickel to the King!" Whether you know it or not, your body has gone to war.

Why war? What's so scary that such drastic action is called for? And who is the foe? For someone with a genuine commitmentphobic response, the foe is the relationship itself. It's the loss of freedom that's frightening. If on some very visceral level you equate commitment with the loss of freedom, then commitment may be anxiety provoking or even truly terrifying. Your body gets prepared to help you escape. It will respond to that relationship the same way it would respond if you were a claustrophobic trapped in an elevator, an airplane, a crowd, or a closet.

DIFFERENT LEVELS OF FEAR

Of course not everyone experiences his or her fear of commit-ment in the same way. Fear can range from severe to more subtle. For example:

• *Overwhelming panic* is the best way to describe reactions that are both immediate and intense. The minute the relationship gets "tight," fear sets in. These men and women can't help but recog-nize what they are feeling.

Adam, a forty-two-year-old photographer, describes the feeling: "With every woman I've been with I've experienced that moment of terror when the relationship suddenly hits the place where I'm no longer a guy trying to get a woman to like me. That's the point where everything turns around—instead of being the pursuer, I'm the pursued. The woman likes me and is making noises like she's thinking of marriage, and I feel like I'm being hunted, and I'm screaming for air. I always find a way out. Usually I have to make some excuse, like I'm moving to Alaska for six months. I try to get out without hurting anyone. Impossible of course. Someone is always hurt, but I have to do it. There is no other way."

Meg, also forty-two, says that she experiences a similar reaction: "Several men have asked me to marry them, and each time I say yes, I stop breathing. The last one was two years ago. I had just turned forty, and I remember thinking, *Go ahead, marry him! Make your parents happy! It won't be so bad. You can have a child right away, and then when the child is fourteen, you can get divorced. You'll only be fifty-five—you can still have some life left.* But I couldn't do it, because after I said yes, I became phobic about everything—trains, buses, cars. One night I made him walk home with me from Penn Sta-tion to Eighty-sixth Street because I couldn't get into any vehicle with him. I completely lost it."

• *Anxiety* ranging from mild to intense is the way many men and women with commitment conflicts describe their feelings. This group rarely feels outright panic, and the symptoms of fear, or phobia, may be so subtle and so seemingly disconnected from the relationship that at first they are only vaguely aware of what's taking place. But when the anxiety hangs around long enough, they become acutely aware of their discomfort. Sometimes this type of anxiety translates into actual physical symptoms, such as headaches, stomachaches, or back pain. Often the symptoms don't emerge until after a commitment has taken place.

Janice, a thirty-six-year-old woman, was recently married for the second time. She told us, "In my first marriage I was uncomfortable and nervous all the time. I felt like I was jumping out of my skin. But I blamed that on my first husband. Within weeks of this marriage I started to feel the same thing. I can't blame my second husband. He's not doing anything. I just feel the walls closing in on me."

Anthony, an accountant, says that although he has never felt actual panic, he is aware of his anxiety. "I know I'm nervous about commitment because I get this anxious feeling in my stomach whenever I let anything get too close. The first time it happened, I was going out with this woman at work, and I thought I had the flu. I felt sick for close to four weeks. Whenever I would go to the office, I would feel sick. When I went home, I felt better. Finally I figured it out. I don't think it was the woman's fault. I just got anxious when she was around. Eventually we broke up, and then two years later, when I started seeing another woman seriously, the same thing happened. It's a real problem."

• *Controlled fear* is the feeling expressed by those men and women who acknowledge their conflicts and who are attempting to lead their lives in a way that compensates for their feelings. Although she is only twenty-four, Debra, who describes herself as the queen of self-help, says that for the time being she has arranged her life to accommodate feelings such as this. She says:

"Right now I'm totally commitmentphobic. I'm afraid, and I know it. I don't want to get involved seriously, and I don't want to make any promises. Looking at different relationships and different married couples, I see that I don't want to be trapped in that little box. It's too stifling.

"I had a difficult childhood, and I've had to work a lot of stuff out. I've read just about every self-help book published, and I attend a twelve-step program designed for children of dysfunctional families. I have to be careful not to be attracted to men with a lot of problems. Because I know me, I know that if I see someone more than a few times, I get involved. Therefore I just won't go out with anyone more than three or four times. I like to date, I like men, I'm just very realistic about what I want, and I don't want commitment, at least not for a long time. The decision not to be in a relationship feels good to me because for the first time in my life I don't feel as if I have to be with someone. I always thought it was expected of me, and I would try even though I wasn't comfortable with it. I like men, but no real promises and no real intimacy—that's what I want. And I don't want any man to try to talk me out of it."

Kevin, thirty-six, says that he has also come to terms with his commitmentphobia:

"I know that I will never be able to be with somebody forever. My compromise: I date only women who feel the same way I do. I don't let it get too intimate. I figure maybe someday down the line I'll be good for limited commitments. But for now, after a half-dozen devastating experiences in which everybody was hurt, I keep it simple and detached. It's working for me."

• *Hidden fear* is the only way to describe the reactions of those men and women whose history clearly indicates that they are avoiding commitment, even though they have no conscious awareness of what they are doing. These men and women are so terrified of commitment that they rarely, if ever, consider becoming involved with anyone who would present them with the opportunity to confront their terror. Because they are attracted to partners who are unavailable or pulling away, unless they accidentally stumble into a committed relationship, they have no idea of the depth of their anxiety. Karen, a forty-year-old musician, says:

"My whole life I wanted to get married and have children, but with every man I went out with, it was the same thing. Something was wrong with every one of them—either they were married or they were petrified of intimacy. I had a couple of relationships that took me a long time to get over. Anyway one of these men, someone who broke my heart about ten years ago, suddenly turned up in my life again. Now he wants to get married—and I'm not so sure.

"I've learned how to live alone, and it seems like a lot of trouble to be with somebody all the time. I have to admit it, now that he's around all the time, I feel that he's pressuring me. I like him, but I don't want him around so much. I feel angry, and I want to scream at him to just get away from me. This is amazing because I fantasized about him every night for years, and if he weren't here, I might dream about him again. But when I'm with him, I have chest pains. This might be my last chance to have a family, and I worry that I should grab it, and him, while I can, but I can't stand feeling this way."

James, forty-four, insists that he has no awareness of any fear and would be thrilled if he could meet the right woman, but his history says otherwise. He tends to go for long periods—sometimes years—without going out with anyone because his feelings are often focused on women who, for one reason or another, are not interested in pursuing a relationship with him. There have, however, been two women who were available and responsive with whom he tried to live. Both times the relationship ended because he "felt miserable."

"I think it was the women in both cases. They both did things I couldn't stand. One of them kept a dog who would always try to get in the bed. She had the dog before I moved in, but I didn't know that it bothered me. The other one played music in the morning that I couldn't stand. In both cases things about the women made my skin crawl. I couldn't take it. I felt as if I had to get away, or I would explode."

IT'S ONLY FRIGHTENING WHEN IT FEELS LIKE FOREVER

"It's the lifetime thing. That's what scares me. The lifetime thing. Whose idea was that anyway?"

—JOHN, forty-two

It's a mistake to believe that someone who is afraid of commitment is by definition afraid of relationships. Men and women with commitment conflicts can be loving, they can be tender, and they can be involved. That is, until the relationship in question looks like it might develop into a "lifetime thing." When permanency is introduced into the equation, fear surfaces. Remember that permanency means different things to different people. Some hypersensitive individuals feel threatened as soon as the first or second date if they believe that "more" will ultimately be expected of them; others may not feel stuck for years.

We have interviewed a fair number of men and women who told us that they were able to sidestep their commitment anxieties because they started thinking about a divorce at the very same moment that they began planning the wedding. But when it became more complicated, when children became involved, or joint property, suddenly they began to feel that there was *no way out.* Here are the most common periods when the claustrophobic fear of being stuck rises to the surface.

No Way Out! The Commitmentphobic Points of No Return

POINT ONE: ONE DATE, NO MORE

Some men and women become unhinged after a good first date, particularly if they feel "more" is expected of them. Unable to relax and allow a relationship to grow, they immediately envision a committed future stretching out in front of them. So they panic.

POINT TWO: AFTER SEX

To many of us sex means intimacy, intimacy means commitment, and commitment means forever. There are those who rarely allow a relationship to develop beyond a brief sexual connection. They are certain their partner assumes ongoing sex represents a permanent bond. Sometimes they assume the same thing.

POINT THREE: WHEN THE EXPECTATION IS REAL

When two people have been going out for a while, there are expectations. Friends, family, the world, and your partner expect you to get married. This is the most common point at which people begin to get scared.

POINT FOUR: THE MORNING AFTER

A fair number of men and women don't react as if the commitment is real until after the wedding, after the couple moves in together, or after the romantic honeymoon haze has faded. That's when they get anxious and/or depressed.

POINT FIVE: THE MORNING AFTER THE MORNING AFTER

This fifth point of no return can occur years into the relationship or marriage. It usually coincides with an event that is associated with "no way out": the birth of a child, the purchase of a home, a fortieth birthday, the arrival of grandchildren, the onset of menopause. Each of these important markers can elicit panic: "If I don't get out now, I'll be stuck forever."

Whether the fear happens in the first hour or in the twentieth year, the need to create distance and shake these unpleasant feelings is frequently intense enough to overlook any feelings of love one may hold for a partner. Getting away becomes the only priority. The fear may be real or imagined, reasonable or unreasonable. It doesn't matter. The key lies in perception.

WHY SHOULD THE IDEA OF COMMITMENT BE SO THREATENING?

Some people might argue that fear of commitment is built into our genetic code, that in the human jungle the mere act of caring for and accommodating to a full-time partner is a threat. After all, it means slowing down, lowering defenses, and becoming less alert to the possibility of danger. The fact is that commitment is scary for a lot of reasons, all of which need to be acknowledged and examined.

First is what we see as the primary conflict—what we feel when commitment threatens our basic and powerful need to feel free. There are those who would even take this a step farther and question whether or not permanent commitment is healthy or even normal. These people question whether humans are meant to form permanent unions with each other. While thinking about this is provocative, there is probably no satisfactory answer to the question of whether people, like swans, are designed to mate for life. And we are not about to argue the merits of marriage versus a single life.

Forever is scary. Commitment—whether in the form of marriage or not—represents an enormous responsibility. Once we commit ourselves, we owe something to another human being. Someone else counts on us, depends on us, relies on us. The notion of this extra burden is frightening. But there is a difference between having commitment fears and being downright phobic.

WHAT THE WORLD TELLS US ABOUT MARRIAGE AND OTHER COMMITTED RELATIONSHIPS

"Four years of therapy has shown me that because of my mother's experiences I regard traditional marriage as a trap."

—SARA, thirty-six

"What I'm afraid of is no mystery to me. I have a brother who is seven years older. When I was about twelve, he got married. His wife immediately became pregnant. By the time I was sixteen, the twins had been born; he had four kids and he was twenty-three years old. When I would go over to help baby-sit, I would feel so sorry for him. It was a madhouse, and he was trapped in it. I vowed it would never happen to me."

—JEFFREY, forty-five

"My mother waited on my father hand and foot. She never had a minute to herself. Every second she was either taking care of me or my brother or chasing around making our father happy. She couldn't even read a book without his asking her to get up and get him something. I love my father, but I don't want that kind of marriage. If I get married, it's going to be to a man who doesn't expect me to be an appendage."

—LISA, thirty-two

We hear about marriages everywhere—on television, in the news, standing on supermarket lines as we glance at the tabloid headlines. We are surrounded by couples we know—parents, family, friends. Looking at these relationships, we have witnessed tension, anger, and sometimes pain in addition to love. As we have looked at marriage, whether it be media portrayals or real life, how have we been affected?

Let's take television marriages. The Ricardos seemed to be having fun, but was this the kind of honest relationship that we wanted for ourselves? Lucy and Ethel were forever hiding the truth from Ricky and Fred. Besides, we all know that the real life of this television couple was even more dysfunctional than the one we viewed on the tube. We may have enjoyed watching the oh-so-normal Cleaver family, but how many young men grew up wanting to be like Ward, and how many young women honestly thought that June was having a perfectly nifty life? We probably looked at couples like Mr. and Mrs. Cleaver and Mr. and Mrs. Brady and thought their lives were boring and dull. The kids had all the fun.

Contemporary television couples such as the Connors or the Huxtables seem to be having a nicer time together, but don't the Huxtables ever do anything without their children? And does anybody actually want a life like Roseanne Connors? Think about the happy television couples like the Keatons on *Family Ties*, and think about the couples from hell like the Bundys on *Married with Children*. Have television marriages made you more or less wary of commitment?

How about your friends in the real world? Do any of them have inspiring marriages? Do you look at them and want what they have? Do you want their conflicts and their anxieties? Do you truly want their brand of togetherness? When you watch them making decisions, do you envy their commitment or are you appalled by the number of compromises each partner has to make? What's the end result? Do your friends give you a positive or a negative view of commitment?

Then there's your family. What kinds of messages did you receive from them when you were a child? Were your parents happily married? Were they happy but disgruntled about the economics of marriage, the sacrifices of marriage, and the compromises of marriage? Was your father burdened and trapped by a dreary job? Did your mother feel hemmed in by the suburbs, or the city, or the country? Did either or both of them make compromises that they resented? Did you hear about it? How about fidelity? Were they in any way running away from each other?

Were they bored? Did life at home seem dull and unsatisfying? Did they do things as a couple? Or were they avoiding each other and hiding out in separate activities?

How about your grandparents, uncles, aunts, and other relatives? What examples did they provide? Sometimes we form certain opinions from observing the parents of friends. When you visited friends' homes, do you remember what you thought or felt about their parents? In short, when you were growing up, what kinds of messages did you receive about commitment?

What about other messages you might have received from the world at large? We've all heard the statistics about the soaring divorce rate. We know that these statistics reflect couples who aren't getting along. We know that couples quarrel about money, sex, religion, cultural differences, and child raising. They quarrel about in-laws, housekeeping, and vacations. They quarrel about who'll do the dishes and whose turn it is to take out the garbage. It's difficult not to have been affected by all this.

We can't help but react to what we read about couples struggling with the economics of maintaining a family. We've seen women carpooling and racing to work; we've seen husbands holding down two jobs. We've seen middle-class families with young children crowded into small apartments because that's all they can afford. This is powerful stuff. Hasn't it made us stop and think about whether we really want a permanent commitment and all it might entail?

At any age, based upon all these messages, you may remember having settled on certain attitudes. If you are a woman, did you decide you wanted a traditional marriage or did you want to maintain a career? Did you vow that you would never relinquish your independence? Did you want a life like your mother's, or did you want something different? If you are a man, did you decide early on that you never wanted to be saddled with all the financial burdens of marriage, or did you dream about making enough to support hordes of children? What about today? Are you a woman who is thinking about the reality of keeping a job *and* doing the major share of housework and child care? Are you a man who fears you will never, ever make enough money to be able to send one child through college?

How have all of these messages influenced your feelings about commitment? Do they make you nervous, fearful, and wary? Or have you decided that they don't matter, because when you finally make a permanent commitment, it will be different? In other words, do you deny that you have commitment conflicts? Or do you know that you have conflicts, but still hope that when the time is right, they will magically disappear?

DENYING COMMITMENT FEARS

"I don't understand any woman who says that she's afraid of commitment. I want it more than anything else. I would get married in a minute."
—LORI, thirty-four

Lori describes her parents' marriage as "deadly." She says her father rarely says anything to her mother that is more meaningful than "pass the potatoes," and hides behind the TV, refusing to pay attention to anything his wife has to say. When Lori was twenty-two, she was married to a man she describes as "extraordinarily unfaithful." The marriage lasted only a few years. Since that time Lori has had only one other serious relationship, and that was with a married man. Lori does very little to improve her social life; if anything, she tends to spend a great deal of time alone. The men she finds attractive always seem to be involved elsewhere. Despite this, Lori is adamant about her desire for long-term commitment. We find it difficult to accept Lori's statements about what she says she wants. We think that she can't help but have a fair number of conflicts she is failing to examine.

For example, written into just about everyone's memory is the statistic that says that fifty percent of all couples end up divorcing. Now, think about it. If someone told you that everytime you crossed the street, there was a fifty-percent possibility that you would get hit by a car, chances are that each of your pedestrian outings would be clouded by anxiety and trepidation. At the very least you would increase your precautions, carefully looking each way, cautiously assessing the cars, the traffic lights, the crosswalks. That makes sense. Yet a large percentage of single men and women, knowing the divorce statistics, knowing—sometimes first-hand—the kind of pain involved in failed marriages, say that they are very anxious to find a permanent commitment and that they feel no fear whatsoever. That doesn't make sense. Considering what we all know, doesn't it seem reasonable that all of us should be at least a little bit nervous about commitment?

A great deal is written these days about denial and the effect it can have on our lives. In psychology denial is defined as an unconscious defense mechanism that we use to allay anxiety by negating important conflicts or unwanted impulses. People in denial are refusing to look at some of the conflicts and problems in their lives. This is a way of protecting ourselves from pain, particularly when that pain gets in the way of living. But denial is also how we stay stuck. If we don't look at the truth in our lives, if we don't honestly examine our conflicts and our fears, then we are denying our experiences, and we don't have a basis from which to make constructive changes.

Women, in particular, have a wide variety of reasons to deny commitment anxiety. They are sometimes under extreme family pressure to settle down, make a home, and produce grandchildren. Even as toddlers they were given dolls and dollhouses and homemaking paraphernalia. It seems to be assumed that marriage and family is something all women are supposed to want. No wonder women who feel the slightest ambivalence bury it.

RATIONALIZING AWAY OUR COMMITMENT CONFLICTS

Like denial, rationalization is a defense mechanism. It is a method that people employ to make unreasonable, or irrational, behavior appear reasonable. In other words we use it to explain away behavior that doesn't always make sense—sometimes even to us. People who refuse to examine their commitment conflicts often find themselves acting out these conflicts. Typically this produces some strange behavior. Rationalization is often an essential tool in explaining this behavior away. Here's how this works:

Six months ago Marc, thirty-eight and once divorced, met Sally, a twenty-nine-year-old divorcée with a four-year-old child. The minute he saw her, he "flipped" over the way she looked. He says he fell in love with her and with her daughter almost immediately.

"This was something I really thought I wanted. My first wife

43

never wanted children, and it was a major issue in our marriage. But Sally loved kids, and her daughter was wonderful. I liked the feeling the whole thing gave me, the sense of being able to take care of them."

Marc told his friends and family that he had finally met the woman for him. For her part Sally—a struggling single parent—saw Marc as a "gift from above." It took very little for him to convince her to move into his house *and* quit her job and come work for him in the small video business he owned. A few days before Sally was to move in, Marc began to experience feelings of "pressure" and anxiety. His anxiety was so intense that he began questioning his judgment, wondering whether he was making a huge mistake. As he began to have these thoughts, he found himself thinking about another woman he had once known and loved, a woman who had rejected him in order to marry another man.

"I had heard that this old girlfriend had gotten separated, so I called her. Coincidentally this was the day Sally was moving in. Two hours before the movers were due to arrive, I met my old girlfriend for coffee, and I realized that I was still attracted to her —*very* attracted to her. I realized that by committing myself so quickly to Sally, I wasn't giving myself a chance. I had only been divorced four years, and I hadn't explored all my options. All in all I was pretty miserable and confused. I went through the motions of helping Sally move in. She was thrilled; I was like the walking dead. I didn't know what to do."

As you can imagine, it was only a short time before Marc's mood —"withdrawn, distracted, and upset"—affected Sally's happiness. Every time she asked him what was wrong, he replied, "It's not you. Don't worry." According to Marc, Sally assumed he was having business difficulties he hadn't shared with her.

"It wasn't Sally, but it was Sally. I had started talking to this other woman on a daily basis, and the sexual tension was unbelievable. Finally, when Sally and her daughter had been in my house for about two weeks, it got too much. I had to tell her.

"I told Sally the truth, that I still loved her, but that I needed to see other people. And I told her that I still had feelings for my old girlfriend and that I needed to get some resolution in this situation. Sally was very disappointed, to say the least. Fortunately she was able to get her old apartment back. She wasn't so lucky with her job, so she continued to work for me for several months while she looked for another job. We went to bed together a few more times, but even though I still cared for her, I knew that I was never going to make a commitment to her.

"This was a very bad period in my life. I definitely wasn't fair to Sally, because I still had feelings for her—you might even call it love. I was afraid that leaving her might be the biggest mistake of my life, and I felt terrible guilt about her daughter. As you can imagine, it wasn't an easy situation. In many ways Sally was very good to me, very caring. I needed that, and I took advantage of her desire to give. It was hard for me to give that up.

"It got very weird at the end. Sally and I would work together all day, then we would go home together, and she would make dinner for the three of us. I would eat, and then I would go out to see the other woman. I would come home to sleep with Sally. Sally would cry. Sometimes I would cry too, because I really felt that way. I mean I had feelings. I'm a very emotional person. As you can imagine, we started fighting. When Sally realized that we were never going to become the family unit she imagined, she was very jealous and very angry."

Now, here comes the part when Marc does some fancy footwork to rationalize his behavior and throws the blame on Sally for being less than perfect.

"I think what happened is that right before the move, I began to see a side to Sally that I didn't really like all that much. She got all tense about moving in and started getting insecure. She kept asking me if I was really certain about what I was doing. I think it was her asking, as much as anything, that made me see my reservations.

"And then she needed help packing, and her mother and one of her older sisters came over. Together they sort of took over, you know. I saw a side to her that I hadn't seen before. She was real sloppy sometimes in her closets. And she was tired a lot. She didn't always get along with her mother, but I could see that in many ways she had some of the same bossy personality traits. Not to mention the same body type, and her mom had definitely gone to pot physically. Yes, I got scared, but I think rightfully so. Of course I hurt her, but it was better that I did it then before things got even more serious. No?"

Shortly after Sally moved out, Marc and his old girlfriend also broke up. He says he realizes that he was probably just "using" her to "get out" of the situation with Sally. His explanation: "I went overboard with Sally, but the way I figure it is if we had been right for each other, it would have worked out."

Anyone listening to Marc's story can see that his behavior was at best chaotic, confused, and irresponsible. One day he is in love with one woman, the next he is ready to sabotage the relationship to pursue an old girlfriend. One minute he is appreciating that someone is making him dinner, the next he is rushing off to see the old girlfriend. After having sex with one woman, he rushes home to cry with another. None of this seems to make very much sense.

What makes even less sense is Marc's method of dealing with the facts of his life. Essentially he manages to deny that he has a problem and to rationalize his behavior by telling himself that Sally is not the right woman. Otherwise he would behave differently. When we listen to Marc, we find it difficult to argue with him. Of course he behaved like a jerk, but maybe what he's saying is true. Maybe if he and Sally were meant to be together, they would be together. That's what the romance novels and movies would have us believe. This kind of logic manages completely to obscure Marc's commitment conflicts and the way in which they cause him to act out.

THE FANTASY COVER-UP

When we hear someone like Marc talking about the problems in his relationships, we may think that he is being unrealistic, but even so we hesitate to tell him so. After all, we may tell ourselves, perhaps Marc is right, perhaps there is a perfect mate whom he is fated to meet. We don't want to burst his romantic bubble. Isn't that what the entire culture of romance has told us to expect?

We think there are some very strong reasons why so many of us use denial or rationalization as ways of masking our commitment conflicts. When our relationships end or founder, we don't look to our commitment issues. Instead we look to romantic fantasies that are accepted and reinforced by much of the world around us. In these fantasies people who are meant to be together are fated. Once their eyes meet, circumstances will conspire to keep them happy forever.

Many people say that they don't have unrealistic fantasies, that they are prepared to accept mere mortals as their mates. They tend to forget that when we fantasize, we think not only about how our future beloveds will look and behave, we also think about how we will feel when we are with them. We think about bliss and trust and sexual desire that doesn't stop. Even when we are prepared to accept our mate's imperfections, we are not prepared to accept our own everyday feelings of irritability and fatigue. We expect to feel close and bonded and perfectly at one with each other—*all the time*. We certainly don't expect ever to feel bored, ambivalent, anxious, or annoyed. If any of these emotions surface, the fantasy is destroyed.

Keep in mind that many single people with serious commitment conflicts never even think about the possibility of dealing with marital quarrels, marital boredom, or marital breakups. They don't think about these realistic possibilities because most of their thoughts about commitment are based on fantasy. In the never-never land of their imaginations, there are no overflowing garbage pails, intrusive alarm clocks, dirty socks, or annoying reading lamps. The partners of their imagination are fantasy images: Like airbrushed photographs, they never get sick, never get old, never get fat, and most important never get real.

Those with serious commitment conflicts are experts in romantic fantasy. They live and love in fantasy land because that's the only place where they can resolve their conflicts. In their dreams, and only in their dreams, can they feel both committed and free. Although they tend to deny it, what they are usually dreaming about is high romance and not everyday, down-to-earth commitment.

FANTASY MODELS FOR A COMMITTED RELATIONSHIP

The mythologies and fairy tales of our culture are extraordinarily limited when it comes to producing models of a committed relationship. The fairy tales of childhood, for example, are not about commitment. Beauty and the Beast, Cinderella, Snow White—these are about romance. They give us no information about what happens once the commitment has been made. Once they were married, did Cinderella and the Prince argue about how to redecorate the ballroom? After the kids were born, did Cinderella reconcile with her family for the sake of the children? Did her rotten stepsisters come around every weekend and make trouble? As the couple got older, did the Prince's sexual enthusiasm wane? Did Cinderella's hormones ever go awry? Did she suffer from PMS, postpartum depression, or menopausal fatigue?

What about Beauty and the Beast? Once the Beast became a mere human mortal, did he lose some of his initial appeal? Once Beauty had transformed the Beast with the power of her love, did she feel as though she were at loose ends? Did she need a new project, a new focus for her energies?

And how about Snow White? Once she was awake and talking, did she say the things her Prince wanted to hear? Or had she spent too many years living with the Seven Little Dwarfs to be able to relate to his world? Did he get bored with her? Did she try to change him? Did he wish she would stop talking so much?

These are answers we will never know, because our fairy tales don't take us past the wedding day. When the idyllic fairy-tale couple walks through the doors to marriage, we don't see what happens next. For most of us, when the initial romance starts to fade, we face reality uneasily. Suddenly everything is no longer perfect, and we lose the hope of ever having fairy-tale perfection. It can feel as though a part of us is dying. Perhaps it is a fear of the unknown, or a fear of repeating the lives of our parents—but it always means giving up fantasies and romantic illusion. Not an easy thing to do for anyone, but particularly difficult for someone with commitment conflicts. Without the fantasy we may feel as though there is nothing exciting left.

EARLY MESSAGES FROM OUR PARENTS

Since we are talking about relationships, we cannot disregard the important messages about relationships that we carry over from our parents' lives. These contribute significantly to our expectations, fantasies, and fears. If one or both of your parents were controlling, you may worry about control; if they were smothering, you may well feel smothered; if they were absent or neglectful, you may be carrying around old wounds and resentments. The messages we received from our parents when we were children all influence our ability to build real partnerships with real partners.

ROMANCE, NOT COMMITMENT

> *"In my head I have committed myself wholeheartedly to some very unlikely men. I mean, really bad-news guys—rodeo riders with drug problems, married men who lived in Japan, temperamental bisexual artists, you name it, I've loved it. In retrospect I wonder what I could have possibly been thinking. The most amazing part is that in each instance I would find myself fantasizing about 'being saved' by these impossible choices."*

> —ANNA, thirty-nine

> *"I become obsessed with the women who've gotten away—women who, for one reason or another, are beyond my reach. I keep thinking they might be perfect for me. Once, for example, I fell head over heels in love with a woman who I spotted from a moving car. I never saw her again, but I carried this picture of her around in my head for years. I was positive that we were meant for each other. My mother, who is pretty disgusted with my single state, recently asked me if I had ever met any woman who I thought I could marry. I asked her to clarify what she meant by 'met.' I told her that if it didn't matter whether or not we had ever actually spoken, then there was this woman in a car. I could have married her."*

> —KEN, thirty-five

Many people with commitment conflicts are incurable romantics with the most traditional views on love and marriage; they may firmly believe that when they get married, it will be "till death do us part." Because they see relationships as tremendous obligations, they typically insist that they respect the sanctity of the marriage vows, even when they are behaving quite differently. If they've never been married before, they make it clear that marriage is something they only want to do once in their lives; if they have married before, they want the next one to be the last one. These people want their love to be forever and they expect a total "in love" sensation all the time. And they don't care how many statistics suggest otherwise. Until reality creeps in, they imagine each of their loves as destined or ordained by karma.

Experts in romantic fantasy, these men and women prefer to live and love in fantasy relationships because real relationships can evolve into real commitment, and that's much too threatening. The problem is that if you follow your fantasies, you can end up leading a very confusing and unfulfilling life.

IS IT COMMITMENT OR IS IT A FANTASY?

Theresa, a twenty-eight-year-old waitress and student, is an example of someone who falls in and out of commitment because of her rich fantasy life. She says, "I've been in lots of relationships. I've lived with four men and I've hurt all of them because I change my mind. At first the man always looks wonderful to me. And then I notice stuff I don't like. My friends tell me that I'm hopeless, but I don't believe it—I believe that someday I'll meet a guy who really is perfect. At the beginning of all my important relationships I've felt as though it was karma. I always dream about marriage and babies, and yes, I guess I do tell the men that I want a family. At the time that's what I feel. But then usually the man starts doing stuff that makes me want to get away."

The "stuff" that Theresa refers to usually involves some form of "pressure" to get more committed. Theresa says that "everyone" also tells her that she is the same with work as she is with love. She came to school in southern California to study acting, but she found it boring, so she dropped out and took a job on a cruise ship. When she returned to shore, she enrolled in a course in management, but that was even more boring. Then she became interested in photography and enrolled in courses. Everyone agreed she had a real talent for it, but she had become more interested in sculpting. Right now she is taking courses in that, and she is thinking of moving to Europe, where she can enroll in art school full-time.

Meeting Theresa, one quickly forgets about her erratic history with work and with men. She appears somewhat shy, and she says that she is very upset by the fact that she has "hurt" the men in her life.

"I sort of abandoned David, my last boyfriend. He's having a difficult time getting over it. When we met two years ago, he was married. I really thought he was the man I was going to spend the rest of my life with. That's what I told him. But living with him was impossible. He was always asking me where I was going, and I just saw that he was different than I thought he was. At the beginning we were always having these romantic meetings because of his wife. It was different when we were in the same house day after day. He would watch football games, and he began to get this little potbelly. He would watch the evening news, and he'd want me to watch it with him. It was like living with my father. I don't want an ordinary life. I don't want to look over and see some guy scratching himself and eating chips. That's not what I want. I know David doesn't understand why I ended it. Of course I still have feelings for him, just not the kind of feelings he wants me to have."

Craig, a thirty-six-year-old high school coach who says that he recognizes both his inability to commit and his capacity for fantasy, told us the following story. It is an excellent example of the use of fantasy to sidestep intimacy.

"Three years ago I met and fell in love with a woman who was all wrong for me. All of my friends told me, but I wouldn't listen. I'm a very laid-back kind of guy, she was a very driven lawyer. I'm from a small town, she's from the city. I'm Catholic, she's Jewish. I don't make much money, she makes tons. And money was very important to her. Nonetheless I decided that she was right for me, and I spent close to a year trying to convince her that this was the case.

"You understand that even though there was an incredible physical attraction, she had thrown up a thousand barriers against our being together permanently. Her job, her therapist, her family, her friends. I decided that if I could just get her away from all that to a place where she could see me at my best, I could work magic in the relationship.

"Years before, I had lived and worked out west. And I loved it. I always dreamed that when I met the woman I wanted to marry, I would bring her out to Glacier National Park, and we would spend an idyllic time camping and hiking. The years that I lived in Montana were very important to me. Living there was addictive. It was a part of my development, and I was incredibly attached to it.

"I figured that she would be knocked out by the environment, by how much mastery I had of outdoor skills, and by my ability to get along in the great outdoors. I figured once I got her there, got her to relax, and got her to take a look at me in a different way, the relationship would move to a new plateau and everything would be all right. So I convinced her to take a ten-day vacation with me.

"Well, to make a long story short, my plan worked. She was totally disarmed by the place, and the strange environment made her totally dependent. If there was a noise in the campsite, I was like the great white hunter—you know, 'It's nothing, honey— probably just a grizzly—I'll take care of it.' She said that having someone take care of her felt wonderful. She was transformed.

"The second day we were there, the weather was perfect—not a cloud in the sky. We took a long hike, and she was thrilled by the mountain goats and the flowers. On the way back we crossed a little stream and there were all these elk standing in the water drinking. That night we went to this lodge overlooking a lake for dinner and we walked back to the campsite in the moonlight— probably not the brightest thing to do considering the grizzlies. I made a small fire and we toasted marshmallows and drank brandy. It was perfect. She was a changed woman—completely accepting and loving, and it was a changed relationship. As I went to sleep, I felt this incredible wave of relief. I was so happy. It was like bliss. That was the night I had 'the dream.'

"I spent the night dreaming about a woman in high school that I had been desperately in love with and that I had never been able to get to first base with. When I woke up, my first thought was that I should immediately do everything possible to find my high school crush. She was the person I should be with. I looked over at my girlfriend, who was still sleeping, and I thought, *What the hell am I doing with someone who is so dependent on her shrink and her family?* She was all wrong for me. I was totally miserable. The face of the girl from high school settled in my head, and I couldn't get rid of it. She seemed more real to me than the woman lying next to me. She was somebody I could really focus on, somebody who was like myself, who wanted the things I wanted. She was the one I wanted. The woman I was with seemed like a foreigner to me, a complete stranger.

"While she was still sleeping, I got up, got dressed, and hiked up to one of the glaciers. It was a long hike—the whole thing, back and forth, took maybe four hours or more. When I got back, my girlfriend was furious. She said I had betrayed her trust. And she stopped speaking to me. That brought me back a little bit, but it wasn't the same. There was so much anger that we cut our camping trip short.

"We resolved things between us for a while, but after that dream I could never get back to feeling the same way. Whenever I was with her, I would begin to feel depressed. It took another six months for the relationship to wind down, but that was the turning point."

Both Craig and Theresa have traditional attitudes toward marriage and commitment. Both say that they are eager to find the right person, settle down, and raise children. Yet, like many people with commitment conflicts, the minute they get a clear sense that another person is genuinely there, they start questioning the relationship and the person. They start feeling constrained and trapped. Those feelings create anxiety and a need to get away. And within a very short period of time—sometimes immediately—they are ready to move on to a new fantasy.

WHEN THE FANTASY FADES

Some people get into relationships and don't think about words like "till death do us part" and "forever." They are able to view relationships as a process, taking them one day at a time, worrying only about one day at a time. Simply put, these people have fewer conflicts and are less overwhelmed by the notion of losing their freedom.

Typically these fortunate men and women understand that people are not always perfect and that any relationship or marriage, even with two well-intentioned partners, can have problems. This attitude doesn't mean that these people don't care for their mates or that they don't work hard at their marriages. Quite the opposite. They may have fears about commitment, but the fears are realistic. Not surprisingly these people's relationships often pass the test of time.

Men and women with serious commitment conflicts are unable to behave in this fashion. When the fantasy fades, they can't move forward in a realistic, loving relationship. They may also believe they should take the next logical emotional step and embrace a settled permanent relationship, but their need for distance prevents them. What they are feeling most strongly is a need to get away, to seek new horizons, and often new partners.

CHAPTER THREE

Runners and Chasers—
Active Commitment Conflicts

Recently Mitch, a self-employed architect, walked away from an important relationship because he couldn't make a commitment. This brought him in touch with his fears. At forty-five Mitch now believes he can review his romantic history with a degree of clarity that wasn't possible when he was younger. Looking back, he sees a pattern; he sees the two women he lived with, proposed to, and failed to marry, and he's aware of the hurt and disappointment these relationships generated. He sees the other women he pursued for a short time before changing his mind, and he realizes that his feelings—and behavior—were contradictory and confusing. He realizes, from all-too-solid experience, that he becomes anxious and critical when anyone gets too close or expects too much. He knows that once he dates a woman more than a few times, he suspects her of trying to trap him into marriage. And most important he can no longer tell himself that this situation will be cured by "the perfect woman," because he has pursued and ultimately rejected any number of women whom he initially thought were "amazing."

Although she is only twenty-nine, Diane, a computer salesperson, is as aware of her commitment issues as Mitch is. She has always found the idea of marriage foreign and a little scary. When she was a little girl, playing with her friends, whenever they discussed the future and their dreams of someday getting married, she would find herself pushing the idea away. She is still pushing the idea away. She knows that she places limits on all her relationships, and although she has an easy time meeting men, she never lets a relationship develop into an easy intimacy.

Diane's pattern is to make her time and space needs known from the very beginning. She has found that men usually resent this; consequently she is often lonely. She doesn't like this, but she also can't handle a romance that places too many demands on her. She doesn't know what the solution is and hopes that someday she will meet the perfect partner with whom she will be in complete accord on how much they should be together and how much they should be apart. Until then she continues to wrestle with her fears.

Patrick, a stockbroker, is much less aware of his conflicts. At thirty-two he doesn't see a clear pattern. All of the women he has loved appear to be very different. He wanted to marry Bonnie, for example, but she was still in love with her old boyfriend. He was very eager to continue his relationship with Suzanne, but she was determined to move back to her native France, and his occupation was hardly movable. Gwen, the other major love of his life, broke it off with him after two years, saying that he wanted more than she wanted to give. Patrick says his problem is that the women he meets don't appreciate nice guys.

Ellen is certain that it is the men she meets, not her, who have a problem with long-term involvement. At thirty-nine she sees commitment only in the context of marriage and says the reason she has never married has a great deal to do with timing and the luck of the draw. There were men who wanted to marry her, but never when she wanted to marry them. She says she expects a great deal from any man she eventually marries, and this presents a problem for some men. Right now she is harboring a secret crush on a married man in the office where she works. The gossip around the office is that this man, who fans Ellen's feelings by being incredibly seductive and flirtatious, is outrageously unfaithful. Despite her high expectations Ellen sees that she has a pattern of "falling" for men who are unavailable, inappropriate, or unable to commit. However, she can't believe that this has anything to do with her own conflicts.

We recognize that there are all kinds of ways to run from commitment, and there are all kinds of people who employ these different ways.

Mitch, Diane, Patrick, and Ellen are all very different. Each has a unique style and way of behaving in relationships. Let's look at these styles, taking gender differences into account, and see if we can find the pattern. All of these people typically have behavior patterns that can be described in one of two ways:

- Active avoidance
- Passive avoidance

The active ways of running away from commitment are fairly obvious. If you recognize that the very notion of commitment makes you uncomfortable, if you never get seriously involved, or always place limits on the amount of intimacy you allow in your life, and if you are always ambivalent, it becomes pretty apparent over time. But there are also passive, or not-so-obvious, ways of avoiding love—ways that don't make you feel as though you have a problem. Active and passive commitment issues manifest themselves so differently in relationships that it's sometimes difficult to recognize that they are both part of the same syndrome.

Although each of us tends to act out in one particular style, if you have commitment conflicts, the potential for both patterns exists. We have all known men and women who clearly flip-flop between the two. Behavior can also change depending upon age, circumstances, or partners.

ACTIVE COMMITMENT CONFLICTS

"I fall in love. And then I fall out of love. Then I fall in love again. Sometimes I don't bother falling out with the first before I fall in with the second. This makes the women you're with angry. There are a lot of angry women in my life. Two women who get money from me every month, one who

thinks she should get money from me, and one or two who just hate me. If making and breaking commitments means I got a problem, I got a problem."
—NEIL, forty-eight

Active avoidance is all about running, and active avoiders find it almost impossible to stand still. Whether they are pursuing a new love or running away from an old one, they are fully active in the relationship arena. When we talk about someone who has active commitment conflicts, we are describing the man or woman whose problems are almost glaring even to the casual observer. He or she never allows a relationship to develop beyond a certain point. On some level the active avoider is always gripped by conflict, and he or she is the one creating most of the turmoil within the relationship.

THE SEDUCTIVE POWER OF THE PROFOUNDLY UNCOMMITTED

Active runners are best described as profoundly uncommitted and highly elusive. Unable or unwilling to allow a relationship to evolve and grow, they are nonetheless highly appealing. Often the very partners whom they have hurt are most persuasive in defending and explaining their behavior. Because runners ultimately convey their ability to walk away from a relationship, their partners are often insecure. This means that within relationships those with active conflicts hold most of the power. Because they control most of the dynamics in their relationships, they are most likely the ones to be blamed for any failures.

A runner's moods control how often the couple sees each other, how often the couple has sex, and how quickly or slowly things progress. The person who is actively running away is setting most of the limits, boundaries, and controlling movement. This man or woman is most likely to be terrified of the *M*-word. In short, by avoiding commitment, he or she is typically identified with the kind of rejective behavior that frequently ends up being extraordinarily hurtful to their partners.

MIXED MESSAGES—THE TRADEMARK OF THE PERSON WHO IS ACTIVELY AVOIDING COMMITMENT

People who are actively running are not always running away. Quite the opposite. In fact active runners are frequently as busily engaged in chasing after new partners as they are in avoiding the ones they have already found. They are totally ambivalent and are acting out their ambivalence. It is the constant activity—looking for love/running from love—that is the trademark of the person with an active pattern. No matter how much these men and women claim to want an easy, uncomplicated love relationship, on some level they are always creating conflict. These men and women will usually be giving their partners a wide variety of intense messages that can best be described as mixed or double. For example:

- Very seductive/very rejective
- Very intimate/very withdrawn
- Very accepting/very critical
- Very tender/very hostile
- Very romantic/very distant
- Very sexually provocative/very sexually withholding
- Very giving/very cold

Within a relationship the classic active runner will move forward, then back, then forward, then back—until it becomes the traditional one step forward, two steps back.

This behavior is extraordinarily confusing at best, whether you are on the receiving end or you are the one acting it out.

Commitment conflict isn't just in your brain. It oozes out of every pore, coloring every moment, every thought, every action, every sentence.

Your touch says yes while your words say no; your body says stay away while your eyes say you care; your tears say you're sorry, but your behavior doesn't change; your smile says you're happy, but your posture says you're scared. There are always two messages; there is always a contradiction.

The thing to remember about commitment fear is that there is a problem committing to yes, but there is an equally overwhelming problem about committing to no. Commit to another person and you feel trapped, disengage from another and you worry about what happens if you change your mind. Either choice represents a limiting of options and a restriction of freedom. And maintaining options and a sense of freedom is what commitment conflict is all about.

ACTIVE COMMITMENT CONFLICTS—THE MALE-FEMALE DIFFERENCE

Until recently we presented active commitment fears almost exclusively in the context of a male behavior pattern. But as society has changed and women have achieved greater equality, they have been presented with scores of situations in which they too can act out their anxieties. Once, women who did not automatically want marriage were thought peculiar. Now many women are realizing that they can support themselves, raise their children, and function successfully in the world without male partners. The fear of being alone is no longer as threatening as it once was. For the first time women are beginning to act out commitment conflicts in ways that we traditionally associated only with men.

However, because of traditional dating patterns, men are still more likely to initiate the classic active pattern of pursuit/panic, and they are more likely to continue it for a longer period of time. The male in our society still assumes the rule of pursuer, and when a man is avoiding commitment, his avoidance is traditionally played out in that style. We have interviewed men in their seventies who were still actively running from partner to partner in the quest for the perfect mate.

The woman who is running away typically has a different style. This behavior might be more correctly described as accepting/rejecting. Here's the difference: a man with active conflicts may initially "come on strong." Then as his fears materialize, he stops pursuing and starts backing off.

A woman with active commitment conflicts substitutes acceptance for pursuit. Then as her fears take form, her behavior also changes. She may express her fears by being less available, less cooperative, and more rejective. Frequently her anxiety shows itself in the number and kinds of boundaries and/or barriers she erects in order to keep the relationship from developing. Sometimes she realizes that she is making a statement about her reluctance to commit. At other times, she truly believes that it is merely a statement about women's issues and that she is only trying to preserve her space and independence.

PATTERNS IN LOVE

If you are involved with someone with active commitment conflicts, you know that it is extraordinarily confusing at best. And if you have such conflicts, you know that you sometimes feel as though you are being ripped apart; any way you move, you feel pulled in the opposite direction.

The conflicting desires—the need to merge and the need to feel free—often create a very specific pattern in relationships. We describe this pattern as the pursuit/panic syndrome. This can be broken down into specific stages:

The Beginning: The Hard Sell (Fearless Pursuit)

At the beginning someone with active commitment conflicts usually appears to be actively seeking a partner. Responding to an intense attraction to someone new, an active avoider will do whatever is necessary to cement an involvement, frequently laying the groundwork for a passionate, complicated relationship. This is not a simple con job; he or she is usually sincere in expressing what is felt—at the moment.

The Middle: The Beginning of Fear

The "middle" begins at the very moment that the active runner starts to feel so secure in someone else's love that he or she begins *realistically* to consider commitment. This often coincides with an event that is associated with a deepening attachment. The decision whether or not to be part of this "event," be it something as simple as celebrating a holiday together or as complicated as the joint purchase of a home, brings on the first rumblings of panic. As fantasy recedes and reality starts to take its place, the active avoider starts placing boundaries and begins to express ambivalence and/or resentment.

The End: Running Scared

At this stage active runners are experiencing claustrophobic symptoms and are out of control in their need to put distance into the relationship. Even when there is still a great deal of feeling, passion, and bonding, they typically erect almost insurmountable boundaries. Because there are still a great many feelings involved, their behavior is confusing to everyone. It often ends up being very destructive to their partners.

The Bitter End: Escape

This is the point at which active runners must find a way out; overwhelmed by commitmentphobic anxiety and the need to get away, their behavior is frequently bizarre. Often they have formed overnight attachments to new lovers. Sometimes their behavior provokes the partner into ending the relationship. Sometimes they literally disappear. Other times the boundaries they have erected are so enormous that there is no way to get close.

KEEPING ALL OPTIONS OPEN—CAN'T SAY YES, WON'T SAY NO

For those with active commitment conflicts, maintaining options is always a need and a major priority. Carl, a twenty-eight-year-old engineer, describes how this need plays out in his life:

"I'm always concerned that something better is waiting for me around the corner. So I'm always trying to make decisions that will leave me open for that possibility. When I'm with a woman, I try to keep it so that if I decide I don't want the relationship anymore, it won't be a shock. In short I try to do nothing that closes any doors and I always make the decision that leaves me with the most options. I guess that pretty much sums up how I think about things."

Carl says that he hates acknowledging this about himself, because he would like to think of himself as someone who can make decisions, but he admits that options are very important in his life. He says that this is one of the reasons why he is never fully comfortable with a woman.

"While I want to be somewhat decisive and have direction, I don't want to have so much direction that I'm limiting myself to only one set of doors. Whenever I decide to date someone exclusively, that's a tough decision. I'm always saying to myself, *How am I going to feel if I see some gorgeous woman giving me the eye?* When I break up, it's impossible because I wonder whether I'll be able to get back with this woman if I change my mind."

Carl says that this attitude of maintaining options affects every single thing he does in life. "This is why I work for myself. I've had wonderful offers for jobs that I turned down because I didn't want to get stuck in a job that might dead-end in a few years.

"It even affects the way I behave in restaurants. I have a tough time choosing a restaurant and then I have a tough time ordering, although I don't make an obviously big deal about it. It's just that every decision is limiting. About appointments? If someone wants to make an appointment with me and they say how about ten o'clock, the first thing I think is, *Is that going to get in the way of something better that might come along?* I think, *Which choice will leave me the most options?* I hate when somebody says to me, 'What time is good for you?' That's hard."

When questioned about it, Carl said that yes, he did feel claustrophobic about decision making. Each yes or no made him feel stuck. This is particularly true of relationships.

"I worry about whether I get out of relationships because it's the right thing to do or because I feel claustrophobic, which I almost always do. Until I was about twenty-three, it was easy going out with women and it was easy making decisions about them, because everyone took it for granted that it was just kid stuff and temporary. But now the stakes have changed. It's a whole different ball game, and that can be paralyzing.

"In college I never felt as though I was closing doors. But now I'm trying to find a person I want to stick with. So I'm thinking, *If I go out with her and we start kissing, what will she think? Will she think we're all wrapped up?* And then next week if I meet somebody else, how will

I deal with that? Now every time I'm with a woman, I'm conscious of whether I'm moving too fast. I feel that I'm closing doors. If I decide to go out with someone, I'm closing the door a little bit. If we kiss at the end of the date, I'm closing the door a little more. We go out more, I'm closing it more. We got to bed, I'm closing it a lot. And if I fall in love with her? Slam! It's locked."

Listening to Carl's attitude, it's difficult to believe that he would ever allow a woman to cross his barriers. But in truth he has formed several intense romantic attachments with women who expected things to continue and who were very disappointed when they didn't. He says:

"Last week I went out to dinner with a friend, and I couldn't decide between the grilled fish, which came with a medley of vegetables, or the fish 'n' chips, which came with a salad. No substitutions allowed. My friend said, 'Don't worry, if you get the wrong one, you can always change your mind the next time.' But that wasn't a good enough answer. The same thing keeps happening with women. I want to pick the right one—the first time. With dinner, the second I ordered, I had regrets. I enjoyed the salad but was disappointed with the chips. So far with women, I've never chosen right either."

Carl echoes something that we have heard from many people. When the decisions are purely business related, he has no difficulty. It's only when it becomes personal that it creates a problem. He says:

"When it comes to business, I'm very decisive. Decisions that have personal consequences I have a hard time making. That ranges from career decisions to what movie I want to see. Decisions that are purely intellectual I can make at the drop of a hat."

FAULTFINDING—WHAT ACTIVE AVOIDERS TELL THEMSELVES

Even though they want to leave their options open, active avoiders have a clear-cut pattern of forming attachments. In order to maintain their freedom they have to be particularly skillful at dissolving these tender ties. How do they justify rejecting partners at whom they may have shamelessly thrown themselves? Once they are involved with someone, how are they able to extricate themselves?

Unable genuinely to confront their phobic reactions to commitment, such people usually throw at least part of the blame for failed relationships on their partner. When you can't explain to yourself why you can't make a long-term commitment, what you do is look for all the ways in which your partner is less than perfect. And everybody is less than perfect. It's easy to find faults. Every person has them; every relationship has them. But to the eye of someone who is experiencing commitment panic, faults in others, whether real or imagined, are magnified and used to justify conflicted behavior.

If an active avoider is frightened enough, nothing is sacred. Such a man or woman can find fault with your values, your religion, your intellect, your height, the way you are in the world, your hairline, your friends, your children, your pets, your job, your style, your habits, your house, your past, your future, your psyche, your mother, your clothes, your debts, your expenses, your small bank account, your large bank account, your profession, or your earning capacity.

It's interesting to note that the "fault" often concerns an intrinsic quality, one the active avoider must have known when the relationship began. We have interviewed a great many people, for example, who keep backing away from commitment because their partners are the "wrong" religion, something they were aware of all along.

This faultfinding has a definite goal: to create distance within a relationship. Those who are actively avoiding commitment have to find something "wrong" with their partners. It provides an easy excuse to end the relationship, should they need it. When someone is looking for an out, any excuse will do.

THE LANGUAGE OF FEAR

> *"My marriage was stifling. I would look out the window at the lawn and I would imagine bars between me and the rest of the world. I felt completely crushed."*
>
> —SHARON, thirty-two

You can frequently spot the men and women with active commitment issues simply by paying attention to the words they use. Often they articulate their fear. They may talk about their need for "freedom," "space," "air," or "room to breathe." When they describe past relationships, they may say that they felt "trapped," "stuck," "boxed in," "caught," "tied down," "stifled," "smothered," "choked," "crowded," or "suffocated."

They may complain about relationships in which they couldn't "breathe." After a relationship ends, they may say, "It's as if someone removed this tremendous weight from my body."

In an earlier era people like this referred to marriage as a "trap." This is the man who called his wife "the old ball and chain" or "the warden." This is the woman who referred to her husband as "my jailer" or "my keeper."

For active runners these words are not mere exaggerations or small jokes. They accurately portray the feelings of intense discomfort that occur whenever someone gets too close.

When people talk about serious commitment problems, they are usually describing someone like Brad. At thirty-nine Brad has been married once, broken one engagement, lived with two other women who hoped for marriage, and has had scores of other relationships he would describe as serious. In between his "serious" romances Brad has had more than a few experiences with women with whom he establishes emotionally intense romances that last only a short period of time. When ending relationships Brad has frequently fallen into the "Houdini" model. Without explanation he stops calling and/or neglects to return phone calls. He may even go so far as to unplug the phone altogether in order to avoid the woman who he *knows* is trying to reach him.

Listening to Brad's history, it is apparent that his romantic life is a mess. But when a woman meets him—when he talks about how he needs closeness and communication—even when she knows about his pattern with other women, she finds it difficult not to believe that with her everything will be different. He says:

"I would be a total jerk if I said that I didn't have a problem. Isn't it obvious? At this stage I've come to see what I do, and I'm trying to change. I really am. However, that doesn't mean that I want to get married in the near future. Maybe someday I'll feel differently, but for now I realize that I don't handle expectations well. I don't want to lead anyone on, so I try to tell women to watch out. I usually do this at the very beginning if I sense that they are getting involved, but to tell you the truth, more often than not they respond as if I were a flame and they were moths. I don't want to hurt anyone. I just don't want to get pressured into anything."

Brad, a dark-haired athletic-looking police detective, is a very attractive man. Articulate and funny, when he turns his full attention to a conversation, women get swept away by his enthusiasm and charm. When women are describing Brad's M.O., the words they are most likely to use are intense, romantic, obsessive, and devastating. They find it difficult to understand when he says he feels "pressured" because at the beginning he is the one doing all the pressuring and seems sincerely interested in a deeply connected relationship. Nonetheless Brad says that with almost every woman he has ever met he has ended up feeling as though someone was "closing in" on him.

"I think a lot of this has to do with the biological-clock stuff. The most self-sufficient-looking woman in the world eventually reaches the point where she starts thinking about baby clothes. And that's it. I don't want it. I know the way I am. If I had a child, I would want to be responsible to it. And I would end up doing time until the child was old enough to fend for itself."

Brad's last relationship was fairly typical. It was with a twenty-seven-year-old woman named Phoebe. He says:

"I met Phoebe while I was still married to Linda. . . . I think because of that I was more vulnerable. My marriage to Linda was a mistake, and it lasted a very short time—less than three years. She's a wonderful woman, but I never really loved her. She was, and is, my good friend. If I were going to have kids, I would have them with Linda. I could always count on her. In my line of work that's very important. But there was never any real passion. She's a nice woman, a schoolteacher. To be honest, she never turned me on. It's not her fault. She's very hurt right now, and disappointed. She needs to find someone who can give her what she deserves. I've told her that, but I don't think she's ready to hear it.

"With Phoebe, on the other hand, it was all passion, and I guess I got carried away and said a few things that Phoebe could interpret to mean that I was always going to be around. When I came down to earth, I realized that Phoebe and I had no real future. Don't get me wrong, she's a wonderful woman. I just don't feature settling down again so soon. I told her this, and I'm trying to restructure a new relationship with her—one where we don't see each other except maybe once a week, with no set schedule. That way maybe I can let her down easy."

Brad's work hours, which are unpredictable and erratic, give him a great deal of leeway in terms of scheduling his dates. He can go on a case for days at a time and basically be unreachable. Sometimes he only comes home to sleep, and there are times when he ends up not even doing that. He says he is aware that he uses this as an excuse for not staying in touch.

"If I decide I want to back away from a woman for a while, get a little space, it's very easy for me to do it. I have a dozen legitimate excuses. I do work long hours. I do get involved. I am unreachable. It's all real. Women get attracted to the cop stuff, but then they resent it. Normally, when I'm really into a woman, I check in regularly by phone. Then if I want to back away, I just check in less often. Sometimes I just don't call someone for a couple of weeks. Then when we get together, she's happy to see me. She's been worried, so she's not likely to go ballistic because I haven't been in touch, and I think I've made it clear that I can't always be accountable."

Even though Brad acknowledges that he manipulates his relationships according to his whims, he prides himself on his sensitivity to women's issues. He believes that one of the reasons women like him is that he is not afraid to express his emotions or to show his feelings. Therefore he is genuinely upset when the women in his life get angry. He doesn't know what to tell them because he is as confused as anyone by his behavior in relationships. He feels so many things. He doesn't like being alone, and he likes the feeling that there is a woman to whom he is connected, someone who cares whether or not he "checks in." But nonetheless he doesn't want her to expect anything or take anything for granted. He enjoys being intensely romantic with a woman, but when she responds by expecting the relationship to continue or wanting more of a commitment, he feels pressured.

When Brad hurts a woman, he feels tremendous guilt, but his behavior is hurtful by definition. He says that he wants things to be equal in his relationships, but because he has set cutoff points and makes all the decisions about how far things can progress, neither he nor his partner can ever get comfortable with each other.

If you look clearly at Brad's story, you see the subtext of a person out of control. He is running from one relationship to another while he perceives all women as potential threats to his freedom. His haphazard behavior can't help but create chaos in the lives of the women he meets, and that in turn creates more confusion in his own.

A WOMAN'S CONFLICT

Women Brad's age have rarely had the opportunity to act out their conflicts so blatantly. Typically they were told, and they believed, that they could do it all—have a career, family, marriage. If their lives have not evolved in this fashion, often they feel as though they have somehow failed. Although they may have some awareness that they are avoiding commitment, they may have fewer opportunities to date as they approach their forties. This obviously affects their perception of their own behavior.

At thirty-eight Regina readily acknowledges that she has run away from more than one relationship. However, it is only within the last year or two that Regina has started to see that she may have issues with commitment. An advertising copywriter, she has a job that has given her the economic security to buy a comfortable one-bedroom condo and a good automobile. Regina has nice clothes, she takes nice vacations, and she has recently started actively putting money aside in the hopes of someday purchasing a house of her own. When she graduated from high school, a woman like her would have been considered an anomaly. She says:

"I come from a real *Father Knows Best* kind of family; it was taken for granted that someday I would be married and have a family. I just didn't know when. The first time I walked away from the possibility of commitment was when I was in college. I went out with this guy who adored me, and everybody assumed we would marry, but I found myself becoming more and more dissatisfied.

He was a very reliable guy, a very nice guy, but I didn't think he was all that exciting, and I have to admit I gave him a very hard time. I would break dates and change plans. I would make excuses so I didn't have to see him all the time.

"My parents were very annoyed with me. They used to accuse me of being too much of a feminist to want a husband. I used to be a real flirt, and there were always guys calling. It made my mother furious at me—she told me that playing the field was going to ruin my chances. Looking back, I realize my fiancé was probably the best man I ever knew, but then I felt as though he was limiting me and that if I stayed with him, I would be missing something. I didn't want to lose him, but I wasn't ready. I wanted marriage, but I wanted it sometime in the future. Now he's happily married, with several children, and he makes tons of money. And yes, I'm sort of jealous."

Regina, who is extremely attractive, has had more than her share of romantic encounters. After breaking her engagement, she moved to a large city, where she says she had a "terrific time" dating a great many men. She says that nothing got very serious and nothing lasted more than a few months, which was fine with her. Then, when she was in her late twenties, she had another important relationship with a man.

"At first I thought this would be 'it.' He was very romantic and at the beginning he seemed perfect, like the Prince, you know. Then out of the blue I discovered that he was misleading me—he was still married. He wasn't living with his wife, but he had never bothered to get divorced, and he had no intention of doing so. I was devastated. Even though I started dating again right away, I was miserable.

"We didn't see each other for a year, and then I ran into him one day on the street, and everything was different. We moved in together, he went through with his divorce, and he asked me to marry him. This time I was the one holding back. The passion was gone for me. And I hated living with him. It felt very confining. I got depressed and nervous and I was hysterical all the time. I felt as though my life was hopeless. I would think about being with him for the rest of my life, and I would immediately start fantasizing about other men. I decided he wasn't smart enough for me and he didn't fit in with my friends. Anyway I guess you could say that I broke two engagements.

"Then for several years there was nobody special, which was okay with me. I complained about not meeting the right men. You know, the usual—the men I liked didn't like me enough to want to get married, and the ones who wanted to get serious, I wasn't that interested in for the long haul. I went out with a great many men, but never for more than a couple of months. For one reason or another I rejected almost all of them.

"Then three years ago I met Philip, who was everything my mother ever dreamed of—successful, bright, the right religion, stable. He was divorced—his wife had left him—and he wanted to get married again. Well, I fell head over heels, but it turned into a sort of a repeat performance of the man I had lived with. After a year or so I got less interested.

"I remember one day visiting his parents; his mother is a very quiet little person, and his father is very structured. Everything in his parents' house has a place, and nothing ever moves—except his mother, who doesn't sit still. . . . She runs around picking things up. She doesn't even let you finish drinking a cup of coffee before she is there whisking away your dish or cup. It's awful. Anyway we were coming back from there in the car and this in- credible anxiety attack swept over me. I imagined that I was Philip's mother, and he was his father. And I thought, that's what my life is going to be like—boring, with a place for everything. I found myself thinking that I understood why his wife had wanted to get away from him. I didn't want to spend my life with him, trapped in that car, going back and forth to places he wanted to be. I knew that if I married him, it would be a big mistake. There are a million women who would want him. I just wasn't one of them. I didn't end it right away—I sort of eased out of the rela- tionship. It was pretty painful at first. We still see each other, but just as friends."

Regina says that at the beginning of all her relationships she has been very receptive. But as they've progressed, she has put up boundaries and created barriers.

"I don't like feeling pressured. I would tell Philip that I loved him, but I wished he would leave me alone. I'm happiest and most comfortable when I'm in a steady relationship with someone whose love I can take for granted but who doesn't expect me to be available all the time. I don't want to be with someone *every* weekend—no matter how much I may care about him. I like being alone. I like being free to do whatever I want. I like the security of a committed relationship, but that doesn't mean that I want to spend all my spare time with someone. I try to make that clear to any man I date."

Regina says that within the last year she has given her relationship history a great deal of thought.

"Now it all starts to make a great deal of sense. The years when I should have been looking for someone who was marriage material, I was more interested in having a good time. Having a good time was my way of avoiding commitment. Then later, when I finally decided I was ready, even then I gravitated toward the wrong guys. And in Philip's case I probably could have had the whole shebang, but I didn't want it. People keep telling me to find an ordinary man and get serious, but I don't know how to do that. I'm not attracted to ordinary men.

"Of course as I get older, it gets more difficult to meet attractive men. Many of the men I'm attracted to now want younger women. When Philip and I split up, I had to face the fact that I might never get married. At least not in the traditional way I anticipated—house, kids, dog."

Regina says that her family, particularly her mother, is very upset that she hasn't settled down, and that she is bothered by this because it makes her feel like a failure.

"I'm more upset about upsetting my mother than I am about anything else. She keeps telling me that she's worried that I'll be growing old alone, but I don't know what I can do at this point. I admit that I've got conflicts. On the one hand, I'm frightened at the idea of never having anybody, but that doesn't mean that I want to settle into a boring marriage just to get married. That's even more frightening. Of course it's lonely having to do everything by yourself, and it gets harder and harder to find friends to do things with you. But if truth be told, I've never liked anyone enough to want to spend that much time with him *or her*. Male or female, I don't like feeling hemmed in by somebody else. I like my space, my privacy, my life.

"I have a friend who says I guard my territory, and I think

that's true. I don't know if I can change. I don't even know if I want to change. When I was young, I thought I would have to get married to get economic security. Now I don't think so anymore. I'm doing very well financially, and it might threaten some men. But the issue of children is different. I keep thinking that I still have a little time. Maybe I should try to adopt a child, but I don't honestly know if I could handle a child.

"I always say I'm lonely, but last week an old friend from college came and stayed with me for a weekend. Now, I really like this woman, and she was no trouble. But it made me crazy to have somebody else around. I couldn't take it. I was so happy to see her leave, it was frightening. Just two days with another human being —taking up closet space, using the phone, watching TV, making coffee—and I got very uncomfortable. I thought, *What would I do if I had a man with me all the time?* The idea is terrifying. Would I be any better with a child? I'm not sure. Being accountable to someone else has always made me angry. I guess you could say I like my freedom."

MARRIAGE JITTERS

Eric, a thirty-four-year-old market analyst, is currently experiencing anxiety attacks at the idea of formalizing an engagement. When he was younger, he expected that his anxieties about commitment would vanish when he met the right person, but so far that hasn't happened. Right now he is trying to decide whether or not he should marry Doreen, the thirty-two-year-old woman he has been dating for the last five years. He says:

"A year after Doreen and I met, I lost my job. She was wonderful about it. She cooked me dinner almost every night so I wouldn't go through all my money. She typed my résumé. She listened to my troubles. She understood when I said I couldn't afford to think about marriage until I was making a living. I guess my dependency gave her some kind of expectations, because now that I'm finally making a living, she thinks it's time for me to start acting like an adult and marry her. She's probably right, but I'm still not ready.

"I know I can't expect her to stay with me much longer without marriage, but if anything, that pressure is making it harder for me to make a decision to go ahead. Everyone is angry at me. My mother is furious because she likes Doreen and she thinks I'm treating her badly. Doreen's family keeps telling her to break it off. Her friends and my friends don't shut up about the marriage issue. The only one who understands is my father. He tells me to take my time and wait until I'm comfortable with my decision."

Recently Eric and Doreen have started seeing a counselor in the hope of ironing out a few problems that Eric says are keeping him from going ahead. The counselor was Doreen's idea, and Eric isn't sure that it's helping bring them any closer together. Because the counselor is very promarriage, Eric says when he leaves the sessions, he feels too much like the bad guy. In addition he feels this process is pointing out to him all the ways in which he and Doreen are different.

"I only want to get married once, and frankly I'm not sure this is it. I would never tell her that. She's very kind, very loving, and would make a great wife, I'm sure. But in some ways she's limited. She doesn't really understand the kind of work pressure I'm under. And besides, she'll want a baby, and that presents a whole series of different problems. I'm only thirty-four years old. I'm not in any rush. Frankly if I don't have a kid for another five years, that's just fine. But that's not fine for Doreen."

In counseling, Doreen agreed to stop pressuring Eric for a commitment and to concentrate on improving the relationship. But they are still having problems because Eric is unwilling to make *any* long-range plans. Last weekend Eric and Doreen had a terrible fight about a vacation that Doreen wants to plan for next spring. To Doreen, Eric's reluctance to make a commitment to the vacation represents Eric's refusal to make any kind of commitment. Eric says:

"I hate to admit it, but she may be right. If I can't spend two weeks with her, how can I think about spending the rest of my life with her? I don't want to plan a vacation, because I think if I do, she'll expect even more and more, and we'll end up right back where we started. I need real space, real time. Sometimes I think that if I just had a year or so to date lots of women, I would get over this and marry Doreen. I was still pretty young when Doreen and I met. Maybe I would outgrow these needs. I can't be sure."

The counselor feels that there are many issues behind Eric's conflict. Eric sees that it is all coming to a head, and he's frightened about losing the relationship and tremendously sad, but not as frightened and sad as he is about losing his freedom. He also wonders whether his doubts mean that Doreen isn't the right woman for him. He is convinced that if she were, he would be the first person in line at the altar.

POSTCOMMITMENT ANXIETY

Over the years we have heard a great deal about premarital commitmentphobia, and the specter of the terrified groom is practically a cartoon character. What we hear less about is the man or woman who starts having claustrophobic responses to marriage *after* the ceremony. We've spoken to a fair number of women who describe this kind of reaction. Alicia is one of them.

Alicia, a forty-one-year-old designer, has been married for three years. She says that living with her husband is making her intensely uncomfortable, and she doesn't know what to do about it. Although she always wanted to get married, once she did, she started to get depressed within the first three weeks.

"All I know is that I became very anxious, nervous, and uptight after I got married. I had never shared an apartment with anyone before. When my husband and I were going out, we were always in each other's apartments, but there were times when he went home or I went home. There was enough time by myself to wash my hair, do my nails, read my magazines, watch television. Those times I had my apartment to myself. Now he's around all the time, and I don't like it. It's not my husband. I love him, I think. But I'm miserably unhappy. What I can't stand is the feeling of someone closing in on me. I feel as if I can't get away from him. It's almost as though he is trying to get into my head. I can't even think without his doing something that interrupts me. I hate it. I can't believe that I wanted to get married. This is awful!"

Alicia says that although she is looking for solutions to her predicament, she finds herself becoming depressed at the idea that she is going to have to stay married for the rest of her life.

"When I think that this is it, I become very depressed. I don't know what I expected, but I didn't expect this. There are too few highs in marriage. I love the highs of getting ready for a date, for example. I love the passion of a new relationship. Of course I'm not sure if the joys of being single are worth the lows of being alone, but at least when you're alone, you have something to look forward to. You have the hope that you're going to meet someone exciting or do something wonderful. In marriage you know that you're stuck with the same old person day in and day out. I never imagined that I would get to feel this way. I keep hoping that these feelings will go away, but it doesn't seem to be happening. I would leave, but I'm scared I'll get depressed when I'm alone.

"My mother and my friends tell me that I'll get used to this, and that if we had a larger apartment or a big house, I would feel better. Maybe that's the solution. But suppose it's not?"

SINGLE AND LIKING IT

Over the past few years we've received a fair number of letters from men saying that they had been "killed" in relationships with young women who they feel are lacking what they perceive to be a "normal" desire to get married and start a family. Many men have been so conditioned to believe in the stereotype of a woman who is sitting on her hope chest waiting for the prince that they don't know quite how to react when women behave differently.

We have been interviewing men and women about commitment issues for about eight years, and when we started talking to people about this, we rarely met women who were *actively* and consciously avoiding commitment. Lately, however, more and more women—particularly women in their twenties—tell us that's precisely what they are doing. These younger women have come of age in a world that is much more accepting of this kind of preference. The dreaded myth of the "old maid" has been replaced by the enviable life-style of a single woman with a large range of options and choices.

Dawn, a twenty-six-year-old who currently lives in Florida, is such a woman. She says:

"My friends tease me about being commitmentphobic, because most of them are at the stage where they are getting married or engaged, and it is the farthest thing from my mind. I want to travel. I want to live in different places, I want to see the world, and I want to do this alone. I don't want to have somebody to take care of me, and I don't want to take care of or wait for anybody else."

Wanting to be alone has nothing to do with Dawn's need to date or be involved with men. She describes herself as a terrible flirt and speculates that her attitude attracts a great many men.

"I date a great deal, and I try to find men I couldn't form a commitment with. I don't want to go out with anyone who had all the things that are important to me because I don't want to have to think about getting married.

"My problem is that my attitude seems to attract too many men. Every guy I date wants a committed relationship. I'm completely honest about my attitude. I start out on date one, telling them how I'm planning to travel, how I'm not looking for a relationship. I even joke about being commitmentphobic. Either they're stupid or they don't take me seriously."

Dawn says she hates it when the men she meets "smother" her by calling on a daily basis or asking her out too many times.

"This week was a great example. One guy I had been out with and really liked called me and asked me out several times. I was busy, legitimately busy, every time. So he calls me and starts hassling me about why I haven't called him, why I'm not reciprocating. I told him that my priorities were my priorities. I was honest—I told him that I wanted to see him, but that other things came first. He was a classic example of somebody who wants to pursue the relationship more than I do. I've broken it off with just about every man I've been with because they made me feel smothered or tried to make me feel guilty.

"Yesterday this other guy called and said to me, 'How's your hand?' I said, 'Fine, why?' He said, 'I figured it must be sore—you haven't been able to return my phone calls.' I told him I was busy.

"I don't expect to always feel this way, but right now relationships make me feel claustrophobic and anxious. If a guy so much as sends me flowers, I get a stomachache. I wonder what he expects of me. It makes me queasy. A lot of guys send me flowers, and I hate it."

Despite her current feelings Dawn is sure she will get married someday. She has had two long-term relationships, and she describes them both as mostly positive experiences. She ended both of them. Marriage was "vaguely" discussed with these two men, but Dawn feels that the conversations were unrealistic.

"I think marriage is a great institution. My parents are happily married. . . . I love my family. I think it's all great. Just not for me, not now. I'm not sure about kids. I love kids, but most of my life I thought I didn't want them. But now I'm not sure. Maybe someday it will be important to me to have children, so I don't want to rule out the possibility. If I did have a family, I wouldn't do what my mom did and stay home to raise them, though. I wouldn't ever want to do that. I would love to be with a man who did that."

Although Dawn says career is very important to her, she realizes that she isn't following a career path right now.

"I had been traveling for the last couple of years, and I came home and had bills, so I took a job. I'm planning to start traveling again probably later this year. I'm also thinking of the Peace Corps. It bothers me somewhat that I'm not on a straight career path. But I think I can wait five more years to settle on a direction. I think ultimately it really won't matter."

Dawn says that among her friends who have married, all have ended up with men that she couldn't imagine spending time with.

"My married friends right now have life-styles that are not enviable. I get on the phone with one of them, and I'm talking a mile a minute about the million of things that have happened to me in the last month. I have a fun life . . . a nonstop life, an interesting life. My friends say things like, 'Oh, we went for a walk, and then we had a barbecue.' They never have any money because they are all saving to buy houses. They can never go shopping. They don't do anything. And the men they've married! I know they love them and all, and some of them are nice guys. But not one of them have I ever had a really intense conversation with. I like intensity. They're nice people, and good people, but I guess I want somebody more exciting. I prefer men who are challenging. If they're easy, they take all the fun out of it."

Dawn says that men don't understand how she feels, and frequently they seem quite hurt when she ends things.

"They call and call. It's like they think I'm going to say, 'Okay, you've whined so much, I'm going to be your girlfriend.' I tried to be friends with one man after we broke up, but he refused because he said he loved me too much to be friends. After a year of not seeing him, we went out for coffee, and it was the same old thing."

Dawn says that she tries not to plan ahead because she has a tendency to cancel things. She owns very little in the way of furniture or equipment and prefers to travel light.

"It's a joke. I tell people I don't want anything I can't pack in a suitcase. People keep buying me things like juicers and toasters. One of my friends got me a microwave saying I needed something to make me a little less mobile."

Many of the women we interviewed for this book referred to their need for their own space. Echoing Virginia Woolf, they talked about how much they would always want a room of their own. Dawn said:

"Yes, I have space issues. I need a lot of space. I think even if I were married and living with someone, I would want my own room. Just a place where I can have the things I like. The things that are all mine. A place to go and listen to my own music and where everybody would leave me alone. That's always going to be important to me."

Dawn is a perfect example of a contemporary woman with commitment issues, but she is following in a tradition that was established by men of an older age group.

"I'VE MET MY MATCH"

> *"I always knew someday I would meet the 'right woman.' Well, I think I have, but I don't know if it's chemistry or pathology."*
>
> —JACK

Remember in the comics when a villain, bent on gaining power over the superhero, tries to create someone with equally superior abilities, someone capable of destroying the hero? When two people with strong, active commitment conflicts get together, their relationship has all the earmarks of a superhuman struggle, sort of a romantic clash of the titans.

At fifty-six Jack, who has a long history of commitmentphobic behavior, has fallen in love with Stephanie, a thirty-four-year-old woman who has no interest in marriage or commitment of any kind. Everyone always helped Jack maintain his belief that once he met the "right woman," he would change.

As far as he's concerned, Stephanie is the right woman, but Stephanie, who feels very strongly about maintaining her own space, limits the amount of time she wants to give to the relationship. This is a shock to Jack's system, because in all of his earlier relationships he was the one who established boundaries and limitations. Now that the tables are turned, he doesn't know what to do. He says:

"All of my life I was perceived as being the one with commitment problems. In my early twenties most of the women I dated wanted to have children and be supported. I would see my friends get married, and I thought they were being trapped into the breadwinner category. It seemed to me that my resistance to marriage and commitment was a perfectly intelligent response to an unfair situation. After all, who wanted to sign on for a big house in the suburbs and a heart attack?

"Anyway, when I was twenty-seven, I met this woman who made more money than I did. She was a doctor. I thought, *Hot dog, I don't have to worry about supporting her. She's never going to give up her career.* She was a beautiful, bright woman, but even so, I grew to hate her. I didn't understand why. All I knew was that I didn't want to be around her. I was like that woman in the movie *War of the Roses.* I hated the way she ate, hated the way she dressed, hated it if she put on two pounds. In retrospect I was despicable, and I have a lot of guilt around it. At the time I blamed my attitude on the fact that she was domineering. In retrospect she really wasn't domineering, she was just a strong, honest, outspoken woman—everything I had thought I wanted."

This marriage finally fell apart because Jack's wife became insistent on having a child. This was not part of his game plan, and he refused to go along with it.

"My wife put up with my criticism, my moodiness, my sulking. I was also having a very discreet affair with a woman, also married, and I wasn't very interested in sex. My wife put up with that. But she couldn't put up with my refusal to have children. She kicked me out."

Jack says that immediately after the marriage ended, he felt two separate and distinct emotions. On the one hand he missed his wife, who had been his "best friend." On the other he felt like a kid in the candy store.

"When I got divorced in the early seventies, the sexual revolution was in full swing. Everything had changed. Women were prepared to go to bed with you at the drop of a hat. I became like a crazy man. I wanted to try everything and everybody. I got myself this terrific apartment, and I was thrilled by the freedom."

But as happy as Jack was with his single state, he couldn't resist getting involved with a woman.

"Within months of the divorce, I had become enmeshed with a woman who was in a different cycle. She was thirty and had never married. We went together for five years, during which time we must have fought and made up a hundred times. She wanted more from me than I wanted to give. She wanted marriage. To get me jealous, she would threaten to date other people, an idea that didn't thrill me. But I still didn't want to make a commitment to her.

"My attitude hurt her very much. I understand that. In the meantime I couldn't stop seeing other women. There were too many of them . . . running around in short little skirts. Everybody was having a grand time. I wanted to be part of that. And I was. I told myself that my behavior was understandable. I had been married for so many years that I deserved this period of total freedom. I wanted to have my cake and eat it, too, because I didn't want to give up my girlfriend.

"One day she issued one ultimatum too many, and we split up. Then I did something very stupid. No sooner had we broken up than I met somebody else. I knew this new woman ten days, and I proposed. And we got married three months later. I think I had to prove to myself that I *could* make a commitment. It made no sense whatsoever, and it was a disaster.

"My second wife didn't know what happened. One day I was telling her that I was madly in love, and we had to get married, the next I was telling her that we had to get divorced."

Jack says that he then compounded the problem by calling up his ex-girlfriend, who had been devastated by his marriage.

"I told her that I had to see her. And for at least a month I went to see her a couple of times a week. It made the whole thing even crazier. Finally she exploded and called my wife. My wife exploded and told me to get my act together. The end result is that I ended up on the street again."

This time Jack says that he learned his lesson. He knew that when he met a woman, he often said things he didn't mean and made promises he couldn't keep; before he knew it, he was in yet another relationship, with yet more expectations. He didn't want that to happen anymore, so he devised a plan.

"From that day forward I vowed I would never again sweet-talk a woman into anything. I would say nothing that gave anyone any expectations. I would tell every woman up front that I was never, ever, ever going to get into another committed relationship. And that's what I did, and that worked fine. I had a couple of arrangements during this time, but nobody got hurt.

"Then this year I met Stephanie, who is really something else again. She was also married when she was in her early twenties, and that was enough for her. She says she is never going to let anybody get that close. I realize she's had difficult experiences, but I'm nothing like her ex-husband. We wouldn't have the same problems. But she doesn't care what I say, she enjoys her life for what it is and she wants to keep it that way."

Jack says that he is also worried that Stephanie might have at least as big a roaming eye as he used to have.

"She hasn't actually said she wants to date other people, but she's sort of hinting at it. When we met, I was very clear that I thought we should both see other people, but now I think it's time to give that up. In fact I haven't been out with anybody else in a long time, so that's reflecting what's actually taking place. If Stephanie is seeing someone, I don't know when she's doing it— although of course I have no way of knowing. She has told me in no uncertain terms that she can't make any promises about fidelity. She says that what will be, will be, and that's good enough for her. I've been with enough women to realize that sex itself is never that different. I've seen enough bodies. It's time to settle down."

Jack feels his age contributes to what is going on. At one time he had no difficulty in maintaining several sexual liaisons at the same time. Now he doubts that he has the energy to do this. He's scared that Stephanie is still young enough to want variety in the same way that he once did. And he worries that Stephanie will eventually prefer a man closer to her own age.

"I think I'm the best man she could find. I can make her life better in all ways. I find myself saying the things to her that were once said to me about love and togetherness. I remember one woman I went out with years ago who always used to stare at me, and I would ask her why she did that. She'd say, 'I'm trying to figure out what's going on inside your head.' Well, that's what I do with Stephanie. I'm trying to understand what she wants and give it to her. I make a good living, and we could have a nice life. Her child is a teenager already, so we could travel, do things. Stephanie doesn't want it. She says I keep spoiling things—why can't I just leave things the way they are?

"A few weeks ago it was her birthday, and she wanted to have dinner with a girlfriend. It's a ritual with her. Even so I don't understand why she wouldn't want me to join them after dinner. I felt very excluded. The same thing happened last Thanksgiving. She went off to dinner with her mother and child, and she didn't want me along. Sometimes she makes me feel like a kid with his nose against the window. And when Stephanie makes her mind up about something, it's nonnegotiable. For example she doesn't want me to just drop in on her. And I can't assume that I'm going to be with her on weekends. I've got to ask every damn time. So I'm caught up in this dynamic of when will she let me see her again?

"This is the first time in my life that I haven't wanted to hold back with a woman. I tell Stephanie not to hold back, not to be afraid. It's fun to relax and give. It's ironic that I've changed, that I feel free enough to love wholeheartedly and I meet someone who is holding back."

HAS JACK CHANGED?

Jack probably hasn't changed that much. But times have changed, and women have changed. Stephanie, who is significantly younger than Jack, has a different agenda than the women he used to date. For the first time in his life he is in a relationship in which he isn't holding most of the power. Stephanie's commitment issues are so strong that they are effectively canceling out his own. Of course Jack feels able to love for the first time. Knowing that no one is about to tie him down leaves him free to open his heart and feel as enamored and passionate as he wishes. Stephanie will never call him on it because she has more issues with commitment than he does.

Jack's pattern with Stephanie points up something that we have seen a great many times. Often a man or woman with a pattern of active commitment conflicts will meet someone who has no desire whatsoever to settle down permanently. Then instead of being the partner who is running away from love, he or she takes on the role of passive avoider.

CHAPTER FOUR

Victims and Nice Guys—
Passive Commitment Conflicts

"There is something about me that seems to attract married men. I wish I could change it."

—CLAUDIA, thirty-four

"Every woman I meet is still in love with her old boyfriend. What am I supposed to do about that?"

—JOEL, twenty-nine

"For years all I did was focus on the men I was with and their problems. Every single one had a commitment problem. Then one day I woke up and said, You know what, I have a problem too. *It all became crystal clear to me that if a woman keeps finding herself involved with men who are running away from commitment, then she is running away too."*

—CORETTA, thirty-nine

Some people look as though they are able to commit. In fact, they may even appear obsessed with getting a commitment. Overwhelmingly focused on love and loving, they claim to feel no fear and maintain that they are longing for a permanent relationship. But even though they are capable of falling head over heels in love and of swearing undying devotion, they do so with people who are ultimately unable or unwilling to reciprocate.

If you are acting out your commitment conflicts in a passive fashion, it's true that you may not be running away from a permanent relationship. In all likelihood you are instead pursuing someone else who is. Passive avoiders are rarely in relationships in which their love is returned in kind. That's what it means to have passive commitment conflicts.

How do you know if you are passively avoiding commitment? The best way to tell is by looking at the people to whom you are attracted. Do they want commitments? Do they share your feelings? Are they appropriate? Are they available? Or are they usually dancing off in the opposite direction? Let's face it, it's very "safe" to say you want permanency if everyone you get involved with is incapable of responding in kind.

Because they are often so emotionally overwrought trying to "work out" unworkable love situations, men and women with passive commitment issues are rarely in touch with their own fears. Instead their fears remain hidden, even from themselves.

Allison, a thirty-six-year-old writer, is one such person. At the moment Allison's life is fairly well taken up by her sessions with her therapist and the codependency meetings that she recently started to attend in the Los Angeles area. Allison, who has a fourteen-year-old son, is trying to recover from the depression caused by the breakup of her relationship with Josh, thirty-four, also a writer. As Allison puts it:

"Josh was the classic 'commitmentphobic.' He had lived with a couple of women before he met me, but he had never been able to make a commitment. On his first date he told me all about himself —how he had never been faithful and how he had never been able to stay in one place for very long. I guess I knew it all up front, but I didn't really pay attention to much of it.

"For one thing Josh had a drinking problem that he had worked through, and I thought this meant that he would be able to work other things out as well. Then the sex between us was so good . . . that was the thing about him—he always wanted to make love—and he acted like he was in love with me. He told me I was beautiful and that we would grow old together; he said we would shock people by making love in the senior center.

"Josh is very beautiful. He's tall and thin with elegant hands and a great neck. I always loved his clothes—the way he wore them. I was crazy about him—I am still crazy about him, and I can't seem to forget about him, even though I know he is poison.

Even so I have all these daydreams that he is sitting in my living room and we're still together."

Allison and Josh met in early May; by Memorial Day he was talking about marriage. When July came around, Allison's son went off to camp, and Allison, even though it upset her work schedule, moved into the apartment Josh was subletting near the water. Allison saw this as a perfect opportunity to solidify the relationship. Allison says:

"He became very dependent on me. He was working on a new script, and we sort of revolved our schedule around his work. I tried to be a writer's perfect wife—I did all the shopping and cleaning and cooking—so he could have the time to concentrate and finish. It was a mistake, and I don't think he appreciated it. In fact I think he began to resent it, although I didn't 'get it' at the time. He also had all these quirky rules about his things—what could be moved, what couldn't. Even though he seemed dependent, he didn't always seem happy to have me there. I probably should have called him on it, but I was afraid."

By the end of the summer, when Allison had to move back into her own apartment, things were no longer as idyllic. When they would see each other, Josh was as romantic and passionate as always, but he was different. Allison believed that there were realistic reasons for this.

"Because my son was in my apartment, Josh could only sleep over on weekends. So when we started to have sex less frequently, it seemed normal within the context of everything else that was going on. He was also slightly withdrawn. But he said he always got this way when he had to finish a script and that I should just ignore him. Easier said than done of course. Then he started forgetting to call, and he would always be late. One day we had a date, and he didn't show up. I got hysterical, and I refused to see him for a couple of weeks. Then when I did, he had bought me a book of poetry and was very contrite, and we patched things up again.

"In the meantime, you have to understand, this relationship took up my life. I was either waiting for him to call, waiting for him to arrive, or waiting for him to relieve my anxiety. When we were together, though, he was the same as always. He would talk to me for hours at a time about what he was working on, about his problems, about his life, about his parents, about his feelings. It went on and on."

Allison says she concentrated a great deal of effort in trying to prove to Josh what a positive force she was in his life. But her own work got neglected because she was often too anxious to concentrate. He had told her that he was having such a hard time working that he needed to unplug his phone. This meant that Allison could no longer call him. Also the sex had changed. He would still sleep over at Allison's apartment, but they wouldn't have sex. She began to worry that perhaps the two-year age difference was affecting her desirability.

"I really began to get crazy that I had wrinkles or sags, and I started working out every day. It was all I could think of. When Josh was finally finished with his script, he said he was exhausted. I had been reading and commenting on the script all along, so I offered to copyedit it. It was the week before Christmas. I took the script to work on, and when I was finished, I tried to call Josh. There was no answer. There was no answer for three days. Once again I got hysterical.

"It turns out that, for this whole time, he had been going out with another woman. She lived right next door. I had actually seen the two of them together in the summer. I just didn't put two and two together. Then he didn't show up on Christmas Eve, and when he came over on Christmas Day to bring me a present, I exploded. That's when it all came to a head, and he told me about this other woman. Fortunately my son was at his father's, because I was a basket case. I cried and cried and cried. So did Josh. He apologized, he promised it would all change, he promised he would work his problems out, and he promised we would be together.

"He goes to group, and it turns out that he had discussed everything that was going on, and they were very hard on him. They had already pointed out how manipulative and unfair he had been. There was nothing I could say that he didn't already know.

"To make a long story short, he promised he would stop seeing the other woman, but he never did. I didn't believe that he could lie to me like that, but he did. We went through another couple of months of getting together and getting apart, and finally we both said enough is enough. It's now June, and I can't seem to resolve my feelings. He wants to be friends, but I can't do it. He and the other woman have found an apartment together, and it's killing me. I can't figure out what happened. We ran into each other one day, and we both started to hyperventilate. I know he still has feelings for me. I can't believe this has happened. The truth is that as angry as I am at him, I would take him back in a minute. I just miss him so much."

When we first heard this story, we were immediately sympathetic to Allison. She was so well intentioned in this relationship, and she tried so hard to make Josh happy, it's natural to want to run to her defense. Josh is a creep, no two ways about it. But just because Josh is a creep doesn't mean that Allison doesn't have a problem. Consider all the things she knew about him from the very first—his attitude toward fidelity, his attitude toward permanency of any kind, his attitude toward romantic commitment. Yet Allison chose to continue without being appropriately cautious and self-protective. Why would she do this? As a single parent the last thing she needs in her life is more instability.

Why did she move into his apartment so early in the relationship? Why did she expose herself to the potential for this kind of turmoil? Once he started to show signs of withdrawing, placing barriers in her path, why didn't she notice? Why is she, even now, prepared to "take him back" if he asks? Why did she have so few appropriate reactions and so many wrong ones?

THE WRONG RESPONSE

Passive avoidance reveals itself in a series of inappropriate responses. Where those who are actively avoiding commitment are busily engaged in running away and setting limits on their love, passive avoiders seem to do everything they can to bond themselves to their love objects. But consider the people they choose to focus their feelings on. No wonder they have no sense of becoming "trapped" in a permanent union.

Greg, a thirty-four-year-old golf pro, describes one of his more painful relationship experiences:

"No matter how much I recognized her problems, no matter how twisted the situation got, no matter how clear I was about the potential downside, I was incapable of extricating myself. I felt as though we were somehow predestined to be together. I felt that I had no choice but to go through the experience—to play it out. To me there was no way around it. And nothing anyone said or did could help me."

The affair Greg is talking about is one he recently had with Ava, his employer's wife. Ava is eight years older than Greg, significantly wealthier, and amazingly cynical about her extramarital romances. When Greg met her and she started flirting with him, every ounce of good sense he had told him to stay away. Instead he catapulted toward her, falling madly in love, in the process jeopardizing not only his emotional well-being but also his job. This type of behavior is typical of Greg, who has a history of getting involved with inappropriate partners. It is his way of avoiding commitment.

If, like Greg, you are passively avoiding commitment, here are some of the ways in which your responses are guaranteeing you a safe way to avoid a committed relationship:

- *You are drawn to inappropriate or unavailable partners.*

This is the most efficient way of avoiding commitment. When someone with passive commitment issues falls in love, it is almost always with someone who is emotionally, physically, or circumstantially unavailable. Having found this person, who typically has even more serious problems with commitment, the passive avoider is free to go all out in an attempt to win an unattainable prize.

- *You make inappropriate commitments and are too quickly won over.*

It's certainly normal to be flattered by the interest of someone new. But men and women with passive commitment conflicts are more than just flattered. They can have an all-encompassing romantic response to someone they barely know. It's important to note here that this response is not only sexual—it is also profoundly emotional. Describing their reactions, passive avoiders typically use words such as *soul mate, karma,* or *fate.* These intense responses can keep someone tied up in romantic fantasies for an extraordinarily long period of time.

• *Your responses are so strong that you seem to lose all ability to establish reasonable boundaries; this is particularly true when your love object is busily placing barriers in your path.*

Instead of merely opening yourself up to the possibility of slowly building a stable relationship, you immediately position yourself for a complete merger. This means that you are physically available, sexually available, and emotionally available for any and all demands that your love object makes. Without doing anything concrete to prove his or her value to you, the other person becomes thoroughly incorporated into your fantasies, and the hold on you becomes so intense that it seems as though it has a life of its own.

The degree to which you allow your boundaries to fall is often in direct proportion to the number and types of barriers being placed in your path. This is a very important characteristic of those whose commitment conflicts are acted out passively.

If, as is often the case, the object of your passion needs distance and is made uncomfortable—or actually phobic—by the expectations of others, then your attitude and behavior serve to intensify his or her fears. Instead of realizing this and backing off, you almost take pride in your power to evoke such strong responses.

• *You have inappropriate responses to negative information.*

He's married. . . . "So what, that could change tomorrow."

She's moving to Japan. . . . "Who cares, we'll write."

He's got twelve children. . . . "It's a small adjustment, that's all."

She has overwhelming medical problems and no health insurance. . . . "What's the problem? I'll get a second job."

He's been divorced three times and has a substance-abuse problem. . . . "Poor guy, it must have been those first three wives."

She's chronically promiscuous. . . . "Not an issue now that she's going to be mine."

He's completely unfaithful, singularly untruthful, and totally disreputable. . . . "Nobody's perfect, he just needs to get more in touch with his feelings."

He never speaks. . . . "Not to worry, I don't need that much attention."

We could go on endlessly with the exercise. The fact is that once someone with passive commitment conflicts is turned on by an inappropriate or unavailable partner, nothing seems to be able to quench that ardor. Totally in love and totally out of touch, they will do whatever is necessary to protect their interest in impossible dreams.

- *When rejected by your love interest, you typically have inappropriate responses to the pain.*

No one enjoys rejection, and few of us handle it well. But people who are passively avoiding commitment seem to have particularly unfortunate responses. Instead of looking for a more requited love, passive avoiders frequently fall into a mode of living that can best be described as round-the-clock yearning. Thus they have a full-time excuse to stay away from real relationships, favoring fantasy and dreams about what could have been. Clearly unhappy and miserable in the "yearning" state, they are nonetheless so totally engaged by their nonrelationships that they are often incapable of looking elsewhere. Time and again, for reasons they don't understand, they find themselves playing out the role of victim, and they don't know how to change this.

"WHAT SHOULD I DO?"—LOOKING FOR ADVICE

After the publication of our first book, *Men Who Can't Love*, we found ourselves inundated with letters and phone calls from women who wanted to know what they could do to resolve their relationships with the commitmentphobic men with whom they were involved. The only advice we could give them was advice that, for the most part, they didn't want to hear. When the relationships were self-destructive, as they usually were, we told them to pull away, take care of themselves, develop their own sense of self-worth, and become more self-protective in the future. We told them that pursuing someone who is running away almost always fails. We told them that when a man feared commitment, he genuinely felt a sense of being trapped; and engulfing him with more love or understanding or acceptance rarely worked.

Just about all of the women we spoke to ultimately extricated themselves from the feelings that were connecting them to hopeless situations. But then a fair number of the same women got in touch with us to describe still other hopeless situations with still other reluctant partners. It was these women, most of them loving, intelligent, perceptive, and sensitive, who brought us face-to-face with what it means to act out our commitment issues in a passive fashion.

Unlike many of their actively commitmentphobic partners, these women could not be faulted for causing pain or unhappiness. They were never rejective or withholding. They placed no unreasonable barriers between themselves and those they cared about. All they did was continue to fall in love with men who were walking disasters as far as the potential for commitment was concerned. And they were unable to see the pattern in their own behavior. The defense they often used, and one that, we must admit, we helped them use, was that men are wary of commitment and that as women they were unwitting victims.

At about the same time we began hearing from men who had read the book. They described the way they, too, had been hurt by women who behaved according to the seductive/rejective pattern described in the book. Each of them typically explained away the problem by saying that "women don't appreciate a nice guy."

These men sounded just like the women. Clearly both sexes had histories indicating that they were infinitely more attracted to partners who were running away than to those who were available.

A HISTORY OF ROMANTIC PAIN

It doesn't take an Einstein to know that a pattern of finding the wrong partners leads to a great deal of unhappiness. Because they are often depressed and lonely, passive avoiders find it difficult to believe that their own actions contribute to the distress in their lives. The vast majority of these men and women are capable and well-intentioned. They are often high achievers and successful at their work; they don't like to think of themselves as self-destructive or masochistic. Yet in almost every instance, when you look at the partners they choose, it seems inconceivable that they couldn't have predicted the outcome.

To better understand how devastating a long history of passive avoidance can be, let's take a look at Andrea, a thirty-six-year-old fabric designer who has a clear pattern of passively avoiding commitment.

Andrea, a tall pretty redhead, tells everyone she meets that she wants to get married. In fact she spends at least an hour every day talking about this, either to her friends or to her mother. She says that the only thing missing from her life is a committed love relationship. People who meet her don't understand why she doesn't have one. Andrea is artistic, charming, smart, feminine, and highly intuitive, and it seems difficult to believe that she hasn't been able to find what she says she wants.

Her history offers some insight into her difficulties. Right after college while her friends were getting engaged and picking out silverware patterns, Andrea—who thought all of this was very provincial and dull—met and fell in love with a young man who was on a brief visit to this country. After several highly charged dates he returned to his native France, promising to write and promising to return someday. He was no sooner in the air than Andrea began to write him the first of hundreds of long, intense letters. She says:

"The letters were my only way of staying in touch. I wanted him to know who I was and what I felt and believed in. I wrote to him steadily for about six months. He would also write, but not as frequently—perhaps one letter or a postcard every couple of weeks."

Andrea excused his less-than-enthusiastic correspondence by telling herself that because English was his second language, he was not very good at expressing himself. What she found more difficult to excuse was the primary barrier to their ever getting together—his family's attitude.

"I was very much in love with him, and I think he was with me also, but it wasn't very simple. He was Catholic, and his family was opposed to the relationship. We talked, in our letters, about getting together, and finally I went to France. His family wasn't very nice to me, and he had changed. He was very withholding."

Despite the cool reception she received, Andrea continued to hold out hopes for this relationship for close to two years. During this entire period, while she was in her mid-twenties, Andrea went out on no other dates and made no attempts whatsoever to meet anyone else. In other words she was behaving like the typical wife, only without a husband. She stayed home much of the time reading; she took a course in European cuisine so that she would be able to cook for her beloved when they finally got together. She also took several courses in French literature and tried to learn to play the piano. Her career flourished, and most of her pleasure came from her work and her rich fantasy life. During this period Andrea met at least one other man who had an interest in her. She toyed with the idea of seeing him, but decided, even though she found him attractive, that she didn't want to be unfaithful, in spirit or in deed, to the man five thousand miles away.

After she recovered from this infatuation, Andrea vowed never again to fall for someone who didn't live on the same continent. And she didn't. Instead she fell in love with someone who worked in the same industry. Gary, her new love interest, was appropriate in all ways except one. He was, by his own description, sexually ambivalent. Although he dated women, he confessed to Andrea that sexually he was drawn primarily to men. Nonetheless Andrea was overwhelmingly attracted to him, and she was sure that he felt the same way about her.

"Gary and I quickly became best friends. We did everything together—everything except sleep together, that is. He would tell me that he had never really been sexually interested in a woman, but I found it difficult to believe. When we were together, there were sexual sparks all over the place. He was very open about his sexual conflicts and his preferences. But I guess I didn't really believe him. He was very attractive to me, and we had a very good friendship. It's true that because of our involvement, I didn't look at any other men."

Gary was offered a job in California, and although Andrea had hopes that he might ask her to go with him, he moved by himself.

This move crushed all of Andrea's dreams, and she sank into a deep depression that lasted another year. At the end of that year she entered therapy and transferred all of her feelings onto her young male therapist. Andrea stayed with the therapist for a year and a half, during which time she made no effort to meet any suitable partners. While in therapy she found herself more and more involved with fantasies concerning her doctor. When he got engaged, bought a brownstone, and moved his office into his home, Andrea could no longer avoid the reality that he had a personal life that did not include her. She became very angry at herself and at the therapist. She decided that she had been spending a great deal of money for few results and she terminated treatment.

For the next year and a half there were no men in Andrea's life and few fantasies, and she was quite happy.

"This period was definitely one of the best in my life. My work was good, and my life was quite full. I have always had good women friends, and I spent time with them. Not being involved with anyone, not being depressed about anyone, and not thinking about anyone can be a very good experience. My head was free just to enjoy life, and for the first time that's what I did. Then I met Martin."

Andrea and Martin, a highly flirtatious forty-two-year-old doctor, met at a Christmas party. Martin was in the process of divorcing his second wife, and he was immediately taken with Andrea. On their second date he told Andrea that he had been unfaithful to both of his wives, as well as to just about every other woman he had ever been with, and that he didn't plan to marry again unless he was sure that the sexual attraction was so great that he would never, ever consider an extramarital affair. He also implied that he was so attracted to Andrea that she might indeed be the woman who would fulfill this need. Andrea took on the challenge, and although the sex was already "fantastic," she tried to be even more provocative and sexually interesting. She invested a small fortune in lingerie, she bought harem costumes, she took up belly dancing. It wasn't quite enough.

When the relationship was less than four months old, Andrea discovered that Martin had resumed having sex with his second wife, who had become more "interesting" to him after the divorce.

Now Andrea is totally distraught and devastated. All she knows is that Martin is the love of her life, the "prince" she always dreamed of. She is in pain and feels overwhelmingly obsessed.

Hearing Andrea's story, it's easy to see that she becomes too quickly involved with the wrong men. Clearly she disregards the warning signals that should inform her of dead-end choices. Furthermore, even after she sees the problems, she stays involved, hoping for a miracle.

PASSIVE COMMITMENT CONFLICTS AND THE MALE-FEMALE DIFFERENCE

Passive behavior patterns are traditionally associated with women, and passive commitment conflicts are no different. Traditionally it is an easier role for women. As painful as it may be always to play the victim within your relationships, a woman has rarely had to accept blame. As long as she assumes the passive role, she can continue to point a finger at the many "difficult" or "commitmentphobic" men who have relentlessly pursued her, only to turn tail and run. If nothing else, her dramatic relationship history doesn't automatically read like it's her fault. Can she be blamed if the only men she meets have a lot of problems? There is a great deal of cultural support for any woman who continues to find herself in such a role.

For a man with a passive commitment pattern it is a very different story. Men generally are expected to be the aggressors, the pursuers, the hunters. This gives them much more control in the way relationships begin. How does a man pursue a woman passively? How does a man justify all of his bad choices? He can't say, "The wrong women keep asking me out." The "wrong" women may keep making themselves available to him, but he is still the one doing the choosing. He is not waiting for someone to ask him out, and he is not reluctantly giving in to an ardent pursuer. He *is* the ardent pursuer—the ardent pursuer of women who put up unreasonable boundaries, women who don't want a commitment, women who are emotionally, physically, or geographically unavailable.

Nonetheless men with passive patterns often blame all women

for their misfortune, saying that the average woman doesn't appreciate a nice guy. But friends and family are rarely that sympathetic. Get into more than one difficult relationship, and it isn't long before they start saying things such as, "You like to suffer," "You like difficult women," "You don't want it to be easy." Your friends may not understand the dynamic that keeps drawing you to the women you choose, but it's impossible not to notice that you are asking out "all the wrong women."

Recognizing the countless similarities in the passive-male and the passive-female patterns can be the first step in understanding how passive commitment conflicts reveal themselves.

Timothy is a good example of a man with a passive avoidance pattern who seems to prefer highly problematic partners. However, he tends to see himself as a victim and his role as purely circumstantial. He says:

"Women always talk about how difficult guys are, how insensitive guys are, how uncommitted guys are. But I don't see it. I think women are the ones with the problem. Take the last woman I went out with, Nicole. She was crazy. I'm sorry, but there is no other way to describe her. I met her at this big party, and I guess we were both drunk. At first when she started talking to me, I thought she was with another guy, but it turned out that she was involved with a guy, but not the one she came with.

"She's a perfect example. It seems as if every woman I meet is involved with some guy who is brutalizing her, but she keeps going back. That's what happened with Nicole. She kept complaining about this guy, but she kept going back to him."

Timothy says that he can't remember the last time he met a woman who genuinely wanted a committed relationship. His friends point out to him that he only dates models and actresses, who are intent on their careers, and is usually attracted to very young women, sometimes women who are still in their teens.

"It's true. I like beautiful women, and they are often looking for work in the entertainment industry. But that doesn't mean that they have to be crazy. My last really important relationship was about a year ago with a woman named Janine. I should have known better—she was very young, just eighteen. But she was very mature for her age. She had a lot of experience, but she was really unclear about what she wanted. She kept me totally off balance and gave me problems from day one. I could never count on her for anything, even a regular weekend. It was like a nightmare going out with her. I remember once we made a plan to go to the beach for a couple of days, and she showed up with two of her girlfriends. I drove them all down to this cottage I had rented, and then all three of them spent the weekend flirting with other guys on the beach. She was crazy, that's all."

Lloyd, a thirty-eight-year-old lawyer, also has a passive avoidance problem. However, the women he chooses are nowhere near as colorful as those Tim dates. In fact, often the women Lloyd goes out with seem very appropriate. The main drawback: They almost always indicate their anxieties concerning intimacy and closeness early on in the relationship. Typically this is why the couple eventually breaks up. Lloyd says that he is trying to work out a relationship with his current girlfriend, Elizabeth, a film editor.

"She has this thing about needing her own time and her own space. What that means is that she doesn't always want to stay at my apartment, and she doesn't want me to stay at hers. She has lots of restrictions about when we can see each other. We spend a lot of time together, but it's not sequential time. For example, we may go out on Saturday afternoon and do something. But if we are going out on Saturday night, we can't just hang out together from, let's say, four to seven. She needs to be alone for those three hours. It sounds strange, but I know what she means. I need time too. But she is so rigid about it. It makes for a very controlling atmosphere. I always feel as though I am about to be dismissed or something, and it's not comfortable."

Lloyd says that Elizabeth is also very reluctant to plan ahead, preferring to keep things spontaneous. This puts him in the position of always waiting for her to make up her mind. He says this "ruins" weekends and every other plan he tries to make.

"On Tuesday I'll ask whether she wants to go away for the weekend. She says, 'How can I know what I'm going to want to do now? It's too early.' I'll ask again all through the week, but it's still too early. Then on Friday night or Saturday morning she'll decide she wants to go away, and it's too late. By then we can't get a car, or we can't get a reservation—or by the time we do, half a day is gone. This is very upsetting, and I think it's destructive. Elizabeth calls it spontaneity; I call it a major pain."

Lloyd says he is beginning to question everything about this relationship because Elizabeth makes it all so difficult. According to him, she puts up tremendous barriers against intimacy.

"Even talking to her on the phone can be exhausting. I called one night this week to say hi, and she told me she was busy, would I please call back in ten minutes. I did, and she asked if I could make it an hour. I called back in an hour, and she was watching a special on television. Finally I said, 'Why don't you just call me when you're ready?' She got angry and said I was trying to make her feel guilty.

"She wants a relationship, but she doesn't want to have to do any of the work. She makes me do it all, and then she gets annoyed because it seems as though I am always pushing for something. I don't know what to do. She's really a lovely person, and I care about her, but I'm beginning to feel deprived here. She's just not giving enough. I have a tough job, and I need some support. It's not coming from her. Minimally I need to know somebody is happy to be with me. She always acts like I'm bothering her. It's too much work."

Although Lloyd claims to be pretty much fed up with Elizabeth's behavior, he admits that he has been saying the same kinds of things for the two years they have been together. His friends and his family keep asking him why he doesn't find himself someone who appreciates him. There are other women who find him attractive, why doesn't he do something about one of them?

A HISTORY OF AVOIDING THE RIGHT PERSON

Always finding the wrong partners means that you are also very skilled at avoiding the right ones. Erika, a forty-one-year-old music teacher, has emotionally pledged herself to unfaithful men and unkind men, men who were profoundly uncommitted and men who were profoundly unavailable, men who slept with her friends and men who wouldn't sleep with her. Erika is smart, pretty, accomplished, sophisticated, good-natured. Is it possible that she never, ever meets anyone who is as interested in marriage as she says she is?

Like Erika, Russell—a thirty-seven-year-old photographer—has a long history of partners who either wouldn't or couldn't make a commitment to him. He has pursued relationships in which there were insurmountable religious differences, political differences, age differences, and cultural differences. At one time every woman he asked out was about to get engaged to someone else, but a series of unhappy experiences have finally convinced him to stay away from women who are living with or about to marry other men. Russell is good-looking, interesting, articulate, and knowledgeable. Russell is also a nice guy. What is his problem? Why can't he find someone who will appreciate him for what he is?

How do men and women like Russell and Erika meet so many wrong "significant others"? Is there some secret signal that they are giving off?

We believe that Erika and Russell, and others like them, are usually genuinely unaware of what they are doing. Nonetheless the minute they spot an appropriate, available potential partner, they look the other way. In truth they are more concerned with finding "interesting" partners than they are with finding suitable partners.

RUNNING FROM A "SETTLED" LIFE—THE PASSIVE PATTERN

If you have a passive pattern, then avoidance is written out, loud and clear, in your own romantic history. Chances are that in your twenties, while your peers were settling into long-term stable relationships, you were either trying to get out of one or chasing rainbows. Think about it. Were you honestly looking for commitment and marriage, or were you looking for romance? Were you looking for stability, or were you looking for adventure?

Think also about the potential mates whom you may have discouraged. Looking back, is there any one person who fits that description? Someone about whom you now think, if I'd only known then what I know now, I might have behaved differently? Maybe you never even went out on a single date with this person.

Maybe just hearing him or her described by friends was enough to make you decide against it.

Here's what you probably thought at the time. You probably rejected meeting or dating these men or women because they looked too settled, too stable, too adult. You decided that you simply weren't ready for your life to be that settled. What you were telling yourself, even though you didn't know it, is that you weren't ready for a real adult commitment to a real adult.

You may also have thought that people like that were too uncomplicated; you may have decided that you were better suited for someone who was more conflicted, someone who could not only understand your conflicts but also provide more of a challenge. Maybe that feeling didn't feel like fear of commitment at the time, but think about it now.

Paul, thirty-seven, who wrote to us recently to describe his situation, provides a perfect example of someone who frequently withdraws from women who are available. He said:

"I'm a single parent with two little girls. My wife left me a few years ago in order to marry someone else. In the past three years I have been involved with several other women who have commitment problems. But I realize that all of these women, who were clearly chasing after me at the beginning of our relationships, also gave me warning signs that they were not available. One, for example, went out of her way to have friends arrange a date. The first time we went out, she told me that she had a terrible crush on me and thought of me as the 'perfect man.' She said she never thought she had a chance with me and that going out with me was her 'dream come true.' This dream lasted maybe four torrid weeks before she started breaking dates. One, a date to get together with friends at my house on Thanksgiving Day, she broke at eleven o'clock Thanksgiving morning. She said something had come up. She told me after we split up that she can only really be sexual with someone if she doesn't like him or if she feels he doesn't like her.

"But what has occurred to me lately: While every woman with a commitment problem broke up with me, I broke up with every woman who didn't seem to have a problem. One woman, I remember, for instance, really liked me. She would make all these excuses to come over to my house and do things for me, and while

I was very attracted to her, I didn't want her there so much. One day she called and said that for my birthday she wanted to come over and cook dinner. She asked me for the keys, saying she would pick up my daughters and then when I came home, she would have given them baths and gotten them ready for bed. All I would have to do is relax.

"I remember walking in the door and being hit with the smell of a nice roast beef cooking. She was in the kitchen. My children had on their pajamas and were playing a game at the kitchen table. The dog was sleeping on a rug in front of a fire. And all I wanted to do was to turn around and walk out. I felt like I was married . . . like I was coming home from work to the perfect family. My reaction was to want to leave. It's sad really because she was trying to be nice. I just wasn't ready for that scene. I felt she was trying to show me what a good wife she would make. It made me very anxious. I split up with her for another commit-mentphobic woman shortly after that."

When men and women with passive conflicts fail to notice, or actually turn down, suitable partners, typically they say that they don't want to "get stuck" with someone who may not be as "interesting" as they would hope. They don't want a boring life. No matter how lonely or unfulfilling they find their current life-style, they would prefer to keep searching for someone who fits their criteria, particularly if they are determined either to broaden their paths or to find high adventure. They want to continue to maintain their options, and in that context they don't want to choose mates who are going to narrow their horizons. In short, they are never quite ready to fit into a settled groove with a settled mate. Whether they realize it or not, that settled groove represents commitment.

COMMITTED TO DREAMS AND FANTASIES

Anyone with commitment conflicts is vulnerable to fantasies. Passive avoiders particularly tend to dream wonderful dreams about long-term commitment. In their minds, and in their imaginations, they are capable of a thousand and one commitments. Given the nature of their elusive partners, and the obstacles that stand in the way of their relationships, they are rarely called upon to test their ability to hang in for the long haul. Their fantasies typically fall into one of three categories:

Committed to Fantasies About What Is Really Taking Place

Passive avoiders typically are unable to assume a realistic attitude toward either shortcomings and imperfections in their partners or weaknesses in their relationships. While someone who is actively avoiding commitment can take a perfectly good relationship and pick it apart, finding fault with everything a partner may be doing, the passive avoider does exactly the opposite. He or she can take the most ordinary of mortals and elevate this person to a godlike status. Instead of being committed to a real person, the passive avoider is usually incapable of seeing a partner's reality. The same is true of "the relationship." Everything that is said, everything that is done, every conflict, every disagreement, every missed meeting, every missed word—it is all aggrandized, blown way out of proportion, until it assumes mythological dimensions.

Much of the passive avoider's commitment to the relationship revolves around a commitment to somehow change one's partner. Altering a loved one's destiny by changing his or her internal attitude is a favorite fantasy.

In this fantasy scenario the barrier to commitment is seen as the loved one's "problem" or "self-destructive" behavior. Problems frequently include an acknowledged fear of commitment. In these instances much of the enormous amount of energy that the passive avoider is giving to the relationship is devoted to encouraging a partner to "get more in touch with feelings," "get over the need for multiple partners," "get counseling," "get help," or "get sober."

What this means is that the passive avoider is unable to accept a partner, or a relationship, as is. In all of these instances, although the passive avoider may feel fully committed, he or she is usually more committed to a full-scale effort to surmount an insurmountable barrier than to the actual partner—who may want no part of this effort. Until the barriers are overcome, there is nothing to fear. Since it is unlikely to happen, there is no reason to feel afraid.

Committed to Fantasies About the Future

"He has a lot of reservations about marriage now, but I feel certain that once he agrees to it, he's going to be a terrific husband and father."

"All our problems revolve around her sleeping with her exboyfriend. Once that relationship is resolved, we'll be okay."

"From the way she behaves sexually, I'd say she was abused somewhere in the past. If we can get over those barriers, and I'm sure we can, I think she'll open up to the idea of marriage."

"If I can get him away from his family's influence and he starts giving me the kind of attention he gives them, then we can discuss moving in together."

"I have this feeling that if I could get him to spend two or three consecutive weeks with me in a vacation setting, he would realize that we should get married."

For passive avoiders the phrase *in your dreams* has special meaning. While they may believe that they are one hundred percent committed to a person or a relationship, what they seem to be more committed to is a vision of how that person or that relationship will be in the future once some obstacle is overcome.

When these men and women talk about being committed, they are not always saying that they are committed to the situation as it exists. They are saying that they want to be committed to some improved, yet-to-be-realized relationship. In short they are committed to their own vision of the future.

This fantasy frequently also includes a partner who needs saving in some way. More often than not this partner is resistant to being saved, and this resistance is the major obstacle in the path of the future fantasy. The passive avoider's role is that of Joan of Arc or Savior. For example: "He's struggling with his inner demons." "She's wrestling with her inner child." "His car was repossessed, and he has financial problems that preclude commitment." "Her landlord is about to evict her." "He's drinking again." "She's smoking too much dope." "His ex-wife and child are camped out on the lawn." "Her ex-husband is destroying her life." "He needs a new therapist." "She doesn't recognize her problems."

Trying to play the magical role of rescuer leaves very little room for real commitment. When you're involved with someone with a chaotic life, you're not worried about getting married. You're not worried about commitment. You're worried about getting past next Tuesday. When someone has a drama-filled life, be it by design or just bad luck, you can get very, very involved—without having to think about the future. These situations may be exciting, they may be gripping, and they may be romantic—but they are not necessarily committed.

Committed to Fantasies About What Might Have Been

There are two major ways in which passive avoiders act out in this way. The first reflects those magic, brief interludes, usually with unavailable partners who represent fantasy models against which all other relationships can be measured.

With the right filters these episodes of chasing dream partners —episodes best described as brief encounters or "ships that pass in the night"—are incomparable. The feelings you felt, the potential you sensed, it all becomes unmatchable.

At forty-six Glen has never come close to being in a long-term committed relationship, but the relationships in which he has felt most willing to make a commitment are those in which his brief-interlude fantasies combined with a woman's unavailability. Describing one of these relationships, he says:

"I fell in love with Tanya from the way she looked from behind. That's how it started. I was driving on Madison Avenue, and I see this woman carrying shopping bags turning the corner. I didn't even see her face, but what I saw was so striking, it was instant death.

"Just then—it was like fate—a parking space opened up. I pulled in and started racing frantically looking from store to store. Then suddenly I saw her through the window of a jewelry store. I immediately headed inside, and I'm trying to think of what I can be doing there. What happens when the saleslady asks me if she can help me. Then I think—earrings, that's it. I want to buy earrings for my sister.

"Anyway I see the woman, and she's even better from the front. I am immediately lost in the chemistry. But completely lost. The salesperson asks me what I want. I say earrings. Just then Tanya gets up to leave, and I'm stuck with this tray in front of me. I run out of the store after Tanya, as she's getting into a cab, and I yell after her and ask her for her phone number. The cab starts up, I figure I'm dead, but just then it stops. She rolls down the window and yells out a number to me, and the cab drives away. I'm hysterical looking for a piece of paper, praying that my memory works.

"I called her and found out her story. She was separated from her husband, but not divorced. We went out for two weeks, and I was like a crazy man. Being with her, I was so anxious, I couldn't stop hyperventilating. I used to go out and run five miles before each date just so I could get my anxiety under control. Within two weeks she told me that she loved me. It was heaven, this incredible-looking woman, looking at me and saying, 'I love you.' She said she was going to divorce her husband because of me.

"Four weeks into the relationship I had to go out of town for three days. The minute I got back, I phoned her, and her voice was different. We met for a drink, and no sooner did we sit down than she said, 'We can't do this anymore.'

"She said that she was no longer sure that she wanted to end her marriage. She said she couldn't see me anymore because the intensity of our relationship was too threatening to her marriage. She had decided that until she was sure that she was going to get divorced, she was going to go back to seeing an old boyfriend whom she didn't feel that passionate about. She said it was safer. And that was that. The dagger came out, and I was dead.

"You have to understand, it wasn't like I created this whole thing in my head. All along she was the one who was talking about our future together. It was the only time I truly wanted to plan a future with anyone.

"The whole thing was like a month on drugs. I was fifty thousand feet into the air, the floor opened, and I start free-falling. When Tanya told me that we couldn't see each other anymore, I couldn't believe it. It was months before I could have sex with another woman. Months."

Today, six years later, Glen still has a difficult time believing that the main component in his encounter with Tanya was fantasy. There's a difference between a magic moment, or a magic month, or even a magic year, and a solid, steady relationship without a built-in fail-safe mechanism. Glen knew his relationship with

Tanya couldn't last. He wasn't even sure if he wanted it to last. But that's enough to make anything feel perfect.

When ships pass in the night, a big part of what makes them look so good is the fact that they're passing. If we stop to get a very good look at each other, to see the human frailties, the disappointments, the incompatibilities, the mood swings, the clingy mothers, the overprotective sisters, the snoring, the belching, the temperamental outbursts, we might not be so overwhelmed by the drama of what might have been.

The second and perhaps most prevalent way in which passive avoiders focus on fantasies of "what might have been" is when they are so invested in the dream that they are unable to recover from a lost love. For example:

> *"I don't know how he could have treated me the way he did. We were so close. It's not just the relationship, it's more. I feel like I've been betrayed by my best friend."*
>
> —JOANNE, thirty-one

> *"I've talked to all her friends. Nobody understands. Until the day she broke up with me, she acted like we were the perfect couple. People keep telling me that's just the way she is, but I don't believe it."*
>
> —CHARLES, thirty-three

Joanne and Charles, and other men and women with passive issues, usually find it exceptionally difficult to recover from the loss of a love. The last thing we want to do is question the feelings of someone who feels betrayed or spurned by a lover. But if you have passive conflicts, it's essential to get a bit of distance from the past.

We all need to grieve the loss of important relationships. It's unhealthy not to do so. But when we put these relationships and our lost loves on pedestals and stop ourselves from finding a new, more loving partner, eyebrows must be raised in suspicion. It sometimes seems as though there is no more perfect partner than one who has lost interest—or left town.

Often passive avoiders imbue their past relationships with magical qualities way beyond the reality they experienced. They deify the ex-love and protect the relationship from scrutiny.

It is fascinating to hear how much authentic information spurned partners often reveal as they discuss these "past perfect" relationships. These relationships were sometimes brief; frequently they were tortured. They were almost never even and easy. Typically the partner whose behavior brought about the breakup had active commitment issues. Almost always there was something disruptive in the relationship, something keeping the couple apart, even when they were together. These "perfect" partners were usually unavailable before they ever became officially unavailable. And the fantasy of a perfect love was nothing more than that: a fantasy.

ALWAYS INVOLVED WITH COMMITMENTPHOBIC MEN

Recently we've spoken to a fair number of women about their tendency to get involved with men who have serious commitment problems. As they get older and wiser, they tend to recognize that this pattern is also protecting them from commitment. Typically these women are very much aware of not wanting to be bored. Melissa, thirty-six, said:

"I've attracted a lot of commitmentphobics. Not creeps. They've been really nice guys—fun and interesting. They just can't go the distance. I think I may be the same way. I'm easily bored. I've finally figured out that I'm usually involved in a mutual dance from commitment. Maybe I don't have the depth, or whatever it is that people have, that allows them to commit.

"When I was young, I dated guys I could control. They bored me. So I started dating men who didn't bore me, and none of them can commit. Many of the men I date now understand the problem, and we can talk about it. I go out with this one man, very evolved. His walls look like the self-help section of a bookstore. He has a real problem with commitment, and he knows it. He warned me from the very beginning. So it's been my choice to hang around. Yes, deep down I'm probably afraid of having some kid screaming at four o'clock in the morning, and he's more afraid than I am. When I met him, I was not as much in touch with my fears. I didn't see how my choices were my way of backing off.

109

"But this man doesn't bore me. He's fascinating, he's wonderful, and warm and loving, and I drop dead when he walks into a room, he's so cute. We keep waffling and breaking up, because I think I should get on with my life and have a child. I would marry him in a minute, but he's not available for commitment. This is my dance."

Like many women with passive commitment conflicts, Melissa attracts men who come on like gangbusters and then draw back suddenly. Melissa describes one such encounter.

"This incredible thing happened to me. I went to see this psychologist give a lecture. He was witty and clever, and I was completely captivated. The next day at work my phone rang. It was the psychologist. He said, 'Look, this borders on malpractice, and I really shouldn't be doing this, but since it was just a class, and we didn't have any direct personal contact, I'm willing to run this risk.' He made it sound as though it was really important to him. He said, 'Could you have dinner with me, because I just thought you were the cutest thing?'

"Well, I just nearly dropped dead, and of course I went. For the next month he wined me and dined me. He took me out with his parents, took me out with his boss. I was running out of cocktail dresses. He treated me with great respect. I thought, *Hey, this is it. This is the one.*

"Then of course, at the end of the thirty days, he said, 'You know, this woman I used to be involved with is coming back to town, and I would like to see her for dinner one night.' Then he calls me a few days later and says, 'You know, we decided to get back together. It was great, thanks, good-bye.' It was fascinating. Most interesting of course is that he was a shrink, and I wouldn't trust him with yesterday's newspaper."

Melissa says that one of the reasons she has become aware of her commitment conflicts is because of her difficulty making decisions.

"I can't deal with too many options. In a restaurant I find myself going inert from the choices. Right now I'm planning to do volunteer work because I'm feeling this tremendous need to be of help in the world. So I'm thinking of joining a service organization. But which one? I'm thinking, *Where do I go?* Do I go to a hospital, do I do babies, do I do old people, do I do blind people, do I serve soup on Sundays? My head feels like it's going to explode from the possibilities. I get totally stuck. I even get stuck when I go to the video store. . . . How do I buy electronics? I close my eyes and point."

Melissa is ahead of the game because she is becoming aware of her problem, but many more women have not given this enough thought.

"I STILL DON'T BELIEVE I HAVE A PROBLEM WITH COMMITMENT"

We are extremely sympathetic to passive avoiders because we know how painful and thankless their role can be. Nonetheless we also realize that those with passive conflicts are often experts in denial. Because they are doing nothing "wrong," nothing that could hurt anyone, they find it easy to hang all their problems on their partners' stuff. Until passive avoiders prepare to shoulder their share of responsibility for their choices and understand how and why these choices are made, they are doomed to repeat the same painful patterns time and time again.

Whether you are a passive female whose pattern draws tremendous empathy or a passive male whose pattern draws friendly fire, it is no longer viable to dismiss these convoluted relationship dynamics as being nothing more than poor choices or bad luck in love. Whether you are male or female, the struggle with commitment is driving you to share a common experience. You can't portray yourself as the well-intentioned victim or the abused nice guy when your history suggests that your own commitment issues are providing the siren song that draws you into so many painful relationships.

CHAPTER FIVE

"I Love You, but . . ."

DEFINING THE COMMITMENTPHOBIC RELATIONSHIP

There are a whole range of terrific reasons why any of us might want to be part of that bonded unit known as a couple. There are equally valid reasons why each of us might prefer to live the unencumbered life of a single person. At one time or another every one of us has probably struggled with this decision, and some of us struggle a lot.

There is a big difference, however, between struggling with the implications of commitment and hurting others because you can't handle those implications. Act out your conflicts within a relationship, and somebody is going to get hurt. That's why it's so important to understand and work out these conflicts without inflicting pain on ourselves or others.

Whenever commitment conflicts provide the primary theme between two people, we define it as a "commitmentphobic relationship." We can understand why some of you might be uncomfortable with this term, and we want to apologize to anybody who is inclined to consult Webster or Fowler about the word *commitmentphobic* or its usage. However, this is a shorthand term that we find descriptive, accurate, and useful. If one or both partners are as concerned with maintaining freedom, distance, and space as they are in sharing time, interests, or intimacy, we call it a commitmentphobic relationship.

PEOPLE WITH COMMITMENT CONFLICTS FIND EACH OTHER

There is something deceptive about these pairings. In these relationships one partner's conflict, or fear, is always more obvious than the other's. Someone always wants "more" while the other wants "less." We refer to the partner with the more glaring commitment issues as an "active" avoider. This is the partner who seems to be calling most of the shots in the relationship, the person who we can observe "actively running away from love." The other partner, whose only apparent fault appears to be one of choosing, or loving, the wrong person we call the "passive" avoider.

The passive partner is expending extraordinary energy caring about someone who is running away and is the person who is most likely to be labeled "the victim." Throughout the relationship the passive avoider accepts the "runner's" behavior with an unusual degree of understanding and even sympathy. In fact it sometimes appears that a shared desire to feel "free" is one of the underlying bonds between the couple.

After years of observing these relationships, we have reached three conclusions:

- The passive partner is often as anxious about commitment as the active avoider.
- During the course of the typical relationship, partners often switch roles at least once, if not more.
- The passive avoider in one relationship is frequently the active avoider in another.

Although the active avoider appears to be responsible for much of the pain and confusion, using labels such as "victim" and "perpetrator" masks the fact that the underlying fears of either player may be identical. If you are the passive partner, the one who always seems to be most hurt in your relationships, it may be difficult to understand how you are also avoiding commitment. But if you're going to change both your behavior and your future, you must come to terms with the ways in which you, too, are running. More often than not the ways in which you are connected to your "soul mate" have as much to do with fear as they do with love.

With that in mind let's take a closer look at the dynamic of the typical commitmentphobic relationship.

FROM SEDUCTION TO REJECTION

The commitmentphobic relationship is one of extremes. The same person who can't get enough of a partner one day can't get far enough away the next.

If you are a "passive avoider," and if you are in love with somebody who is vacillating from total affection to complete withdrawal, you will find yourself in a dizzying blend of pain and confusion. How could someone who wants to be with you so badly suddenly want to get away? It makes no sense. If it's not the relationship that's causing your "soul mate" to act so strangely, it must be something else.

So you start digging around for an explanation. Perhaps there's a problem at work, a problem with the family, trouble with the law, sexual abuse or another secret from the past, a hidden compulsion, an overbearing mother, a controlling father, an emotional response to closeness that is so extreme that you can help solve the problem—your mind runs wild with possibilities.

Meanwhile the active avoider typically is unwilling, or unable, to articulate the real reasons for his or her behavior. Instead you are being bombarded with a plethora of mixed or double messages. You hear the ones you want to hear, believe the ones you want to believe. While the active avoider may vaguely mumble something about "fear of commitment," for the most part his or her silence and confusion passively supports your belief that there is some deeper secret. You will never hear the whole truth about the degree of ambivalence, fantasy, and anxiety your partner is feeling. This behavior is part of what goes on in a commitmentphobic relationship.

We believe that the commitmentphobic relationship goes through several separate and distinct stages. In all of these stages the man or woman with active conflicts appears to be in control of the relationship. He or she is setting most of the rules and establishing most of the boundaries.

Here is an outline of the various stages of a commitmentphobic relationship:

STAGE ONE—THE BEGINNING

The seduction phase when love, lust, and excitement are so intense that they overshadow any fears. There is a great deal of fantasy attached to this period, and one person—typically the active partner—is doing everything possible to convince the other to let down his or her boundaries and become fully involved in the relationship.

STAGE TWO—THE MIDDLE

The first rumblings of commitment panic are experienced. This stage starts when there is a definite shift of power in the relationship. The active avoider realizes that the partner appears to be won over and has expectations for a more committed relationship. Switching direction, the active avoider responds to this by erecting boundaries and establishing limits. During this entire period the active avoider is sifting through his or her conflicts and doubts about the relationship. Consequently there are a great many mixed and double messages, as well as a certain amount of push-pull and back-and-forth activity. As the active avoider pulls away, the passive partner becomes more and more insecure as well as determined to get more of a "commitment." Sometimes this stage is brief, but it can also drag on for years.

STAGE THREE—THE END

The active avoider, feeling trapped by anxieties, expectations, and demands, may feel as though both physical and emotional space are being invaded. The sense of being trapped is so acute that it often produces a whole range of phobic reactions, including anxiety, palpitations, and stomach distress. Getting away and creating distance becomes more and more of a priority—this is frequently expressed by hostile and selfish behavior. Often the behavior becomes so provocative that a confrontation is forced.

STAGE FOUR—THE BITTER END

The active avoider is experiencing so many conflicted feelings that his or her behavior appears not only rejective but also bizarre and out of control. The fear and conflict are so intense that the active avoider is incapable of thinking about anyone else's feelings. Active avoiders may appear angry or hostile; they may refuse to take phone calls or be pinned down in any way; often they immediately become involved with someone else in a way that seems "inconceivable." Consequently the passive partner is devastated by cruel and thoughtless behavior. Instead of moving on, the passive partner may become increasingly committed to a fantasy of the relationship and may find it extraordinarily difficult to recover.

STAGE FIVE—CURTAIN CALLS

Once the active avoider has exited the relationship, the level of anxiety falls off so dramatically that he or she is often left only with a sense of longing for the abandoned partner. When that happens, contact is frequently reestablished, and there are mini-replays of the entire relationship.

Let's take a look at some commitmentphobic relationships and how they are played out. First let's look at some relationships in which a man is the active avoider.

A CLASSIC PURSUIT/PANIC PATTERN

When Brian and Jessica met, he was forty and she was twenty-nine. He had never married, but he had lived with two women. She had been briefly married when she was in college. Since then she had been without a serious long-term relationship.

They met when Brian noticed Jessica in a small local bookstore that they both visited often; Brian involved the owners in assuring Jessica that he was "from the neighborhood" and "safe." For her part Jessica found Brian, a stock trader, extraordinarily attractive, but she thought his interest in her was odd, since it seemed to lack a realistic basis. She gave him her phone number, even though she thought they really weren't suited for each other. Within a short time he was besieging her with "charming" phone calls. For two weeks he was on the phone "proving that he was definitely worth knowing." He also sent flowers, and several books purchased at the little store in which they met.

By the time they actually had a date, Jessica was intrigued, and her defenses were worn down. Who was Brian and why did he like her so much? For their first date he took her to a dinner party at a friend's house. Jessica liked everything about it. She liked his friends, she liked his attentiveness, she liked the feeling of being part of a couple. She says:

"I found him very interesting, very intelligent. But I also thought he was spoiled and he drank a little too much. He told me that he had recently broken up with a woman who was still very interested in him. He said that she had been all wrong for him, but that even though the breakup was a long time in coming, it was painful.

"We went out for two more weeks before I finally agreed to sleep with him. During this whole time he kept bringing me more and more into his world. I met his sister and his friends. I heard all about his life and his childhood. Brian is very sensitive, and I got the feeling that he trusted me more than he does most people."

Jessica says that after she and Brian slept together for the first time, he told her that he had hurt every woman he had ever been with and that he didn't want to hurt her. He asked her to promise him that she wouldn't allow herself to be hurt. Although she thought it a strange request, Jessica assured him that she wouldn't let that happen.

"I wanted to ask him to be more specific about what had happened with the other women, but, lying in bed next to him, it didn't seem appropriate. There was a great deal of chemistry between us, and we spent a lot of time in bed. Within a month or so he began to encourage me to spend more time at his apartment. He always wanted me to stay over, to stay for the weekend. I have a cat, so I had to keep going home. Finally he said, 'This is stupid. Bring the cat and move in with me.' He really pushed me to do this. So I sublet my apartment and moved in. That was my big mistake."

Jessica says that her major error was in not thinking everything through. She says that there were telltale little signs almost from the very beginning that Brian wasn't genuinely committed, but that she hadn't given them proper weight.

"If I'm being completely honest, I have to say that there were ways in which I always felt Brian slipping away from me. It was all very subtle, but it was happening. Maybe that's why I rushed to move in with him. I guess I didn't feel secure enough to let him out of my sight. I thought moving in would secure the relationship.

"I would say that he started overtly changing as soon as I settled in. Small changes. He stopped rushing home. He stopped automatically including me in everything. Some nights he would go off with his friends, and he wouldn't get in until very late. And he started drinking more. When he was home, sometimes he appeared distracted and distant. But he still called me twice a day at work to tell me that he loved me. I thought all the little ways in which he seemed withdrawn were just natural reactions to a new situation.

"Before I moved in, we had discussed living together for six months; if that worked, we agreed we would then make plans to get married. When the six months rolled around, Brian began to hem and haw. He told me that he loved me very much but that the stock market was so unstable, it was making him too anxious to think about marriage. He said he needed more time. It made me nervous, but I didn't want to pressure him. I tried to back off, but it was hard. I had some time off from work, so I went to visit a friend for a long weekend. That seemed to make things better, because when I came back, Brian said he really missed me. I found out later that in the five days I was gone, he had had a brief affair with another woman.

"We went on like this for another ten months. I tried to stop pressuring him, but every now and then I felt as though I had to find out if anything had changed. So, yes, I would bring up the subject of marriage. When we talked about it, he always said he wasn't ready yet. I remember one night he said he still loved me but he didn't know if he was 'in love' with me. We talked about it, and I thought we decided that his feelings were normal—that's what happened when you had been living with someone for a while. That made sense to me.

119

"Finally what happened is that I don't *know* what happened. We continued as we were; we made love two or three times a week, I made dinner two or three times a week, we went out to dinner on the weekends. We seemed to be having a reasonable life together. In fact it felt so committed already that I had stopped thinking about marriage, and we hadn't mentioned the *M*-word in months. Everything seemed really cozy and solid.

"Then one weekend we went to the beach with a married couple. They were his friends, but I had become quite close to the wife. I thought we had a nice enough time, but on Sunday afternoon he seemed a little distant and went off for a walk by himself. That night, when we got back to the city, we both had sunburns, and the apartment was an oven. He turned on the air conditioner, and I went to get the cat, who was staying with neighbors. When I got back, he said we had to talk. He told me that the relationship was 'over for the time being'—that's how he put it. He said that he needed his space back. He said he was sorry and he knew this was a great strain for me. He thought I should try to get my apartment back.

"That night we slept in the same bed, but we didn't touch. I must have cried all night long. The next day Brian said he couldn't 'take it' and left to stay with a friend until I got myself more together. Finally after a couple of days of this I asked the neighbors if they could watch the cat, and I moved in with my sister and her husband until I got my apartment back. After I moved out, Brian called me and said that he still loved me and that he hoped we could be together again someday but that right now he wanted to be alone. He said that the breakup was difficult for him too.

"He never called me again, and I heard from friends that he was already serious about another woman. The same friends told me that he said that he loved me but that it couldn't have worked out because there were too many ways in which we weren't similar. I don't know what he means by that. I remember that we could talk for hours and that we both liked the same things. I remember all the fun we had—and the sex. I can't tell you how much this hurts me. I guess I still expect him to come back."

Obviously Jessica has been deeply wounded by this aborted relationship. One day she was planning her days and spending her nights with a man she loved; the next she was alone, with her cat, looking for a place to live. Yet Jessica acknowledges that she had a sense of Brian's ambivalence throughout the relationship. In fact she agrees that she might not have been so quick to move in with him if she had been feeling more secure. And what about Brian? We've heard many variations of this same story over the years; every time we do, we ponder what was taking place in the man's head. How could he be so casual about ending what appeared to be an important relationship? How could he encourage someone to alter her life without thinking about the consequences? Even if he changed his mind, how could he be so rejective and coldhearted?

LOOKING AT A RELATIONSHIP FROM THE OPPOSITE POINT OF VIEW

We recently spoke to Michael, a thirty-four-year-old attorney who has his own practice in Chicago. He described his relationship with Cheryl, a twenty-eight-year-old woman. It provides a glimpse into how a man with active commitment conflicts feels in this kind of situation, and we can very clearly see the different stages.

THE BEGINNING

Michael lived in Chicago, about five hundred miles from Buffalo, which is where Cheryl was working. When they met, according to Michael, there was an "amazing" attraction. He quickly began flying or driving to Buffalo every week to see her. Within a month they started seeing each other every other weekend, and spending a great deal of time on the phone. He says:

"At the very beginning, when we were highly attracted to each other and very fond of each other, she expressed her willingness to move to Chicago should a job opportunity arise. I remember I said, 'That's an awfully big step. If it doesn't work out, you could end up feeling very frustrated. Are you sure you're prepared to deal with that?' She said that *I* shouldn't worry about whether or not she could take care of herself. I took that to mean that she's

121

mature emotionally and had things under control. I figured she knew what she was doing.

"Later as the relationship developed, I wanted to find out how compatible we were because seeing somebody under these conditions was not a very good way to get to know a person. At the time she moved in, no question about it, I was definitely in love with her. But it would have been better if she could have moved to Chicago to live in her own apartment. However, it was clear to me that she wasn't going to come to Chicago unless she moved in with me. To tell you the truth, I wasn't sure if I was ready for that, but in my head it came down to choosing between having her move in with me or ending the relationship. She didn't say that, but the feeling was implicit in our conversations.

"When she moved in, although I was happy about it, I was also filled with trepidation. I was nervous about making a level of commitment I didn't feel I was ready to make. Unfortunately I didn't express any of this to her because I didn't want her to think that I didn't love her. I hoped she was moving with the understanding that if it didn't work, it didn't work. I don't remember if we specifically talked about that, either, or if I just hinted at it.

"I knew that she was leaving a very good job, but neither one of us properly evaluated how difficult it would be for her to find an equivalent situation in Chicago. I just figured she was a mature adult who knew what she was doing."

THE MIDDLE

"At first I was delighted to have her in the apartment, but very soon I began to have these nagging little feelings of incompatibility. We had different attitudes about some stuff. It may have had something to do with sharing my apartment, which is pretty small. She was also worried because she was having a tough time solidifying a job offer. As I think about it, I realize that I can't remember anything that big that we disagreed about, but I felt it."

Michael says that although there were many things that he and Cheryl did that were a great deal of fun, there were also times when he feels they didn't "click" as well as they should. He says that at this point he realizes his sense of being cramped for space was affecting him in general.

"The more I talk about all of this, the more I begin to wonder if some of the things I think bothered me had less to do with those specific things and more to do with my feelings of being claustrophobic. I know that I began to feel caged in.

"Seeing each other every other weekend worked so well. It was like a vacation when we were together. It was purely for fun. Once we were together day to day, we didn't always agree about everything. What finally happened is that after about six or seven months my father got sick and I had to fly down to Florida to see him. That made me think about a lot of things, such as family. I decided that part of my problem with Cheryl was religion. She wasn't Jewish, and if I had kids, I would definitely want them to be raised Jewish."

THE END

"When I came back, I was happy to see her. We talked a lot about what I was going through, and the question of children came up. I guess I voiced my concerns. She said she would be willing to raise our children in the Jewish faith if that's what I wanted. Later that night I found myself lying wide awake in bed thinking, *What the hell is going on here? This isn't working.*

"I realized that she was waiting for me to propose to her, and I couldn't tell her that I was going to be able to make that commitment any time in the next twenty years, if ever. And that's when it began to crumble. I couldn't have felt any more trapped. It was nice to know that she loved me enough to have my children and raise them any way I wanted, but it didn't overcome what I felt. In fact that conversation confirmed that neither of us really understood each other's position when she moved to Chicago. She was ready to get married, and I wasn't—and I might never be ready. The knowledge that we were on totally different tracks built up and built up, and it was too much to deal with.

"For the next couple of weeks I spent a lot of time thinking. I was feeling tortured because I knew the right thing to do was to break up with Cheryl, but I didn't really want to do it because I had so many feelings for her. I was looking for all the differences that would make it easier for me to decide to split up. I still loved her, but I was having these anxiety attacks that forced me to resolve the situation. Finally one evening I decided that I had to do it."

THE BITTER END

"I told her when we were on our way to falling asleep. There was no preparation—I just told her. She was very upset of course. She didn't really have any clear sense about how I had been feeling. She knew I was having some problems, but the idea of breaking up pretty much came as a surprise to her. And she had to move again, which was a great strain on her. Afterward she was angry, resentful, sad, and weepy. I felt both relieved and terrible. Terrible for putting her through that, but relieved because it was such a burden off me. I didn't enjoy making her life miserable, but once she was out of the apartment, I felt as though this weight came off me. She didn't want the relationship to end, so I felt bad that she was so unhappy."

CHANGING ROLES

Michael is one of those people who seem to switch back and forth between active and passive commitment conflicts. In other words he is either running away from an available partner or running after someone who is unavailable. Soon after Michael's relationship with Cheryl split up, he met Mary Lou, whom he says he was "crazy about." In this relationship she was the one who was resisting commitment, and he was the one who wanted more. It's ironic that Michael felt so strongly about staying within *his* faith, because Mary Lou, a Protestant, was clear from the beginning that she wanted to stay within *her* faith. He says:

"When Mary Lou and I met, we were both in heaven. I really flipped for her. She was the kind of person who appealed to my imagination. She was driven, strong, dynamic, and intelligent. It was so hard to pin her down that I was blinded to other women. She said that I was very different from the other men in her life. What I think she meant by that is that I tried always to treat her with respect and dignity. I tried to be supportive and sympathetic. I think that's what she needed, but she didn't place any value on it."

Michael says that this relationship was very brief, and it ended because Mary Lou suddenly turned on him.

"She began to get very argumentative. I felt picked on a lot. It seemed as though she was hunting for ways to find fault and hunting for ways to get me upset, and I always felt as though I was being pushed into a fight. Finally she announced that we were totally incompatible, and she dropped me like a hot potato. One weekend she was telling me that I was everything she ever dreamed of. Then all of a sudden I felt as though she had turned into a monster. It was so sudden and so total that I was stunned."

Michael says that he recognizes that what Mary Lou was feeling was very similar to his reactions to Cheryl.

"It was very close to what I had done with Cheryl, so I understood it. But it still didn't feel good. It didn't make me heartbroken at first, just heart bruised. But every now and then I find myself thinking about Mary Lou, and I get this knot in my stomach."

THERE WERE ALWAYS TWO VOICES IN MY HEAD

Oliver, a tax consultant, talked to us about a relationship that had a similar dynamic, but the relationship stretched out for several years because Oliver was unable to resolve his ambivalence.

"When I met Louise, a divorce lawyer, I thought she was incredibly sophisticated and glamorous. She knew exciting people, she went to chic restaurants, she wore designer clothes. I thought, *I want that.* And I chased her like crazy."

Louise was five years older than Oliver, and for that reason, among others, she wasn't sure she and Oliver had a future. Oliver says that nonetheless he convinced her.

"I planned a campaign, like a little war, to win her over. I did everything I could, until I convinced her to go to bed with me. The minute I did, she changed, or I changed, or I saw her differently. Within a few days it was a whole different relationship, and I wasn't so sure this was what I wanted."

"For one thing it turns out that Louise was really a homebody. She worked hard all day, and she wanted to come home and relax. She was a fabulous cook, and she would make me these incredible meals, which I should have appreciated. And I did. But —I wasn't sure I wanted to be in a real relationship; it felt too much like playing house. I had feelings for her, but I didn't feel right."

Oliver says that almost as soon as he "won Louise over," he started having serious doubts. He says:

"We would spend three or four days at a time together, and I remember how tormented I used to be every time I left her house to go home. I always felt as though I should break up with her at those times. On the one hand I loved her; on the other I would wish that I could tell her that I wasn't really committed. I would be having these conversations with myself about all her good points and all her bad points.

"The relationship lasted two years, and during the entire time I was struggling with trying to make a commitment. She sensed my ambivalence—that made her insecure, and she wanted some assurance that the relationship was moving forward. I would have these sobbing sessions with her in which I would promise that soon I would be able to make more of a commitment. She would give me ultimatums and threaten to end the relationship, and even though five minutes earlier I was trying to find a way to exit gracefully, once she made that choice real, I would cry and beg her just to give me more time.

"By the end I was really in so much conflict that I couldn't move. I would invent excuses so that I didn't have to see her so often. When I would come over to her house, she would make dinner and wait on me, and I would sit around feeling and looking uncomfortable. We would have these awful conversations about when we were going to make a commitment. Through it all there were always two voices in my head. I would tell myself that she was a good person who loved me, she was somebody I could count on, she had an interesting life, interesting friends, and she was my best friend. . . . I could do a lot worse. The other voice would be saying, *Get out, date, meet new women; live, see the world, you're too young to die.*

"When I was with her, I would invariably start thinking about all the different kinds of women I might be interested in. She was tall, so I started fantasizing about petite women. I looked at women who didn't have careers, women who didn't cook, women who were different from the way she was. In short any woman who didn't make me feel as though I was suffocating, which is how being with her made me feel. Of course in reality I probably wouldn't want to marry any of these women, either, but at the time I felt as though Louise was keeping me from meeting them. That made me more than a little angry.

"I think what I hoped was that some miracle would happen and make me feel different. I hoped I would somehow suddenly 'grow up' and be happy about making a commitment. But it didn't happen. What finally did happen was that I started withdrawing sexually. We went on a vacation together for ten days in Europe, and we only had sex once. Every night I'd roll over and pretend to sleep. I had decided that if I didn't stop having sex with her, I was going to have to marry her. I know that's crazy, but that's the way I felt. That's when she got most upset. She said I made her feel ugly and undesirable. She said I was torturing her. Again I cried and begged.

"Then about two weeks after we got back, one night I had one of those 'If I don't get out now, I'll die' thoughts, and I followed through on it. I announced that I couldn't be in the relationship anymore. She said I had given her no real warning. And in many ways I hadn't. She had sensed my ambivalence, but when she'd tried to talk about it, I would basically deny it. I always told her that I loved her. And I did. My reservations I kept to myself because if I told her about them, she might have done something to change.

"This sounds awful, but I knew I didn't want her to remedy anything. I wanted to get out. That's all. If she had tried to do anything else for the relationship, or me, I would have felt even more guilty. I didn't want it to work. I wanted to be free. It was that simple.

"After all that the relationship still wasn't completely over. Believe it or not I was still ambivalent—only less so. We continued to see each other off and on for another year before she finally became totally fed up. I don't blame her."

"I LOVE YOU, BUT . . ."

As Oliver points out, his relationship with Louise is an exercise in ambivalence. He always felt as though he loved her, but. . . .

In fact there is probably no better example of commitment ambivalence than the use of the simple phrase "I love you." Some men and women with commitment conflicts never say it. They might say, "I really care for you," or "I feel very strongly about you," or "I really like you a lot"—but never the big one. They can't even fake it.

But many more people with very obvious conflicts have no problem saying, "I love you." They love saying it, at least for a while. In fact at the beginning of a relationship they may bury their partners in the phrase. Then, when the relationship gets serious, there's a shift. As commitment begins to be expected of them, they stop saying, "I love you" and start saying, "I love you, but . . ." For example:

"I love you, but I need more time."
"I love you, but I can't live with you."
"I love you, but we're too different."
"I love you, but you're too good for me."
"I love you, but I love Andrea/Andrew more."
"I love you, but it would never work out."
"I love you, but I have to marry someone else."
"I love you, but I need to work things out."
"I love you, but I need to be alone."
"I love you, but my career isn't far enough along."

And let's not forget the classic "I love you, but I'm not *in love* with you."

Frequently men and women with active commitment conflicts don't articulate any of the *but*s. They say "I love you" to their partners; the *but*s they reserve for their conversations with themselves.

What's particularly unfortunate about these conflicted sentiments is that even when those with active conflicts do articulate all their reservations, their partners are likely to mishear or misinterpret. They hear the "I love you," but they rarely pay adequate attention to the reservations.

SHORT-TERM FEAR

Of course not all commitmentphobic relationships last long enough for people to ever get around to discussing permanence. Joy, a thirty-five-year-old photographer, describes a brief relationship she had with Aaron, a forty-three-year-old college professor. This provides an excellent example of a short-term relationship that fits into the pursuit/panic mold. In it Aaron's attitude goes through an amazing transformation. Many women have experienced this kind of brief and confusing encounter. Joy says:

"Aaron must have asked me out about two hundred times before I said yes. When he first started asking, he was married. That's why I said no, even though he must have called me once a week for a year. Then I stopped hearing from him. I heard about him, though—from mutual friends. It seems he had started this heavy affair. That's what made his wife ask for a divorce. After he separated, he developed this really terrible reputation around his office because he was going out with two women at work as well as a few more that he had met at academic conferences. One of the women from work was said to be very, very upset and making scenes in the office.

"I knew he wasn't being wonderful to them, but I met two of those women. One I didn't think was that bright, so I figured that was his reason for dumping her. The other had really dirty, stringy hair, so I figured she was a slob, and I excused his behavior. Little did I know.

"Finally we ran into each other again at a party, and this time there was no reason for me to say no. I was with a man who was just a friend, but I found out later that Aaron didn't know that. He was with a woman, and he told me they were just friends. It later turned out that they were 'sleeping together' friends. Anyway, I was dancing, and he came over and asked me to dance. He said, 'I feel as if I've spent my life waiting to dance with you.'

"The next day he called me and we went out for the first time. He seemed thrilled and excited to be with me. I asked him about all the stories I had heard about him, and he said he was probably going a little crazy after being in a bad marriage for so long. He convinced me that he wanted to start a serious relationship with me. He couldn't stop telling me how much he loved looking at me and how much he loved talking to me. We went to bed after a few weeks, and then all he could talk about was how much he loved sex with me, how much—how much.

"Once we slept together, the relationship lasted only a few more weeks before he stopped calling regularly. I talked to our mutual friends and found out that he had started seeing yet another woman. He told people in the office that he planned to see the two of us at the same time. The next time he called, I said no, and I told him why, and I asked him not to phone again. He didn't call again, and I couldn't believe it.

"I sound calm about this now, but at the time I was very, very upset. A couple of years later I ran into him at a conference, and we had coffee. He said that he realized that he had never been committed to his wife and that he didn't want to be committed to anyone. He said that he was learning to be less of a 'bastard' with women, but that things had moved too quickly with me. He said that it had been obvious that I had wanted more from him than he was prepared to give. He said that one of the reasons he was attracted to me was that he thought I was very free and not likely to get dependent. That's what he liked about me—that sense of freedom—and he said he was really surprised when I got involved emotionally. That's not what he wanted. He didn't ever again want a relationship that was connected."

EVEN BRIEFER ENCOUNTERS

Sometimes all the stages of a commitmentphobic relationship seem to be played out in the course of one or two dates. We have spoken to some men, for example, who told us of going on blind dates, falling "madly in love" within minutes, and establishing a connection that was sufficiently intense that by the end of the evening they felt that the next step would have to be marriage. Rather than think of that possibility, they decided that the relationship would have to end before it began.

So many of us, particularly women, have been on the receiving end of this kind of behavior. We go out on a date with someone who seems so totally smitten that it lowers all of our defenses and creates powerful expectations that don't seem unreasonable, but then the phone never rings again. Where do all these Houdinis go? Are they all together in a room somewhere swapping stories? These are the kinds of jokes women make when they are together.

If you have ever wondered what went wrong when everything seemed so full of promise, it's important to understand the dynamic that makes someone run when things are going too well.

WHEN A WOMAN IS THE ACTIVE PARTNER

The man isn't always the active avoider within a relationship. Often it is the woman who is playing that role, but with a difference. Because we are accustomed to thinking of men as the pursuers and women as being pursued, more often than not we find ourselves acting out these stereotypical roles as we establish new relationships.

Men have been socialized to chase. They have been told they should be the hunters. Even though they often resent this position, they can be even more resentful of any woman who tries to reverse the roles. Women are still socialized to be "caught"; they are conditioned to wait for the man to act. They give indications of their interest—signals of their availability—but rarely feel comfortable pursuing a man in the same fashion a man would pursue a woman.

What does a woman with active commitment issues do? How does she set up a relationship in which she is doing much of the initiating and setting up most of the boundaries? Unlike a man, nobody expects her to make a thousand phone calls, send flowers and candygrams, play guitar under her beloved's window. When a man does this, it's considered acceptable male behavior.

Women with active issues typically set up a different style. When the relationship begins, they appear accepting or downright seductive. They end the relationship by withdrawal and rejection. In between they call the shots by setting up rules and boundaries that are impossible to overcome. Many men have been conditioned to believe that all women, by definition, are anxious to get married. When these men meet a woman who doesn't fit this mold, they are often confused and shocked by what is taking place.

Andy says that he has a pattern of attracting women with commitment problems. He told us about a relationship that he says went through very definite stages. He describes Crystal as bright, beautiful, and self-sufficient. Unlike many women, Crystal seems relatively comfortable about assuming the role of pursuer.

He says:

"I met Crystal through my job. She worked for a company that I was doing business with, and for a few months I was in their offices on a regular basis. She came up to me in the hall and said, 'I've heard about you—who are you anyway?' So I introduced myself, and we started chatting. Every time I was there, we would talk a little bit."

Because Andy was dating a woman with whom things were becoming serious, he made no attempt to ask Crystal out. But she had other ideas.

"One day she came up to me as I was walking out the office door and said, 'You know, I really like talking to you. How about if we go to lunch sometime?' We went to lunch and ended up spending two and a half hours together. I started walking her back to her office, and she said, 'Some friends of mine are going out on Friday night. I wonder if you would like to join us.' I was very flattered by her attention, so I said yes.

"We went out with this group, and we went to a place where there was dancing. Crystal and I danced together most of the night. The next day, Saturday, she phoned me and said, 'I just wanted to make sure you had a nice time last night. Did you?' We ended up talking on the phone for hours. Before we hung up, she said, 'You know, the company takes over a country club for a day every year'—this was going to happen the following week— 'Would you like to be my date?' I said sure. So we went, and we had a terrific time. It ended up with more dancing. During the evening she told me that she had two tickets to a concert by a group I had said I liked. She asked me if I wanted to go. It was on a night that was tough for me, but I said I would adjust my plans, and I did.

"Then she called me and asked, 'How do you feel about me?' I told her that I liked her a lot. She asked me why I never asked her out. I told her it was because she never gave me half a chance— she asked me to do something before I could get the words out of my mouth. I said, 'Give me an opportunity and I'll ask you out. In fact I'll ask you out right now.'

Andy didn't want to go out with two women at the same time.

"I was very up front with Crystal. I said, 'Look, I'm seeing this woman, and we're sleeping together.' She said, 'That's okay.' But she kept pursuing me. She sent me things. I was going away for a long weekend, and she sent me half a dozen little cards telling me to behave while I was gone because she was waiting for me. She would call me and leave these messages on my machine saying that she had called to hear my voice. Everything she did and everything she said made it very clear that her feelings were 'Boy, you are the man I've been searching for.' I found this very appealing. She is also a very, very desirable woman.

"Finally Crystal and I went out to dinner one night, at her suggestion, and in the course of dinner she said, 'I feel we're emotionally very close right now, but you're not very physical with me.' I repeated that I was sleeping with someone else, and besides, I told her, I like to establish an emotional base in a relationship before it gets sexual."

At about this point, Andy says, he realized that he was tremendously attracted to Crystal, and she seemed really to like him. Therefore he decided (a) to break things up with the woman he had been seeing, and (b) to move to a new plateau with Crystal and start a sexual relationship. What he didn't know was that Crystal was *already* sleeping with someone—an old boyfriend for whom she later said she had no feelings.

"Well, once I broke up with the other woman, I started trying to move the relationship with Crystal in the direction of sex. But as I became more interested in developing a sexual relationship, Crystal changed. It took us a month to get to bed, because every time we saw each other, she had reasons why she didn't want to have sex. When we finally did, she was very different from what I would have imagined—mechanical, technique oriented, and essentially emotionless.

"Two weeks after the first time we went to bed, it was my parents' anniversary party. I asked Crystal to come as my date. We went, and she appeared to be having a good time, but about a week later she told me that she had started having these 'pangs' and feeling uncomfortable when she was with me. She said she wanted to get out of the relationship, but she realized that she had pursued me to such a degree that she had a hard time telling me she had changed her mind. I was hurt, but I said she should do what she was comfortable with, but then she called me and said something else. She said that she had trouble when she cared for somebody and would I please give her time.

"The relationship continued for another couple of weeks. Then one Friday night she was supposed to come over to my apartment after work. She never showed up, and she didn't call. I called her apartment. I called some of her friends. No one knew where she was. I left messages on her machine, but she didn't return them. Finally on Sunday she called. I was understandably very concerned and worried. She said that she had decided that we were better friends than lovers—there was no 'chemistry.' What she wanted was to continue seeing me, but she wanted to see other people too. She said that she needed that freedom."

Andy says that Crystal was the master of the double message. For example, she told him that she thought that he was the perfect man for her, that he was everything she ever dreamed of, and that he had every quality she ever wanted in a man. The only problem was that Andy was "too emotional"—although she didn't think that was such a big problem because she felt she needed to become more emotional herself.

"One minute she said I was everything she ever wanted. The next she said that there was no sexual chemistry. Anyway, I told her that if that was the way she felt, it was okay with me, and I basically withdrew.

"In the meantime, however, we had made plans to go down to Mexico for a week. We had the tickets and a deposit down on hotel reservations. She said that she would still like to take this vacation, but just as friends—no sex. I said okay, that I thought that we could do that. So we went down, and I made no overtures to her whatsoever. On the third night we got into an argument. I said, 'You know, I don't buy this sexual-chemistry thing. Something else is going on. What is it?' She said, 'You know what it is, really? I just can't tolerate the obligations and the expectations that come with a committed relationship. I can't tolerate the feeling of having to do something because I'm expected to.'

"The next night she got into bed with me and seduced me. It

was better sex than any we had had up to that time. Afterward she said that she wanted me to understand that this didn't mean that we were having a relationship. I said, 'Okay.'

"The next night we went for a walk on the beach, and she was hanging all over me, and we had sex on the beach. It was great. But the next day she told me that she was angry that we had sex. She felt that she had established these guidelines, that we were going to just be friends and I had ruined that. I was flabbergasted. She said that we'd better not have sex that night. So I said okay, and I stayed away from her for the rest of the vacation.

"When we got back, she immediately started dating somebody else, and we went back to being just friends. . . . But she vacillates. Sometimes she becomes very dependent on me and calls every day. She told me that she felt that she needed two men in her life. I was the emotional man, the other guy was the sexual one, and that she was purposely orchestrating her life to keep both parts separate. Sometimes this takes some very odd twists and turns.

"Even though she was seeing some other guy, we decided that we would have a drink to celebrate Christmas. She showed up at my house totally dressed up. Makeup, short skirt, the works. It was weird. And seductive. So I sat her down and said, 'Look, this isn't working out. You're giving me all these mixed messages. You act seductive, I respond, then you say no, and I can't handle it. I don't think we should be seeing each other anymore.' Well, she started to cry. She said, 'I love you so much. I couldn't stand being without you. Don't break up with me now.' I said, 'This is really crazy! You said we weren't seeing each other anymore. We're not even having a relationship to break up!' She said, 'Don't say anything more. Let's just get through the holidays.'

"A month or so later we went out. We hadn't slept together in months, but all of a sudden she started talking about getting married. I said, 'Married! You can't even sleep with me.' " She said that she could, and just to prove it, we went back to my apartment and had sex. Then she called me the next day and said, 'You know, all of that talk about marriage—let's forget it.' I said fine.

"We slept together a couple more times, but then we stopped altogether. But she is still always flirtatious and sexual. And she starts up with me physically—a lot of foreplay, no sex. And she still buys me presents, sends me little cards. You know the kind of thing a woman does if she really likes you. She tells me I'm the most important person in her life. Since we're not together, that doesn't seem to mean very much."

SHE HAD TO SAY NO BEFORE SHE COULD SAY YES

Wes, a thirty-four-year-old advertising executive, says that he was devastated by a woman who he believes had serious commitment problems. He met her while he was in Washington on business.

"At that time I had a client in Washington, and I was there more than I was in New York. One weekend I stayed in Washington.

"I went out with a group of friends, and she was there—very pretty, very quiet . . . tall . . . sort of a Julia Roberts look. We all went out to dinner, and she didn't say anything to me. Then we went dancing. The others all moved off together, so I asked her to dance. You have to understand this woman and I had never exchanged a word, but we hit the dance floor, and suddenly she was all over me. There was such intimacy in her body language that it knocked me over. *Wow*, I thought, *this feels really close.* We truly didn't exchange five words that entire evening. Afterward we went out for coffee. Same thing. She didn't speak, but when we got out on the street, she took my hand. She seemed shy and yet very aggressive and forward sexually. It was a completely disarming combination. So I asked her out.

"We went out to dinner, and it was very hard to talk to her, which made me think that it wasn't going to work between us. One thing I remember is that she said her friends all told her that she was afraid of intimacy. I didn't pay too much attention, though. Going home, on the street, she took my hand and sort of plastered herself up against me. She seemed so comfortable when she was close to me. It seemed very intimate to me. We kissed good night, and I was very turned on.

"We had talked about a magazine article I was reading, and the next day I called her and asked if I could bring it over. She said sure. When I got there, she was wearing this old T-shirt and short shorts. She kept calling attention to her body, apologizing for her shorts. She made me coffee and she kept touching me. It was intoxicating to have that kind of physical attention. She suggested we go for a walk. It was a gorgeous spring day, and we walked down to the park near the river, and again she reached for my hand. When we got there, we sat on the grass, and she put her head on my leg. All of this stuff made me think, *Shit, this woman really likes me.* A big part of me wasn't clear why she seemed to like me so much. We had exchanged very little information. And yet I was flattered. I remember thinking, *Oh, my God, I'm going to be spending my weekends this summer visiting her in the Washington heat. That's even worse than New York.* I remember telling her that I was nervous about having to spend the summer working in Washington.

"The next time I went out with her, when I got to her apartment, she made this big deal about having just bought a new bathing suit, which she insisted that I see her in. She was talking about how we could go to her beach club in the summer. It made me feel as though she had bought the bathing suit just to please me—to keep me happy in Washington. After dinner we went back to her apartment, and she sort of jumped me. Even though there was a lot of physical contact, we didn't have sex. I was uncomfortable with it. In my head I had a very traditional scenario that included waiting and going through stages.

"In the meantime she kept acting like we were going to be together. You know, she would talk about things we could do together, and trips we could take. During this part of the relationship she included me in her life: She introduced me to her family; she included me in her little decisions—like where to move the couch and how to put up her shelves. She asked me to meet her in a store so I could see this present she wanted to buy her mother. She wanted my advice about everything. She asked me to help her pick out some furniture she was buying for her bedroom—she wanted to have me check out the mattress. And the sex, which happened very quickly, was incredible.

"For about a month we had a very casual intimacy. It was easy and close. I was doing most of the phoning, but she was definitely waiting for my calls. And we were seeing each other every few days.

"Anyway one week I had to go back to New York. I was gone maybe five days. We talked every night, but when I got back, she was resistant. I didn't get the sense of someone who was waiting to see me. In fact she told me that I called too often and she didn't like it.

"That's when there was a definite shift in the relationship. We started to have little disagreements, mostly because she was finding fault with me. There were a whole bunch of things about me that were suddenly not to her liking. She said I was making too many assumptions and that I wasn't giving her enough time to herself. I tried to back off. This made it better, but whenever we got closer, she would withdraw. There was about a month of this kind of little back-and-forth stuff. I thought maybe if we took one of those trips she talked about, things would improve, so I made plans for the two of us, which she agreed to.

"Well, the 'trip' weekend came, and she said she'd changed her mind. She had 'stuff' to do. We hadn't had a whole weekend together in several weeks, but at the last minute she couldn't go away because she had to do laundry and paperwork. I was nuts. I felt totally slammed and hurt.

"So I fought with her about it, and that's when her attitude really changed. She told me that she had never agreed to go anywhere with me. She said she needed her space and that she didn't want to see me for a while. She blew me away.

"I guess she pushed the wrong buttons, because I became obsessed. All I wanted to do was talk. I needed to know what had happened to change the way she felt. I wanted her to face what went wrong and talk to me about it. I believed she still cared about me, but that she had problems. I thought we could work them out together. So I would call her every five or six days, pretending to be casual, looking for an opportunity to resolve our problems. When she didn't see me for a while, she would warm up.

"Sometimes she would ask me over. She would tell me that she wanted to make it clear that if she saw me, we couldn't sleep together. Then of course we did. It was like she had to say no before she could say yes. Or maybe considering the beginning, she said yes before she said no. It was very confusing.

"She was willing to see me, but she had lots of rules. For example, she didn't want any planned dates, and everything, from sex to whether or not we went out to dinner, had to be spontaneous. You can imagine, living in another city, how spontaneous I could be. I had to reconstruct my life. Figuring out how to see her under these conditions took up most of my thoughts. I got so scared of offending her that I just stopped initiating anything, particularly sex.

"We would watch television on her couch, and I would pretend to be disinterested in her and interested only in what was on the tube. I knew that if I looked disinterested enough, she would move over to me and start something. I would feel frozen, as if I couldn't make one move because if I did, everything would be over. One night, I remember, she asked me to please spend the night. The minute I got into bed to sleep, I knew it was a mistake. When I woke up the next morning, I was right. She seemed angry and annoyed to have me there. A week or so later she told me that it was over. She said she was unhappy about all these things about me. For example, even though I was several inches taller than her, I wasn't tall enough and I wasn't really her physical type. It was incredible rejection.

"A year later I saw her at a party, and she started the whole physical thing again—rubbing against me, taking my hand. I was tempted, but this time I stayed away."

BREAKING THE SEXUAL BOND

Sex is one of the most powerful ways that two people can be bonded. When there is a powerful attraction and a passionate sexual connection, it seems to make sense that both partners would want it to continue—particularly if there is nothing else that's going wrong in the relationship. Yet men and women who are feeling intense commitmentphobic anxiety are sometimes able to break this bond in a manner that shocks their partners.

Barbara, forty-two, recently ended a relationship that had become uncomfortably close. Until she and Stan moved in together two years ago, she had always lived alone. It was her dream to find a partner with whom she could build a life. She was therefore quite surprised by the anxiety she experienced when she finally started living with a man. She says:

"When I met Stan, I had just about given up on all men. I had had so many destructive relationships in my life. Most of the men I went out with had obvious commitment problems, and I had been seriously hurt. Stan seemed different. We had a lot in common. At first we also had very nice sex. There was a strong and very sweet physical bond. That was the hardest thing to break away from. I knew Stan loved me, but I couldn't stay with him.

"I knew I should be grateful that Stan was so devoted, and I was. I didn't want to be alone, but having somebody around all the time, and I do mean all the time, is no picnic either. Maybe it was Stan, maybe it was me. All I know is that I reached the point where if he walked into a room, I felt so cramped for space that I had to walk out. I would get headaches, and I felt as though it hurt to breathe. I know it wasn't fair, because he didn't do anything except occupy space, but this made me so angry that I became a real bitch.

"I started trying to avoid sex because if we had sex, I thought I was expected to be more emotionally connected. I mean, I got guilty if we had sex, and then I just wanted to be alone. I stopped sleeping in the same bed with him. It was sort of a gradual thing, and eventually we were always in different beds. He kept suggesting that we get counseling, but I didn't want to do it because I thought then I would never get out alive. You know, when you're in a relationship, even with someone you love, and you find yourself thinking that you won't feel human again until you get rid of him, it's not a good thing.

"Finally we talked about it, and he agreed he should move out. The funny thing is that the day he moved out, I almost fainted from the pain of ending the relationship. I was so upset, I couldn't see straight. Of course I miss him physically, but when I think about the way I felt when he was here all the time, I know that I had no choice."

Since Barbara had spent many years in relationships with men who treated her badly, one can't help but wonder why she was so resistant to seeking couple's counseling. Why was she unwilling to try to fix her relationship?

140

"SHE NEVER SAID, 'HOW DO *WE* FIX THIS?' "

Jeremy, twenty-nine, told us that the most frustrating thing about his ex-girlfriend is that she would do nothing to try to improve the relationship. He said:

"There wasn't that much going wrong between us. Just small disagreements about where to go on weekends or whether to use her car or my car. Nothing major. Our values were pretty much the same. All we had to do was do some accommodating. But she wouldn't do it. And she wouldn't talk about it. She never wanted to try to improve the relationship.

"Our biggest problem: She never wanted to make plans. What that meant is that if it was something she wanted to do, we would plan for it. If it was something I wanted to do, she would say, 'Let's not overplan.' If I wanted to take a trip or see a play, it was murder. I would try to find ways to compromise, but she wasn't having any of it. When we fought, I was always the one who had to accommodate her. Although she kept telling me she loved me, she made it clear that the only way to have a relationship with her was to do things her way.

"I thought we should see somebody to talk about *our* problem, but she wouldn't have any of it. Finally she told me that she had always had a problem with commitment, and that I was making her uncomfortable. Basically, she said, she loved me, but she wanted her space much more than she wanted to work on a relationship."

Men and women who are working to maintain space and distance within a relationship want to continue doing just that. Typically unless there is some dramatic turnaround in attitude, they don't want to resolve the problems in the relationship. To work on "fixing" a relationship is the equivalent of making a commitment. Think about it from the point of view of the person with active commitment conflicts: If you feel that you are in jail and your warden asks you to help him make your cell more secure, how are you going to respond?

HOLIDAYS, BIRTHDAYS, SPECIAL EVENTS

"Everything was fine until my sister's wedding, and my boyfriend refused to go with me. It meant so much to me to look like a normal person with someone who cared about her, I couldn't believe that he would leave me alone at a time like that. But he did."

—ASHLEY, twenty-six

"We spent Christmas together, but I could tell she was distant. Then a couple of days later she told me that she wanted to be alone—with friends—on New Year's Eve. You can imagine how I felt."

—RODNEY, thirty

"Harv and I went out together for five years. For every one of those years he disappeared regularly on my birthday, my son's birthday, Christmas Eve, Thanksgiving, Valentine's Day. He said they didn't mean anything to him. They meant something to me, though."

—SYLVIA, thirty-six

You will notice from many of the stories in this book that men and women with active commitment issues can be particularly adept at causing crises around those moments that most of us like to think of as special. If you are involved with someone with active commitment issues, holidays and special occasions are almost certainly going to set off the conflict. The reason: Most of these events involve family and togetherness. Consequently they can be perceived as setting up tremendous expectations and obligations, which the person with active conflicts often doesn't want to meet. One man we interviewed describes his feelings:

"I know I really hurt her on Christmas and New Year's—several years in a row. But I couldn't help it. I felt that if her family saw us together on those days, then I would have to marry her. I didn't want that. I didn't want the world to think of me as her husband —tied up with her for life. I didn't want to think of myself that way."

WHY IT ENDS WHEN THE BEST HAS JUST BEGUN

The commitmentphobic relationship is far more likely to fall apart when the going gets *good* than when the going gets tough. People with active conflicts may get unhappy when their relationship isn't working, but they only panic when their relationship is working too well. They may be uncomfortable when there's too much distance, but they're paralyzed when there's not enough. Sometimes the better the relationship, the *worse* they feel.

The active avoider thinks, *If it gets any closer, I'll never be able to leave.* An overwhelming amount of fear rushes to the surface. The avoider starts thrashing about. Next thing you know, everything is in pieces. If you don't have a commitment problem, this makes no sense. If you have a commitment problem, it makes perfect sense. Commitmentphobics *have* to have an out. As their avenues close one by one, they feel worse, not better. The exits are all being sealed off. Loss of freedom is inevitable, and that is unacceptable. It's a matter of survival.

What most active runners never adequately consider is how painful this can be to their partners. When you leave a relationship at its peak, the effect is devastating. Indeed some people never fully recover from this kind of loss.

HOW COMMITMENTPHOBIC RELATIONSHIPS END

Commitmentphobic relationships typically end in one of three ways:

• *The active avoider precipitates a major confrontation and provokes the more passive partner to break it off.*

When it's a relationship of some duration, with a real history and many complications, the active avoider may end it by pushing his or her partner up against a wall, using provocative behavior such as infidelity, or boundaries that become ever more unreasonable.

Although it may not appear that way, the active avoider is usually aware of what he or she is doing, but would prefer not to assume responsibility.

• *The active avoiders withdraw slowly, setting up boundaries all the while, until there is no relationship left.*

Slowly but surely—some commitmentphobic relationships just can't end any other way. One woman told us, "He just kept seeing less of me. It was still passionate, it was still intense, but there was less relationship and more space. Finally it was all space and the only relationship that was left was a once-a-week phone call, every Wednesday night. Why Wednesday? I used to think it was because we met on a Wednesday, but who knows?"

• *The active avoider ends it suddenly, disappearing like Houdini, offering little or no explanation.*

The person who announces without warning that the relationship is over and then sets it up so that there is no further contact is totally panicked. This can happen early in a relationship, or not for years, but when it does, it is brutally difficult for the passive partner, who may be completely unprepared. Over the years we've heard so many disappearance stories that we refer to this phenomenon as the "Houdini Syndrome." We've heard of active avoiders leaving while their partners were taking showers or talking on the phone. We've heard stories of men ending long-term relationships by getting out of bed after particularly passionate sex, saying they needed a little air, and then never returning. We've heard stories of men and women suddenly announcing, "It's over," and refusing, from that day forward, to take phone calls.

RUNNING TO A NEW PARTNER

Since active commitment conflicts are all about running, the active avoider often ends an important relationship by running off to a new partner in what seems to be record time. The passive partner, on the other hand, typically retreats and takes a very long time before he or she is able to recover.

AFTER IT'S OVER—UNRESOLVED, UNEXPLAINED, UNEXPLORED

The lack of real resolution is the most frustrating thing about the end of a commitmentphobic relationship. One partner—typically the passive one—or both, are left with an extraordinary sense of it not being over. Too much was left undone, too much was left unsaid. Partners wonder, If the communication was extraordinary, why did it end? If the sex was wonderful, why did it end? If the values were so similar, why did it end? There are many unanswered questions, and many ways in which the good elements of the relationship were never fully explored. It feels frustrating and sad.

CHAPTER SIX

Getting Distance

Those with unresolved conflicts typically either find a relationship with distance built into it or they try to manufacture distance in the relationship they already have.

Some people manage this by getting involved in relationships in which there are actual physical boundaries separating them from their partners. They pair up with people who live far away, or they turn a close relationship into a long-distance relationship by moving themselves or traveling frequently. For others even thinking about moving away is enough to ease the threat. Escape fantasies, such as joining the Peace Corps, are not uncommon.

Some people create distance by hiding in their offices and "getting lost in their work" or by seeking out relationships with other workaholics. Others hide out at the gym or on the golf course or in the basement with their stamp collection. Some people create obstacles that limit relationships: They may have schedules that limit their availability or seek people who do the same; they may have needs that limit their availability—sleep requirements, dietary requirements, and so on; they may always have more than one romantic interest or find partners with other romantic entanglements; they may exclude their partners from certain key areas in their lives. Whatever the choice, it accomplishes the same thing: distance.

Psychological boundaries can also give commitmentphobes the distance they need. Perhaps they erect emotional walls or seek partners with emotional walls; they may use language that is intentionally distancing; they may withhold sexually; they may find fault with their partners, creating distance in their minds and in the minds of their partners; they may flirt or fantasize about having other partners; they may find partners they can never completely trust to be faithful.

LOOKING FOR SPACE

Here are two examples of people who are struggling with the need to distance their partners:

"I love my husband. Honest. But I can't stand having him in my kitchen. It makes me want to kill. The kitchen is my space."
—JANE, thirty-seven

"My wife has the damnedest habit. Whenever I'm watching the news on television, she comes and sits next to me. I don't like it. I don't know why, but when I'm watching television, I want her to stay away, at least twelve feet or so. Otherwise I'm uncomfortable."
—ALAN, thirty-nine

Everyone has physical and psychological boundaries that they prefer not to have crossed. To make things even more complicated, these boundaries fluctuate. The same person who craves closeness one moment is nowhere to be found the next. The man or woman who spends an ardent weekend in bed with a lover may feel an overwhelming need to spend the next two weeks alone. All of us are constantly regulating our space, both physical and psychological. It is part and parcel of being a territorial animal. Some, however, take this to extremes.

Men and women with commitment conflicts can be unusually sensitive to their own needs for space and have far greater requirements than your average Joe or Joan. Ongoing physical closeness makes them uncomfortable, nonstop emotional closeness makes them feel put upon. Hence they are often "space talking": "I need my space," "I need *more* space (room, time)," "You don't give me any space (room, time) for myself," "Don't crowd me." These phrases may sound like tired clichés, but the feelings expressed are usually genuine and heartfelt.

Some people can't handle *any* intrusion into their physical or emotional territory; everything feels like a violation of their boundaries. Many of these people manage to make their feelings known. Others feel almost as uncomfortable, but they don't articulate it. Still others are highly sensitive to having their space "invaded," but they aren't really aware of what's happening. They experience their discomfort as some kind of low-level anxiety or mild annoyance for which they can't find a cause. All of these people may put up with their discomfort for the sake of having a relationship, although their feelings may resurface as anger or resentment.

Vicki, a self-employed public relations consultant, exhibits just about every symptom associated with commitment anxiety, but she is most sensitive to her need for space. At thirty-eight Vicki has been married twice. She says that she finds men in the nineties too "needy" and that this makes it difficult for her to sustain a relationship.

We interviewed Vicki in the large two-family house she shares with her sister in northern California. She occupies one five-room apartment, her sister the other. Because of the proximity, and because it's her sister, she considers this a roommate situation. She says:

"I know I can't handle too much intimacy. With my sister in the upstairs apartment, we never get in each other's way, and we each have our own place. But it's nice knowing she's there if I really want someone to talk to.

"I don't ever again want to have a man living in a place that I consider my house. Let him live in his own. Maybe he'll have a boat—let him live in his boat. When somebody's around, I start to get crazy. That's just the way I am."

Years of trying to relate in a more traditional fashion have convinced Vicki that she needs to have her own place in order to have a relationship.

"Unless I stay centered, I can't give anything to a relationship, and I can't stay centered unless I'm alone a great deal of the time. The man I'm seeing now wants to be with me all the time, and I keep telling him that doing that makes me crazy. I need to read *my*

149

books, listen to *my* music, have *my own* peace. I have to do that. Maybe some people can be with someone else all the time and stay centered. Some people can be tied down. I can't."

In terms of her work Vicki also resents feeling tied down. She feels she is a workaholic, but she can't work on any set schedule.

"That's one of the reasons why I prefer being in business for myself. In fact that's how I got successful. When I worked for somebody else, I felt like a caged animal, like a lion in a cage. I can't be..r being confined in an office or to a routine. That's why I went out on my own."

Despite her problems in relationships Vicki has never really been without one. Her first marriage took place when she was twenty-two. She says:

"The day after the wedding I panicked. I woke up and I simply panicked. I said I have to go home to my parents, and that's what I did—drove to the airport and got on a plane to my parents' house, twenty-five hundred miles away. I stayed with my parents about a month before they talked me into going back to my husband.

"Don't get me wrong. I really liked my husband; we were great friends. I just discovered I was unhappy sharing space." At first Vicki was able to handle her feelings because she and her husband were fortunate enough to find an unusually large house.

"It had about twenty rooms, and we used every bit of it. My husband also needed a lot of space because he had different interests. We each had lots of little rooms. I had a room to read in; he had a room to read in. I had a room to watch television in; he had a room to watch television in. We never had to be together. But separation of course makes you grow apart, and that's what we did. Anyway we lost the lease on the house, and eventually we got divorced."

Within a few years Vicki married again.

"Both times I got married, I knew it wasn't going to be forever. With my second husband I said, 'Let's get married so we can end this relationship.' Some relationships you have to take full cycle, and this was definitely one of them. We were very much in love, but I knew it wasn't going to last. We were married for two years."

Vicki says that before marriage the relationship wasn't confining because they kept breaking up with each other. For example, he would start seeing someone else, or she would. Or she would stop paying attention to him, or he would do something to "push her buttons." She found the "on and off" quality very "comfortable."

When Vicki and her second husband moved into an apartment together, that made the marriage all the more difficult. To compensate for the lack of space, she started devising little gimmicks that would make her feel more as though she were alone.

"I felt smothered; I couldn't breathe. I told my husband how much I hated it and how much I hated coming home. In fact I tried to stay away as much as possible. When I did come home, I would make him sit around the house, poor guy, with headphones on while he was watching television so I could feel like he wasn't there. The only way I could stay calm is if I could forget that he was there. People thought I was crazy because I made my husband sit around with headphones on. But after a while he stopped minding it. The really bad thing is that my husband started liking the feeling of being alone. He stopped wanting to talk to me or spend time with me." Even when we went out to dinner, he started taking his headphones with him—so he could listen to the radio. It turned very crazy."

After the marriage ended, Vicki found herself remembering how it was with her second husband when they were just going together and breaking up at regular intervals.

"I liked that—so I began looking for the same kind of relationship with a different man. I decided the answer was distance. I found a man who lived in Denver. That way I wouldn't get into the emotional traumas that come with closeness. For a while it was great. We would meet in New Mexico or Europe or Canada. All romance. But it didn't last."

Recently Vicki's current love interest insisted that she take a vacation with him. After much resistance she agreed to a short trip, even though she feared that she would start feeling smothered. When they got to the chosen spot, she discovered that he had rented a country property with two houses:

"I was thrilled. We used both houses. One I used as my very own. I would go there to be alone and relax in. I thought that maybe this could be a solution to my problems. Maybe this is the way I could live with a man. In two houses on the same property.

If they were both big and beautiful, it might work. It's an idea, no?"

If you are thoroughly sensitized to your need for space, life is not easy. If someone uses your towel, it makes you uncomfortable. If anyone borrows something without telling you, it makes you nuts. If they rearrange the refrigerator, it's grounds for murder. Of course you may have control issues as well as commitment conflicts. When that is the case, the combination produces such feelings ∪ʄ rage and resentment that it's often impossible to stay with any one partner for very long.

Close, but not too close. Far, but not too far. People like this want to be near the ones they love, but they also want to be alone. They want a relationship, they just don't want to have to relate. Not all the time anyway. And certainly not in shared space.

NEEDING DISTANCE/NEEDING INTIMACY/NEEDING CONTROL

It's also important to look at the need to maintain distance from a slightly different perspective: gaining control and losing control. Men and women with commitment conflicts are often control freaks. In order to regulate distance and intimacy, they need to control much of what goes on in a relationship, including their feelings and the feelings of their partners. There is too much at stake if they can't. The need to control distance, and consequently the amount of intimacy in a relationship, is very much part of the push-pull dynamic of a commitmentphobic relationship.

In the beginning of a relationship both partners are strangers, and the bond is fragile. Without control, lovers can feel that they are on pins and needles the entire time. They're lost and unsure of where they stand. This may sometimes be fun and exciting, but it's also frightening. Typically this is the point at which someone with active conflicts begins to do everything possible to get some sense of control. Intimate letters, gifts, phone calls, sex, words of love—whatever it takes to know that this other person could be yours, should you want it that way.

Being in control affords the active partner the luxury of scrutinizing the relationship. He or she can think, *I don't like this, I'm not attracted to that, I'm not sure about this, I'm not wild about that. What will this be like in a year . . . five years . . . ten years . . . fifty years?* Assured of control, it is easy to find three thousand reasons that the relationship ultimately won't work.

What happens when the relationship feels too close and one partner needs to create distance? That depends on how much distance is needed. But it can be extremely destructive when one partner wants to build a relationship and all the other wants to build is a wall.

For the active partner there is of course always the risk of creating too much distance because if your partner responds by pulling away, you may discover that distance makes your heart grow fonder. Without the ax poised right above your head, the relationship looks a lot more appealing. You start seeing your partner in a very different light, appreciating everything about him or her instead of obsessing about everything that is missing. You realize how much you care. You realize how special your partner is and how comforting the relationship is. Naturally these feelings draw you closer.

If only it stopped here. But it almost never does. Instead this is usually just the first of an endless series of backing-and-forthing. It's always too close or too far, and you're always trying to make adjustments in one direction or the other, always trying to balance fear and longing. Controlling the relationship becomes a full-time job, with no rest for the weary. It's more stressful than controlling air traffic at JFK. Very few people do a good job. Most swing from one extreme to another. They get close until they can't stand it anymore, then they run away or force their partners to run away till the distance is unbearable. By the time they've finished, the relationship is a shambles, and no one has escaped tremendous pain. Maybe they don't lose their freedom, but they definitely lose.

BOUNDARIES FROM DAY ONE

Setting up and maintaining boundaries are the primary ways in which people with commitment conflicts keep their distance. For example:

"He never let me meet his mother."

"She wouldn't go to parties with me. At first I thought it was because she was shy, but soon I realized that she didn't want to go public with me."

"She wouldn't spend the night in my apartment."

"He took me out every other Saturday night, and every Wednesday—never any other time."

"He wouldn't spend holidays with me."

"A year into the relationship she still wouldn't let me buy her dinner because she said it might obligate her into a commitment."

"I never get to meet any of his friends."

"There were incredible boundaries around sex."

"He wouldn't go on a vacation with me—ever."

Often boundaries such as these exist from the beginning. Other times they are introduced gradually. The same person who has dated you every weekend for two years refuses to share a vacation or a holiday weekend. The same woman who has made mad, passionate love with you for over six months refuses to let you meet her family. The same man who has brought you into the inner world of his psyche severely restricts the amount of time you can spend together.

These boundaries usually feel unnatural because they don't accurately reflect the emotional bond that exists between the couple. In a relationship with restrictive boundaries both partners are always conscious of the sensitive areas. The problem is that boundaries are a little too effective as a means of maintaining distance. They become like little land mines that stand between both partners, and the resentment and anger that are generated frequently destroy the relationship.

SEXUAL CONTROL/SEXUAL BOUNDARIES

"The first couple of months were great, and then he started having this desire problem."

"We have wonderful sex, and then she doesn't want me to spend the night."

"He has all these silly rules. We can't have sex on two consecutive days because that's like being married."

* * *

Commitmentphobia isn't about sexual conquest for the sake of putting another notch in the belt. Yet sexual seduction often plays a key role in the way active avoiders attempt to establish control of the relationship. Sex can be used to establish intimacy, and it can also be used to avoid intimacy. Sex can bring a couple closer together or push them farther apart. In short, sex is probably the most effective way of controlling both intimacy and distance within a relationship.

At the beginning of a commitmentphobic relationship men and women with active conflicts tend to be overwhelmingly seductive, typically establishing an intense and frequently obsessive sexual involvement. This is not necessarily limited to the act of making love, although men and women with active conflicts are often stellar lovers. It is a romantic, fantasy-driven sexual connection that partners typically describe as obsessive.

The level of sexual interest and involvement usually stays relatively high until the person with active conflicts begins to feel stuck or trapped. Then we are sometimes reminded that there is another way to use sex to control a relationship: withholding it. Behaving in this way can create a huge obstacle on the path to commitment. And it's deceptive, because it rarely appears to be motivated by commitment issues.

Withholding sexually can be far more complicated than "having a headache." For example:

- He or she may be highly seductive and yet unwilling or unable to be sexually engaged.
- He or she may suddenly lose interest or "desire."
- He or she may place restrictions on frequency or duration or suddenly behave in a more repressed manner.
- He or she may be unfaithful as a means of distancing a partner or reducing intimacy within the primary relationship.
- He or she may begin to communicate sexual dissatisfaction.

Since this behavior usually reflects a major change in attitude, it typically causes the other partner to become extraordinarily anxious and insecure about the relationship. Remember that some of the most powerful double messages in a commitmentphobic relationship revolve around sex.

Zack, thirty-three, describes a relationship in which a changed attitude toward sex presented an insurmountable boundary. You will also note that his story contains a great many sexual mixed messages.

"When Helene and I met, sex was definitely the major component in our relationship. The first three months we were together, the sex never stopped. I was traveling a lot at the time, and whenever I'd get back from the road, we couldn't get enough of each other. Daytime, nighttime, my car, her car, my apartment, her apartment, the Jacuzzi, the bathtub, the floor, the kitchen counter. She wanted it more than I did—though I definitely did want it. That's what made the whole thing seem so nuts.

"There was something else about her that was weird. She had this picture of some other guy on her bedside table. She would keep telling me that I was the best lover she ever had, so I asked her once why, if that was the case, did she keep some other guy's picture there. She said she loved me, but she wouldn't move his picture. It was almost as if she did it on purpose, to keep me on edge. When we made love in her bed, I would make her turn it toward the wall.

"The sex between us stopped being great almost from the moment that I stopped traveling. That's when she stopped wanting it. First she said she was depressed. Then she said that her needs had changed, that sex wasn't as important to her anymore. We went from making love every available moment to making love once a week, twice at the most.

"First I was sympathetic, then I got crazy. It made me want her so bad, it's embarrassing to think about it. I would scream, I would beg, I would buy her presents like it was going out of style. Nothing worked. At one point I actually had to get her to make appointments to be with me for sex. Otherwise she would avoid it completely. I felt tortured. Sex became the focus of my day. My work came to a standstill.

"The pitiful part is that I didn't need to have sex that much. I just couldn't handle the change in her. I didn't understand, and it made me a basket case. The only thing that had changed was my availability. Once I stopped traveling, I was there for her. Looking back, I realize that was what had turned her off. She liked me better from a distance."

INFIDELITY AS THE ULTIMATE METHOD OF GETTING "DISTANCE"

"We had incredible sex every day for three years, until one day he walked through the door and said the relationship was over because he was 'in love' with someone else. We haven't seen each other since that day."

"When she told me she had started sleeping with someone else, I couldn't believe it. The chemistry between us was so thick, you could cut it. How could she do that? I don't understand it."

"I always thought that when people were unfaithful, it was because they were dissatisfied. I swear my boyfriend wasn't dissatisfied. He couldn't stay away from me. So why did he start sleeping with someone else?"

Infidelity is a common ingredient in relationships in which a true commitment has never been made. But in commitmentphobic relationships, even though there is no commitment, there is usually a tremendous amount of passion, intensity, and bonding. These feelings can be so strong that the faithful partner is stunned when he or she discovers that there has been a sexual betrayal. It's like being poisoned by your soul mate. When so much has been shared, how could there be this level of betrayal? What do you think? How do you recover?

It probably doesn't help the pain to know that your partner is out of control. The intimacy that existed between the two of you generated such overwhelming fear and anxiety that your partner had to do something to create more distance.

But knowing that doesn't change the facts. Even if the relationship gets back together, you feel as if your sense of trust has been destroyed. What happened sits between the two of you like an enormous barrier. And what if the relationship ends? Suppose your partner leaves you for this new person. What then? You feel you can't walk down the street without running into the two of them. You feel as though you can't even phone your ex-lover without worrying that you might hear that new person's voice on the phone. Suddenly you become the outsider, and your lover is sharing all those special moments with someone else. The new person in your lover's life has become more than just another human being. This new person has become an obstacle or a road-block between you and the one you love. And that's the whole point. It's the ultimate way of creating distance. The ultimate boundary.

ANGER AS A DISTANCING TECHNIQUE

"He is the one who rejected me. He is the one who is making me unhappy. He is the one with the whole new life that doesn't include me. So why is he so angry at me?"

"I told him that it doesn't matter that we don't get married right away. I still love him, and that we'll work it out. But he's hostile all the time. He's getting what he says he wants, why is he annoyed all the time?"

"My wife started getting angry at me within months of our marriage. She's always mad. She says I'm crowding her. I'm not doing anything except living in the same house."

Sam, thirty-eight, has been in the same relationship for the last three years, and he has a great many feelings for Kathy, the woman with whom he is involved. He should; his ambivalence has created a situation in which she has put up with a great deal. The relationship is very sexual, very interdependent, and very compli-cated. Sam loves Kathy, but he is also very, very angry. This anger takes many forms. In his head he is usually either finding fault with Kathy or arguing with Kathy. His problem: In his words he feels "boxed in" and he would like to end the relationship.

What is the obstacle stopping Sam from doing this? According to Sam it's Kathy, and the way he feels about her. The way Sam explains it, as crazy as it may sound, is that the woman he loves is standing between him and his freedom to pursue other women.

Sam can no longer properly evaluate what is going on. If Kathy makes him dinner, he thinks she is trying to trap him. If she buys him a present, he thinks she is trying to trap him. If she is unusually nice, he thinks she is trying to manipulate him in order to trap him. Kathy can't win. Because of the way Sam feels, everything makes him angry.

When those with commitment conflicts reach the point where they feel an inexplicable fury at their partners, it is a reflection of a clear-cut commitmentphobic response. Active avoiders can reach an extreme where all they can think about is how to "get out." They feel so entrapped and so totally enmeshed in the relationship that they don't know what to do. They are searching for the exit, and in the process of scrambling to find a way out, they can be cruel; they have little sensitivity left for their partner's feelings. They know that their attitude and behavior are unreasonable, but they feel they can't help it. In the meantime the anger serves another purpose. It is a means of further distancing and alienating their partner.

Anger sometimes surfaces in a rather peculiar form of behavior we call gaslighting. If you saw the film *Gaslight,* you will remember that Ingrid Bergman played a wife being driven mad by her husband, who keeps telling her that she is imagining things.

Gaslighting is a hostile way of making someone else assume responsibility for your feelings and your problems. It's making someone else feel confused in order to achieve your own ends. It's mean and it's destructive.

Some people with commitment conflicts gaslight their partners because they can't bear being so full of guilt. They want to end the relationship, but they want to shift the blame. They can't assume responsibility, and they want to believe it's not really their fault. If they can convince you (and themselves) that you have a problem, they don't have to feel so bad about their own cruel behavior.

The story told to us by Gloria, forty-four, provides an excellent example of commitmentphobic "gaslighting":

"Lennie swept me off my feet. From the minute we met, he told me I was his precious love. He thought everything I did was wonderful. I realized he was unrealistic, but we were both over forty, so I thought he must have some sense of what he was feeling. We got married within six months.

"By the time we were married a month, he was a changed person. He told me that he didn't love me the way he once did because I was such a crummy housekeeper. I tried to point out to him that he was being overly critical. I may not be the best house-keeper in the world, but I'm far from the worst. Besides we were both working—why didn't he clean, or we could hire somebody. He couldn't stop talking about my sloppiness as well as a whole bunch of other stuff that he said I did wrong.

"I realized that he was out of control, and I suggested that maybe he was having a reaction to living with me that had more to do with commitment than it did with dust. He told me that I was crazy, that I was the one with the problem, and that I was trying to drive him away. I wanted to go to couple's therapy, but he would have none of it. Not only did he refuse to consider that he might have a problem, he refused to accept any responsibility around the house. He would come home at night and start examining surfaces looking for dirt or clutter. He was so mean. One night he called me a stupid, dirty bitch. I just started crying and asked him to leave. He said it was proof that I wanted to get rid of him all along."

Some people with commitment conflicts truly believe their excuses, distortions, and manipulations. They've buried their ambivalence and their guilt about it, so they are genuinely unaware of what they are feeling. They don't feel guilt, shame, or remorse. They feel anger. People like this are in deep denial. They are so cut off from their conflict, they don't even realize they have a conflict. This makes them so convincing that it's hard for anyone not to believe them. And that makes them truly dangerous.

There is no winning with someone who is in this kind of denial. Relationships with these people are confusing, frustrating, and hurtful. Healing only comes through recognition of what has really taken place.

The following statements are all examples of people who have been "gaslighted" by partners with serious commitment conflicts. Note the hostile twist to each ending:

"He did everything he could to put me over the edge. Then when I snapped, he told me he couldn't spend time with someone who couldn't control herself."

"She did everything she could to make me jealous. Then when I lost it, she said she couldn't stay with me because I was too jealous."

"She did everything she could to make me insecure, then told me I was too insecure to have a relationship with."

"He did everything he could to make me angry, then said he couldn't deal with my anger."

PARTNERS WHO ARE ALREADY DISTANT

When all you are feeling is longing and yearning, there is no room for feeling cramped and trapped. That's why some men and women find it easier to fall in love at a distance. Yes, there is some question as to whether or not what you are feeling is really love. And there is certainly some question as to whom or what it is that you're falling in love with. But it sure feels powerful while it lasts.

Some men and women seem to have an almost uncanny ability to find partners who are about to move to another part of the country or the world. This gives them a green light to pursue their fantasies, to exhibit their finest courting skills, and to thoroughly submit to this fleeting vision of a relationship. It's a perfect setup. Then of course the lover actually moves. The one who is left behind pines, grieves, and is consoled by friends. Poor Alice/Alex, this always happens to her/him. Will either of them ever meet somebody who hasn't bought packing tape by the gross?

Of course with distance built into a relationship, it's more likely that you're falling in love with a fantasy than with reality. When there's distance, partners look more perfect. Your time together feels more perfect. The highs are much, much higher. And the lows either escape you or are so strong that they bring you closer together.

There are many ways in which distance can be built into a relationship, and it isn't always about mileage. What does it mean when someone is distant? Whether it is a lover who lives six thousand miles away on another continent, a married lover at work, or an uncommunicative spouse in the next room, the partner who is distant is someone who is unavailable to you.

Here's what typically happens when you choose a "distant" partner or distancing circumstances. First, you feel good because the distance increases the fantasy and reduces the threat of intimacy. It feels safe. You don't feel suffocated. So you're free to let yourself go. You feel yearning and romance and desire. It's easy to open up, to be vulnerable and get more in touch with your feelings. So you have this incredible, intense, compact relationship—a lifetime of bliss in only a few short months or weeks or days. And the next thing you know, you're at the airport with tears in your eyes.

A relationship in which distance is a given usually presents the following problem sooner or later: The distance is too great for one of the partners. He or she wants to get closer. While one partner's feelings may have changed, the terms of the romance have not. When people choose a relationship with built-in distance, these choices often come back to haunt them.

FINDING THE DISTANCE YOU NEED IN FANTASY PARTNERS

"My sister is a really terrific person, but she's crazy. She keeps falling in love with these guys on television, or some guy she'll see in a store. Her last big 'crush' was on this gay guy at work. She won't even look at anybody who might be interested in her. She has found something wrong with every single guy who could be interested in her. She thinks my husband is a jerk because all he does is take care of his family."

—KELLY

Kelly's sister has found the distance she needs by focusing on fantasy. What makes a fantasy partner so attractive, so desirable, so easy to relate to? Is it what you read in the gossip columns, what you see of her breasts on MTV? We doubt it. We think that with certain men and women their greatest attraction is that they are totally, completely, undeniably unavailable to you. They are at such a distance that thinking about them is unquestionably "safe," and you will never be asked to make a real commitment.

"DISTANT" AND MARRIED

Lots of men and women with very serious commitment problems get married. Lots. Every single day. And their problems don't go away. Typically they get worse. A lot worse. And they hide it all behind closed doors, behind the illusion of a marital contract.

Many of the men and women we interviewed talked about a partner's postmarital transformation. From Dr. Jekyll to Mr. Hyde. Many never saw Dr. Jekyll again. Whatever commitment problems were evident before the marriage paled in comparison with the ones that came after. So much for the "If I can just get him to the altar" myth.

The most insidious thing about commitment conflicts among marrieds is that it's the last thing you would suspect. People who can't commit don't get married, right? Wrong.

Marriage can have everything or nothing to do with commitment. You can be married and still feel and act ambivalent, or you can never sign a single piece of legal paper and be the most committed partner on the planet. But how does somebody who is married act out commitment conflicts? That's easy. It's done with distance.

The spouse who has an affair, the workaholic who never comes home, the mate who is still carrying a torch for an old flame, the "statue" at the breakfast table, a newspaper where a face should be, the lump in the living room interrelating with a television set, the gadabout who continues to hang out with friends, night after night. There are all kinds of ways to maintain distance in a marriage—without ever leaving home.

When we talk about commitment and marriage, men usually get the worst rap. We hear about how they break engagements and leave their brides at the altar, about how they won't "grow up" and how they spend every waking moment hanging out with the guys. Until recently we heard very little about women who panicked at the idea of marriage.

Stories about the anxious bride and the claustrophobic wife used to be very, very rare. Yet now we hear them all the time. Whether these women are only now coming forward and admitting to what they are feeling or whether this is a new phenomenon that reflects recent societal changes, we have no way of knowing for sure. Our guess is that it's a combination of both.

From the women we talk to we've learned how many are genuinely surprised when they discover themselves married and conflicted. What they often do is try to create little spheres of activity in which they are apart from their mates.

For example one divorced woman we spoke to said that while married, she spent much of her time trying to gain distance within the marriage. To do this, she would lock herself in the bathroom and stay there smoking a cigarette trying to get calm. In the meantime her husband would distance himself with the television set. She found that most of the time one or both of them would be involved in an activity that purposely shut the other one out.

CONFLICT, CONFLICT, CONFLICT

How can one adequately describe the behavior of a person with commitment conflicts? It's bizarre, contradictory, perplexing, endearing, and incendiary. It's charming and it's vicious. It's passionate and it's detached. It always makes perfect sense if you remember this one rule about men and women with full-blown commitment conflicts: They can't commit to yes and they can't commit to no. Commitment means forever, it means "Good-bye, freedom," it means death. But saying good-bye to a loved one is also forever. It's also a commitment, a commitment to losing someone from your life. It's a double bind.

That's why so many of these men and women don't say anything. Or they say, "Maybe . . . I'm not sure . . . I need more time . . . I'll let you know tomorrow . . . Maybe in a year I'll be ready . . . I want this to work, but I need some distance . . . I love you, I'm just not sure about the future"—all classic ways of avoiding the end. Saying no triggers the same feelings as saying yes. It represents finality and the closing of doors.

This is why there are so many actions that aren't clear. They ask you out, then they cancel. They say they'll call, then they don't. They take you to Paris, but they won't take you to a family picnic. They ask you to move in, then they resent the intrusion. One action is always canceling out the other.

And in their relationships the need for distance is always canceling out the need for intimacy.

PART TWO

Understanding Your Fears and Facing Your Conflict

CHAPTER SEVEN

Recognizing Your Pattern

Commitment conflicts affect more than your romantic life. They come into play anytime you have a decision to make. That means they can influence the way you handle your career, your money, and your friendships. Deciding to marry means you've chosen a mate. Deciding which VCR, computer, or car to purchase means forgoing all the other types on the market. Deciding on a career means turning your back on the other possibilities. The possibility of ambivalence exists every time we decide to choose one course of action, no matter how small, and give up another.

Nothing says that you have to be committed to anything—a person, a cause, a schedule, or even a major purchase, and nobody says that having conflicts is not normal. Complex people have some fairly complex emotions. But by not looking at your conflicts, your insecurities, and your behavior patterns, you're giving your fears more power than they deserve.

BUT . . . IF YOU DON'T WANT A COMMITMENT, DON'T MAKE ONE

From where we sit, this book is not about whether you should make a commitment or whether you need a commitment. The purpose of this book is to make you aware of your conflicts so that you don't make relationship choices that bring you pain. This is about not getting clobbered in your personal life. It's about understanding the kind of people you choose to get involved with and why you make those choices. It's also about handling your conflicts in a responsible manner so that you don't inflict needless pain on others. It's about knowing what you're running away from and what you're running toward. We want you to take a closer look at some of the ways in which your conflicts might be sabotaging you in the nonromantic areas of your life. We want you to be able to decide for yourself whether some of your patterns in and out of love are causing you problems, and we want you to be able to alter your behavior accordingly.

LOOKING AT YOUR PATTERN IN PAST RELATIONSHIPS

Do you have a relationship right now? What's happening in it? What happened in each of your past relationships? What do you want for your future? The best way to lay the foundation for constructive change is to spend some time exploring your relationship history. To get a better sense of your pattern, let's take an honest look at your choices, your motivations, and your behavior.

We think this is one of those times when it helps to get very concrete and specific. For that reason we encourage you to take out a pen and pad of paper and start writing things down.

Before You Start

Going over personal histories can sometimes be upsetting. We all make mistakes, and just about everyone has survived a fair amount of pain, anguish, and shame. It's not fun to look at. Many times we would just as soon forget these relationships—and the way we acted in them. In fact some of us have worked very hard to do just that, and this makes a great deal of sense. The only reason to excavate all this material from our past is to help us shape a different kind of future. Taking this kind of rigorous inventory can be overwhelming, so we suggest that you do it in stages. Let's start by getting a better sense of your pattern in relationships.

As Far As Commitment Is Concerned, Do You Have an Active or a Passive Behavior Pattern?

Everyone has the capacity to act out in both patterns, depending on the partner and the circumstances. However, each of us is usually more comfortable with one pattern than the other. For example:

- John has a long history actively running after—and then running away from—dozens of women. However, in his head he carries a memory of an equally commitmentphobic woman who rejected him.
- Mary is usually found playing the passive role in commitmentphobic relationships with an unavailable man. However, she has rejected any number of available men, who view *her* as an elusive femme fatale.

As you answer the following questions, keep in mind that women are often still more comfortable with a passive pattern and men with an active one. Think about your history in relationships. Which pattern seems most familiar to you?

Are you the active partner?

1. Do you have a history of pursuing—or becoming wildly enthusiastic about—new partners whom you later reject?
2. Are you consciously aware that you are ambivalent or afraid of commitment?
3. Are you convinced that somewhere there is a "perfect" person who will help you overcome that fear?
4. Do you often feel a need to create distance in your relationships?
5. Are you aware of having caused pain to any of your past loves because of your unwillingness to commit?
6. As your relationships become more intense and more intimate, do you often begin to find more faults and reasons why you shouldn't make a commitment?
7. In your relationships are you the one who sets most of the rules including how often you will see each other?

8. Do expectations and demands make you feel trapped and resentful?

9. Once a relationship's initial stage is over, are you conscious of setting things up so that your partner will have fewer expectations?

10. When a relationship has ended, do you allow almost no time to elapse before finding a new partner?

11. Do the demands of a relationship make you feel that someone is encroaching on your space?

Active avoiders will answer yes to many, if not most, of the above questions. Passive avoiders, on the other hand, will answer yes to many, if not most of the following questions.

Are you the passive partner?

1. Do you have a history of getting involved with partners who have serious, obvious commitment problems?

2. Do you spend a great deal of time fantasizing about relationships, often about past partners or unavailable partners?

3. Have you often been attracted or drawn to people who were obviously inappropriate or unavailable?

4. Are you often more committed to the potential of a relationship than you are to a person?

5. Do you feel more powerfully connected to partners when they are miles away, or involved elsewhere, than you do when they are sitting next to you?

6. Are you so afraid of being stuck in a boring, ordinary relationship that you gravitate toward partners who appear to be more exciting, even though their life-styles are less stable?

7. Are you turned on by the challenge of altering the behavior of a difficult partner?

8. When relationships end, do you tend to get stuck in the grieving process for an inordinate amount of time?

9. Are you waiting for something magical to happen to resolve your romantic life?

10. Do you resist taking the necessary steps to meeting appropriate, available partners?

11. If someone doesn't knock down your defenses in a first meeting, do you resist letting a connection develop over time?
12. In many of your relationships was it always clear on some very basic level that it could never last?

Do You Remember What Happened in Your Past Relationships?

You can't learn from the past if you can't remember what happened. So let's examine the most important romantic relationships and/or romantic feelings (crushes, unfulfilled fantasies) in your past. Try to do this in descending order of importance, starting with the past loves who are most significant. *Don't examine your current relationship until you've finished with the past.*

Try to remember back to the very beginning of each of these important relationships and answer the following questions about each of the people on your list, one at a time. Figure that each important person deserves several sheets of paper. As we said before, take your time. Don't try to do everybody at once.

1. What were your first reactions to this person?
2. How do you think this person first reacted to you?
3. If you were not all that attracted initially, do you remember what changed your mind?
4. At the beginning were you the pursuer or the pursued?
5. Was this person appropriate for you or inappropriate? And why?
6. Was this person available for a commitment or unavailable? Why?
7. Looking at this relationship from the other person's point of view, were you an appropriate choice? Why? Why not?
8. Were you available for a commitment? If not, why not?
9. How did your feelings for this person change over the course of the relationship?
   - What did you feel at the beginning?
   - What did you feel in the middle of the relationship?
   - What did you feel at the end of the relationship?

- What did you feel immediately after the relationship was over?
- What did you feel later, after some time had elapsed?

10. For each stage, if your feelings changed, *why* did they change?
11. Do you remember any specific turning points? What were they?
12. How do you think this person's feelings for you changed over the course of the relationship? Why do you think they changed?
13. At the beginning of this relationship, did you have any reservations? What were they? Did any of them come back to haunt you?
14. List all of the ways in which this person may have tried to put distance into the relationship. Were you emotionally shut out? Were there unreasonable boundaries? Were you excluded from important parts of his or her life?
15. List all of the ways in which you may have introduced distance or boundaries into the relationship.
16. How well did you really know this person? What didn't you know about this person?
17. How well did this person know you? What didn't this person know about you?
18. Was this person's behavior at the beginning, middle, and end of the relationship consistent with what you know about him or her? How was it different?
19. What did you want from this relationship at all the different stages?
    - At the beginning?
    - In the middle?
    - At the end?
20. If you wanted different things at different stages, what changed your mind?
21. How honest were you with this person? Specifically, what feelings and what facts, if any, did you conceal?
    - At the beginning?
    - In the middle?
    - At the end?

22. How honest do you think this person was with you? What feelings or facts do you think might have been concealed?
    - At the beginning?
    - In the middle?
    - At the end?
23. In what ways might you have been unfair in this relationship?
24. In what ways might your partner have been unfair?
25. At any stage of the relationship were you critical and faultfinding of your partner? At which stage(s)?
26. At any stage of the relationship, was your partner critical and faultfinding of you? At which stage(s)?
27. What were your fantasies about this relationship? How did they change as the relationship evolved?
28. What are your fantasies, if any, about this relationship now?
29. Was there ever a time when this relationship felt solid, even, and easy? How long did that last? What precipitated the change?
30. How soon after starting this relationship did you know your partner's relationship history? Did any of that matter to you?
31. Did this partner ever warn you about his or her behavior in relationships?
32. Did either you or this partner ever discuss ambivalence or fears about commitment?
33. If this person discussed such conflicts, did you believe what you heard?
34. If you discussed such conflicts, do you think your partner believed what he or she heard?
35. On some level did you always know that this relationship couldn't work out unless there were some major changes in behavior or attitude?
36. What made you believe that such a change was possible?
37. In this relationship were you hooked on the potential as much, if not more, than you were on the actual relationship?
38. How would you compare this relationship as it really ex-

isted with the relationship as you believed it could be if only you could actualize its potential?

39. How did this relationship end? Did you end it? Did the other person end it?
40. What was the major issue involved in the breakup?
41. If commitment was the major issue, what other problems might the two of you have had if a commitment had been made?
42. Do you think you were self-protective in this relationship?
43. Do you think your partner was self-protective in this relationship?
44. Why was this relationship important to you?
45. Make a list of the ways in which you think you should have been more self-protective in this relationship.

After you've finished with your past, take the same quiz about your current partner, if any, and answer all applicable questions. When you're done, try the following exercise:

Make a list of the qualities and characteristics that you consider most important in a partner.

Now make a list of the primary characteristics of each of your most important partners.

How do these two lists compare? What kind of conclusions can you draw from the lack of agreement?

How Rapidly Do You Make Commitments in Nonromantic Areas?

Commitment isn't just about romance, it's about life. If you are hypersensitive to commitment, your struggle is going to emerge in more than one area. There are people so commitmentphobic that all the cells in the their bodies scream out, *Don't tie me down!* Reluctant to do anything they can't undo, worried about making the wrong choice or limiting their options, they can never make choices in any areas of their lives.

This level of anxiety is paralyzing. If every choice, every small commitment—because it limits options—feels like a small death, it's impossible to live a full life.

In this section we'd like to take a closer look at the struggle to maintain options and remain uncommitted in a world full of commitment. Does any of this sound like you? How about the people you've been in love with?

How Elusive Are You?

Do people ever complain that they can't find you when they need you? Are you impossible to pin down? Are you purposely vague and elusive about your plans? Can the people in your life always count on you—do they know that you're always there should they need you—or do you keep them so off balance that they are afraid to ask too much of you?

People with commitment conflicts often work very hard to keep family and friends at a distance. They don't like being that accessible. At a family gathering or party they don't stay in one place too long and prefer to move around. They don't give many people access to their inner world. Even with their closest friends they often don't allow conversations about themselves to become too deep and are experts at changing the subject before anyone gets too close to what they are truly feeling. If they do allow someone to get a glimpse of what they are really feeling, they are inclined to balance the intensity by drawing back or vanishing. Often they don't want to commit themselves to the present because they are saving themselves for something better. Even they are not sure what that something is.

How about you? Are you elusive? Do you resent expectations from lovers, friends, and family because they make you feel locked in? How about your partner? Does he or she change plans, break plans, show up late? This sends out a message to anyone who is paying attention: NO EXPECTATIONS.

Do You Thrive on Anonymity?

Men and women with serious commitment issues hate the idea of looking as though they are committed to anything. Maintaining anonymity is another way of maintaining freedom. Does this need affect you? For example:

Does the thought of joining an organization where you are seen as a committed member fill you with dread?

Is it difficult for you to commit your thoughts to paper, where someone else can read what you feel or think?

Would you prefer to leave letters unsigned?

Do you avoid putting your name on the mailbox?

Do tape recorders make you nervous?

Do you hate having your picture taken because something is never right about the way you look?

When people ask you specific questions about what you do or what you feel, do you purposely keep your answers vague and uncommitted?

Have you ever been in a close relationship that you downplayed in front of friends because it wasn't perfect enough to admit to or to risk being judged by the world?

Can You Make an Appointment Three Weeks from Tomorrow? How About Three Months?

Those with serious commitment issues embrace the concept of spontaneity as if it were a religion. They find it hard to imagine how people can make plans weeks, or even months, in advance. They hate having their life be that predictable. It's all last-minute. Sure, they may miss out on some opportunities, but it feels like a small price to pay for freedom.

Does this behavior seem familiar? Is it painful to make plans weeks or months ahead? Do you make it very clear that all of your arrangements are always "tentative"? Does your appointment book look like a scratch sheet at Santa Anita? Do you try to keep yourself open in case something better comes along—something more important or more exciting? These are all classic symptoms of commitmentphobic behavior.

What Do You Do for a Living?

Do any of these sound like you?

- You're never happy with the job you have, and you're always thinking about making a change.
- You've never held a job for an extended period of time.

- Your work moves you from office to office, city to city, or country to country.
- You've never been able hold a job unless there was great freedom and diversity.
- Your business is so volatile, you never know from week to week whether or not you'll have a job.
- You think of yourself as a free-lancer, even when your work is permanent.
- You're self-employed and wouldn't have it any other way.
- You always feel somewhat detached from your jobs, no matter how long you hold them.

After romance, nothing is more revealing than your pattern in work. If you have commitment conflicts, it's highly unlikely that you will be comfortable holding a stable nine-to-five job in a stable industry. In fact you may always be searching for the perfect profession or the perfect job, much as you search for the perfect mate.

Where Do You Live?

Do you think of your living quarters as temporary, no matter how long you've been there? Instead of accepting your current space as "home," are you always dreaming of where you'll live next? Do you pride yourself on your ability to move at the drop of a hat? Have you ever spent an extended period of time bouncing back and forth from place to place—six months here, a year there, house-sitting here, subletting there, staying with friends here, staying with family there? In your head do you fancy yourself a "citizen of the world," footloose and fancy-free, and think it mundane to be tied to any one place?

What about *buying* a house? For some people, owning their own home is a dream come true. Is it your nightmare? In light of the ups and downs of the real estate market, you have many good reasons to be scared. Renter's pride may be very fashionable right now, but the real question is this: Is it the real estate market that terrifies you, or is it the loss of freedom . . . the responsibility . . . the commitment?

You probably have all kinds of great reasons to justify how you choose to live: It's cheaper, or easier. It's less work, or less worry. It's exciting. It's glamorous. It's more fun. All of these explanations are valid, but in our experience they are often a cover-up for something much larger: the incredible sense of dread you experience at the thought of settling down.

What's Hanging on Your Walls?

Men and women with serious commitment problems sometimes announce their unavailability by the way they choose to live. People who prefer beds that cannot be shared are good examples. Here are just a few of the "beds" described to us: a single cot, a sleeping bag permanently installed on the floor, a single futon rolled up in a corner, and a lumpy couch. These bedding choices clearly announce one's preference for sleeping alone.

Other decorating giveaways:

- Does your living space look unfinished at best?
- Do you have furniture covered in plastic waiting to be returned to the store because you've changed your mind about whether you want to commit to it—yet again?
- Are your walls as bare as your cupboards, which are *very* bare?
- Do you have more furniture in storage than you do in your living room?
- Are your books packed in cartons . . . somewhere?
- Have you never gotten around to buying anything that matches?
- Are you unable to reach a decision about where to build bookcases, where to put the couch, or where to hang the pictures?

If any of this sounds like your home, then it is clear that you haven't made a commitment to living where you are supposed to be living.

To help justify the appearance of your surroundings, you probably have a fantasy of some future space where you'll live very differently. This is the place where you'll buy beautiful furniture and great art. It's the place where you'll design perfect built-ins just for you and your needs. This dream about tomorrow keeps you from committing to the present.

Joe and His Phone—Does This Sound Familiar?

Joe is a worst-case commitmentphobic. The way he uses his phone speaks volumes. Callers never know if he's in or if he's out because at home he hides behind his answering machine, and at work he hides behind the receptionist. His family can never reach him, and his friends realize that the only way to be sure of reaching him is to show up at his door. One day, on his answering machine, he had twelve separate messages from twelve different people, all saying the exact same thing: "Where are you?"

He calls his girlfriend and leaves messages saying, "Call me back." But when she does, he's never where he says he'll be when he says he'll be there. He gets angry because he has so many messages on his machine, but he never returns calls, so people keep trying. When he breaks up with one woman, he gets the next one to record the message on his machine. This is his way of turning away any ex-girlfriends who might continue to call. For Joe the phone is his way of announcing his inaccessibility, and the way he uses it verges on performance art.

Do you know anyone like Joe?

Younger Than Springtime—Does This Describe Someone You Know?

We know a man whose entire life is a statement against growing up. Where he lives, how he lives, whom he associates with, the kinds of relationships he establishes, his attitude toward work, his attitude toward his hobbies—all reflect his insistence on avoiding adulthood. His apartment is the apartment of a young man; his clothes are the clothes of a much younger man. He has two types of friends: one as childlike as he is (either chronologically or emotionally) and the other, parental, who treat him as an adorable child. In his head he still has the potential of a twenty-one-year-old, and that's how he behaves.

Are Pets an Overwhelming Responsibility?

Is the thought of having an animal dependent on you for survival enough to make your heart race? You say that with your lifestyle it wouldn't be fair to have a pet, but maybe you want it that way because you simply don't want the commitment.

When most people consider getting a pet, they think about how much pleasure it would bring into their lives. But if you've got a commitment problem, those warm thoughts can be quickly displaced by thoughts of all the problems a pet can bring into your life. What if you can't get home to feed it? What if you want to go away for a while? What if you want to move to a place that doesn't allow pets? What if it gets sick? What happens when it gets old? There are so many possible complications.

Truth is, there aren't many pets that don't require at least some commitment from their owners. That loss of freedom is enough to stop some serious commitmentphobics from having any form of life in their apartment except carpenter ants.

How Hard Is It to Make Major Purchases?

Does the thought of buying a new car make you toss and turn all night? Are you living without a VCR because you can't decide what features you really need? Do you stay home every year because you haven't decided where to take that big vacation? These are all classic signs of the struggle with commitment conflict.

True commitmentphobes may agonize over major purchases—sometimes putting them off indefinitely. But sometimes a major purchase can't be avoided. And that's when the terror kicks in. What if you make the wrong choice? What if another store has a better price? What if a better model comes out next year? What if your needs change? What if, what if, what if . . .

What About Small Decisions?

Is a ten-page restaurant menu enough to make you wish for a tranquilizer? Do the words *final sale* make you tremble? If a sweater comes in four different colors, do you wind up buying none, or all? Do you change your outfit a dozen times before you leave the house? Decisions, decisions, decisions . . . when will it ever stop?

If you've got a commitment problem, life's "simple" choices aren't simple at all, they're maddening. Getting dressed in the morning can be an arduous task. Going grocery shopping can be overwhelming. Buying presents can be painful. Any choice that's final is a source of torment. You drive waiters crazy, you drive salespeople crazy, you drive friends crazy, but most of all you drive yourself crazy.

Do You Want to Return Everything You Buy?

Thinking of selling the house you just bought?

Trying to find a new home for the dog you just adopted?

Wish you could return the car you just drove out of the showroom?

Exactly how long do you hold on to your receipts, "just in case"? For those with unresolved commitment conflicts, buyers remorse is a lifetime guarantee.

Do You Have Difficulty Getting Rid of Things?

Are your closets full of old clothes? Are your filing cabinets overflowing with papers? Do you have cartons of memorabilia that you just can't toss, even though you know most of it is junk? The inability to part with such things goes beyond being sentimental—it's a commitment issue.

Once you get rid of something, it's gone forever, and commitmentphobes can't face forever. Saying good-bye to anything— even an old shirt—generates tremendous anxiety. What if I need it a month from now? . . . a year from now? . . . five years from now? What if I make a mistake? Such questions torment you, rendering you incapable of cleaning house.

What About Kids?

Almost everyone fantasizes about having children, but if you've got big-time commitment issues, you may wish that it never gets past the fantasy stage. If the thought of buying a goldfish is enough to keep you awake all night, you may figure that parenthood is not such a good idea.

The prospect of children can sometimes produce a commitment crisis within a relationship or marriage. The idea seems too confining and too limiting. However, those with conflicts can take heart in knowing that we've seen from our interviews that men and women with extraordinary commitment issues are often able to become overwhelmingly committed to parenting.

It would appear that commitment issues can get very muddled when they come up against the biological imperative. While some commitmentphobes see children as the ultimate ball and chain, many others aren't nearly as frightened. They can't imagine missing out on being a parent. They see children as a temporary commitment, not a permanent one. And that's a lot easier to handle.

Are you certain you want children, but not sure you want to stay with the other parent? If you have children, are you a committed parent, or do you resent the responsibility? Do your children live with you? Are you the primary caregiver? Do you look forward to the ongoing experiences you share together, or are you counting the days till they go to college? Perhaps both. After all, commitment issues are about conflict.

What's Going on Inside Your Head?

This is tricky stuff. To the outside world you may look solid, sound, and committed. But inside your brain your conflicts are raging, and you always have a contingency plan. The only thing that enables you to make "commitments" are the elaborate escapes you are always plotting. The bottom line here is that just because you don't look commitmentphobic doesn't mean you don't feel commitmentphobic. The only proof may lie safely inside your brain. You may be masterful at hiding your fear, but you know it's there—and that's what counts.

If you have answered the previous questions honestly, you should have a clearer sense of your pattern. Acknowledgment is the prerequisite to effecting some kind of constructive change. The next step is to figure out exactly what scares you about commitment.

CHAPTER EIGHT

Exploring Your Feelings, Exploring Your Fears

COMMITMENT-ANXIETY STEW—A LIST OF INGREDIENTS

The fear of commitment is not a simple fear. It's a complex collection of anxieties, worries, and concerns, and it varies in composition and intensity from person to person. This means that for each of us our struggle with commitment is a reflection of our own unique blend of "anxiety stew." In order to understand what you (or any of your partners) find frightening, you need to get a sense of the many emotional triggers—the "ingredients"—that are part of any individual recipe.

We believe the flight from commitment can be set off by any number of dynamics that might occur between two people. These are the dynamics that trigger feelings one associates with discomfort or stress. Even though you may not relate to the fear of commitment as a whole, you may feel differently about some of the individual components.

We urge you to look at the following series of questions. As you respond, keep in mind that each specific anxiety mentioned in this list may feel vague or unimportant to you. Nonetheless, unexamined and in combination, these anxieties can assume tre-mendous power in your life. These are the primary emotional ingredients that blend together to produce a fear of commitment.

183

How often do you feel the following:

1. I'm afraid that no one will want me because I'm not perfect enough.

Never _____ Sometimes _____ Always _____

2. I'm afraid that any partner I choose won't be perfect.

Never _____ Sometimes _____ Always _____

3. I'm afraid that people will judge me by the partner I choose.

Never _____ Sometimes _____ Always _____

4. I'm afraid of losing the freedom to do what I want when I want.

Never _____ Sometimes _____ Always _____

5. I'm afraid of losing my sexual freedom.

Never _____ Sometimes _____ Always _____

6. I'm afraid of being bored.

Never _____ Sometimes _____ Always _____

7. I'm afraid I'll change my mind and I'll be stuck.

Never _____ Sometimes _____ Always _____

8. I'm afraid I'll end up feeling limited and constrained by the compromises and obligations of commitment.

Never _____ Sometimes _____ Always _____

9. I'm afraid of losing my individuality and my sense of self.

Never _____ Sometimes _____ Always _____

10. I'm afraid of being controlled.

Never _____ Sometimes _____ Always _____

11. I'm afraid of losing control.

Never _____ Sometimes _____ Always _____

12. I'm afraid that I won't have the magic feeling and won't end up with "the mate that fate had me intended for."

Never _____ Sometimes _____ Always _____

13. I'm afraid of growing older.

Never _____ Sometimes _____ Always _____

14. I'm afraid that my life will narrow and I'll die without ever having lived or having done everything I want to do.

Never _____ Sometimes _____ Always _____

15. I'm afraid that I'll love so much that something awful will happen to me.

Never _____ Sometimes _____ Always _____

184

16. I'm afraid that all the things I'm ashamed of will be found out by those I care about, and they will reject me because of it.

Never _____ Sometimes _____ Always _____

17. I'm afraid of being dependent on someone else.

Never _____ Sometimes _____ Always _____

18. I'm afraid of having someone be dependent on me.

Never _____ Sometimes _____ Always _____

19. I'm afraid of making another romantic mistake.

Never _____ Sometimes _____ Always _____

20. I'm afraid I'll make my life more complicated and create more problems for myself.

Never _____ Sometimes _____ Always _____

21. I'm afraid I'll be giving up a life I enjoy just the way it is.

Never _____ Sometimes _____. Always _____

22. I'm afraid of sharing my money.

Never _____ Sometimes _____ Always _____

23. I'm afraid that the circumstances of my life right now are such that there is no room for another person.

Never _____ Sometimes _____ Always _____

24. I'm afraid of the responsibilities that come with marriage and commitment.

Never _____ Sometimes _____ Always _____

The feelings expressed by each of these statements reflect underlying feelings and fears about permanent relationships. To better understand how powerfully each of these can affect your attitude toward commitment, it's worth dissecting and examining the underlying concerns one by one.

COMMITMENT ANXIETIES FALL INTO FOUR SEPARATE CATEGORIES

There are a wide variety of commitment fears. Some are a direct result of being human; these are the universal feelings that touch us all. Others are personal anxieties that result from our own history and experience. Still others are based in fantasy and are fed by media images and Hollywood love stories. We believe commitment issues fall under the following categories:

- Narcissistic Commitment Issues
- Claustrophobic Commitment Issues
- Universal Commitment Issues
- Circumstantial Commitment Issues

NARCISSISTIC COMMITMENT ISSUES

Nobody's Perfect—The Narcissistic Worldview

Are you too "picky"?
Are you too easily "picked" apart?

There are two basic narcissistic commitment issues. Most of us are familiar with the first; worrying about whether or not your partner is the perfect choice. But there is another narcissistic issue, which revolves around the fear that *you* are less than perfectly pleasing. One way or the other, narcissism affects just about everyone, and we could probably all use some help in understanding how narcissistic impulses sabotage relationships.

If you find that you always become "too picky" in relationships, if you spend too much time worrying about whether you are pleasing others, or if you too easily become invested in proving your worth to someone who is holding a magnifying glass up to your real or imagined shortcomings, then you already have some understanding of how this works.

The Quest for Perfection

We all remember the story of Narcissus, who, when staring into a pool, became so absorbed with his own reflection that he fell in and drowned. *Narcissism* is a terribly judgmental term, and when we hear it, we immediately think of a spoiled man or woman preening in front of a mirror. This isn't always a fair assessment. To one degree or another, contemporary society, with its emphasis on image and externals, has made narcissists of us all. We have all been told to expect perfection of others and of ourselves.

Narcissistic personality traits are nothing new, but few of us have thought about what it means to find these traits in ourselves or in our partners. The way that narcissism influences the development or lack of development of a relationship is very much connected to commitment issues. Some of us are always engaged in the quest for perfection; others, acting out the flip side of the same coin, are more likely to be worried that our own imperfections will be found out.

Being narcissistic goes way beyond simply being in love with one's own reflection. It really means that we are often more in touch with the reflection, or image we project, than we are with our own core. What you may not be aware of is how your own need to present a perfect picture can be connected to narcissistic issues.

We have all known some supreme narcissists, men and women who are so fixated on their own reflections (and consequently on the reflections of others) that their inner cores are unavailable. A lifetime of distorted messages has long ago cut these people off from their true values and feelings, leaving them only with what is on the surface.

Anyone who is this narcissistic believes his or her value lies in the superficial external characteristics presented to the outside world. If you can't see it, it has little value. Extreme narcissists are never able to love or accept anybody because narcissism is about perfection, and nobody's perfect.

If your own sense of self-worth is tied in with being a perfect partner—whether that sense of perfection comes from being a perfect lover, a perfect cook, a perfect caretaker, a perfect provider, or a perfect nurturer—you are involved with narcissistic image issues that could be creating problems in your life.

Even men and women with mild narcissistic impulses can become so wrapped up in externals that they can't see their own worth. Instead all they notice are the flaws in the images they present to the world. Consequently they never accept themselves for who they are; and without self-acceptance it's impossible genuinely to accept anyone else.

Keep in mind that narcissistic people see themselves as the center of the universe. That isn't always fun. Narcissistic impulses can make you feel that all eyes are on you all the time. Worrying about what others think and feel about you is a very uncomfortable way to live. That's the main reason why people with intense narcissistic issues may struggle day and night to present perfection.

Part of someone's perfect presentation is the company he or she keeps. The closer you get to someone like this, the more he or she worries about the kind of image you reflect. Just as they must be perfect, so must you be perfect if you are to be part of their world.

If you are involved with a supreme narcissist, you know what it is to be scrutinized for "flaws." If you have ever been subjected to this kind of treatment, you know that your first reaction may be an attempt to improve or modify those things with which your partner is finding fault. Under these conditions there is a tendency to believe that everything will be okay if you just change all the things that your partner doesn't like. If you could only change your body type, make more money, and give away your cat, it would work out. If you could only convert to a different religion, read two newspapers a day, and learn French, it would be okay. But with people like this, it's never okay.

Narcissistic people typically hurt others because they can't tolerate any more hurt themselves. But it would be a mistake to believe that they can be changed by the love of the perfect man or woman. This is not what it's about, and it's not going to work. Such a person will hold any flaws, real or imagined, against you. If you are too pink or green or yellow, or too boring or jealous or angry, or too naive, or too trusting, or too nice, someone with these tendencies might search it out and turn it against you.

We All Have Some Narcissistic Tendencies

Many of us have fantasies about "the perfect partner," and sometimes we actually believe we can find such a person. We want our partners to look good and to sound good. We want them to reflect everything we think we are or everything we would like to be. And many of us carry with us that little narcissistic voice that points out when someone's real characteristics don't quite measure up to fantasy requirements.

It's the narcissistic impulse that causes you to look at a potential partner and think, *Maybe I could do better. Maybe this person is too short, too tall, too thin, too fat, too poor, or too rich.* Where do these critical voices come from? Perhaps you had parents who constantly criticized you, your choices, your appearance, your friends, your friends' choices, your friends' appearances. In fact perhaps you have been surrounded by people—family, friends—with judgmental attitudes. Perhaps every time you go out with someone, you remember this and place your date in the harsh glare of these voices from your past. You think, *Is this person good enough? Is this person rich enough? Is this person attractive enough? What will my family say about me if I'm with this person? How about my friends? How about the world at large?*

I'm the Best/I'm the Worst—The Two Sides of the Narcissistic Coin

The issue of narcissism is tremendously complicated because those with powerful narcissistic voices can reflect one of two extremes and can go back and forth between them. Often they tell themselves that they are wonderful and deserve someone who is perfect in every way. At other times they feel that they have no real value and deserve nothing. It is this flip-flop that dictates the whole projection of their attitude in relationships.

For example, when John wants Mary and she doesn't immediately respond, all of his self-doubts are activated and maximized, and he begins to question his value in the world. But when Mary responds strongly and makes it clear that she is totally involved and available for John, he becomes the perfectionist, questioning *her* value in his life.

Narcissism and Commitment Conflicts Go Hand in Hand

If you are anxious about commitment, if you are nervous about permanency with any one person, your narcissistic voice, wherever it comes from, gives you the methods and rationalizations to help you stay uncommitted. It's that narcissistic little voice inside of you that allows you to look at a perfectly suitable person and resist exploring the possibility of a real connection. It can automatically reject some pretty terrific possible people for a wide variety of reasons, most of them superficial and some of them downright silly.

These superficialities are not necessarily about physical characteristics. They can be about where someone went to school or what he does for a living or what she is wearing. Or they can revolve around some personal quirk or image that an individual may or may not attach to a particular type of education, profession, wardrobe, or life-style.

In other words, in evaluating all romantic situations, instead of applying reasonable judgment skills, those with narcissistic impulses use this to guard the door, making sure that no one who doesn't fit specific fantasy expectations has a chance.

CLAUSTROPHOBIC COMMITMENT ISSUES

What if you make a commitment to someone, and you end up feeling trapped, as though you can't get out? What if you end up feeling "tied down," with all the anxiety and stress this implies? What if another person's presence, needs, ideas, and vision impinge on your territory, crowd your space, and take away your freedom? What if, what if, what if?

The word *claustrophobic* conjures up all sorts of images of unreasonable limits and small, enclosed spaces. That's why any environment that limits choices or freedom can be viewed as claustrophobic, as can any situation that ties you down or keeps you stuck in any way. This includes emotional environments as well as physical environments. On some level we all have a visceral sense of what kinds of environments make us feel claustrophobic, and we try to stay away from them. Sometimes we go to people's houses and we watch the way they live and we think thoughts such as *They seem happy enough, but I certainly couldn't live that way.*

Often what we are responding to is a gut sense that what we are watching would make us feel claustrophobic. We don't want that much closure in our lives because we know that we would start to feel anxious, uncomfortable, and resentful. But we rarely realize this unless we feel stuck in a relationship that is evoking these feelings.

The idea of commitment can produce a whole range of claustrophobic responses. These include:

The Fear of Losing Freedom

Back in the 1950s young men and women didn't view marriage as something that would restrict personal freedom. Quite the opposite. They probably thought they were finally going to be able to act like grown-ups and do things their way without parental supervision. That meant gaining freedom.

For people today it's a lot different. Today most of us are a lot farther down the road. Typically we know what it is to live alone, make our own decisions, and function as independent adults. We know that there are many joys to being single, and probably nothing is more joyous than the sense of being free to do whatever you want, whenever you want to do it.

When you're making a commitment to be with another person, you have to start taking another person's needs into account. You gain something—but you also lose a degree of freedom. But there is also no denying that the anticipation or the idea of the loss of freedom is far worse than any reality. When someone thinks about all the personal freedom that will be lost, typically he or she lumps all of the events that represent freedom into one time frame. They are viewed all together with no spaces in between.

For example, Jay is worried that he will not be free to go skiing with the guys once he is married. In truth Jay goes skiing with the guys no more than once a year and sometimes not even that. Yet the thought of having to take a wife along on all such ski trips makes him feel totally crippled. When he thinks about it, all he can see is the loss of that one weekend a year, and he loses sight of the other 363 days in the year. He also realizes that if he discussed it with his girlfriend, she would probably say, "What's the big deal? So go skiing without me."

In this instance it's also interesting to note that Jay and his girlfriend have taken some wonderful skiing holidays, none of which he would have done if he were still single. He knows this, and yet . . .

It's apparent that what Jay fears is loss of the option to do whatever he wants whenever he wants without consulting anyone. This makes him feel trapped, which, in turn, triggers claustrophobic anxiety.

For some people this concern with the loss of freedom crops up after marriage when they think back to all the things they enjoyed doing when they were single. A woman may think back longingly to the happy dinners she shared with single women friends, even though these kinds of festive events may have only taken place a few times a year. She forgets about lonely weekends and remembers only the glamorous once-in-a-lifetime dates when someone whisked her away to some exotic event.

The Fear of Giving Up Sexual Freedom—What It Means to You

"Suppose I meet somebody else I want to sleep with, what do I do then?"

Some men and women don't think twice about agreeing to monogamy, but many others experience reactions ranging from mild anxiety to total terror. Some of the people in this group feel that they haven't had enough experience. Others know they've had plenty of experience, but they want still more. A fair number of people who openly acknowledge the depth of their commitment conflicts have told us that they have never been faithful to anyone, and they doubt that it would be possible. Whatever the reason, if you admit to a sexual curiosity that has not been adequately resolved, then you may be a poor candidate for commitment.

But some men and women are not so much afraid of monogamy as they are of losing the option to behave otherwise. They worry that as a partner grows older, desire will wane. Some men have told us that they worry about those one or two times they are presented with situations, or invitations, that may be impossible to resist. For this group the idea of losing sexual freedom seems to be more disconcerting than the reality.

The Fear of Being Bored to Death

What could be more claustrophobic than the feeling of being entombed in a dull marriage? Talk to people about their relationship fears, and many will tell you that they can envision nothing worse for themselves than being trapped in a boring life. A boring life is one that is both ordinary and terrifying because it is a lifeless life, a death before life.

If you are convinced that you are meant to have an exceptional life, then you may well be frightened of finding yourself stuck in a marriage that is both dull and ordinary. That sounds simple enough, but it is not the entire story. Our interviewees have taught us that there are a number of very complex underlying factors that lead many people to equate commitment with boredom. This fear is most likely to affect your ability to be in a committed relationship if:

- You are accustomed to having chaos in your life, and you don't really feel "alive" when a relationship begins to get too settled
- You saw your parents' life-style as mundane, stultifying, or repressive; the absence of "life" in their committed relationship makes you fear falling into any pattern that reminds you of them
- You have a very dramatic fantasy life, and unless the same kind of soap-style drama exists in your personal life, it feels lackluster
- You are extremely bright and need a tremendous amount of stimulation from any partner
- You are very emotionally needy, and you expect your romantic relationship to fulfill all those needs
- You lack adequate challenge in your professional life and therefore depend upon your personal life to fulfill the majority of your intellectual and emotional needs
- You question your own depth and complexity and turn to others to resolve any feelings of inadequacy you may have

Whatever the reason, for those with commitment conflicts, the conclusion is always the same: boredom equals death.

The Fear of Physical or Emotional Limitations

Years ago, when we first started interviewing people about commitment, we talked to a man who was in the process of ending a one-year marriage. At the time the reasons he cited for wanting a divorce sounded very strange. Now they make a great deal more sense. He said that he and his wife had lived together for almost five years before they got married. To him these were happy and good years. But when they got married, his wife wanted the relationship to change. She had expectations of marriage that seemed simple enough but that he found terrifying.

You see, marriage to her meant duplicating the kind of routinized life-style that her parents and their friends had. Once married, she expected the following: As a couple they would eat dinner together every night, using the good china. Every Friday evening they would eat out. Every Saturday they would go out with friends. Every Sunday they would join family.

When they had been living together, mealtimes had all been very spontaneous, very unplanned. Some nights they had dinner together; other nights they didn't. There were no set rules about when they went out or how often they went out or what they did. This man told us that within six months he felt as though he was entombed and ready to be carted off to the old-folks home. When he described his marriage, he said, "It was claustrophobic."

People who make a commitment to each other agree that they will make certain accommodations for the good of the relationship. But accommodating another human being can make one feel boxed in and uncomfortable. This can produce a kind of emotional claustrophobia.

For example, immediately after marriage some people fall back on stereotypical role-playing. Women head for the kitchen, men head for the garage. Women do the food shopping, men service the car. Women prepare dinner and gossip on the phone, men watch the ball game and lose potato chips in the couch. This is the American caricature of the way things are supposed to be. But if you don't personally feel like fulfilling your half of the cartoon script, while your partner is very comfortable with the other part, your situation is going to feel repressive.

In other words any situation that doesn't allow you to be who you really are can feel stultifying and claustrophobic. This is frightening, and with good reason. Many men and women look around and are unhappy with traditional patterns. Yet they don't know what else to do. This can produce an underlying wariness of all traditional relationships, which helps explain why we turn to unrealistic and fantasy-based relationships in which we are limited only by our imaginations.

Anything in a relationship that can be perceived as limiting can produce a mild to severe sense of claustrophobia. This in turn can contribute to resentment and a need for distance. Sometimes habits that are really quite innocent may be experienced by one or both partners as confining. The reason? Some activities seem to imply that if you are a couple, you are seen as one entity, with no boundaries between the two of you. For example:

If we're a couple, we take vacations together.
If we're a couple, we go to all parties together.
If we're a couple, when we go to parties, we stand together.
If we're a couple, we spend all our weekends in shared activities.
If we're a couple, we share the same bedroom.
If we're a couple, we share the same bathroom.
If we're a couple, we never disagree with each other in public.
If we're a couple, we go to sleep hugging each other.
If we're a couple, we present a unified front to the world.
If we're a couple, we have to have sex *x* number of times per week.

Even people who are loyal, monogamous, and *in love* can feel constricted by the idea of living this way. These men and women want the freedom to act differently in a relationship. Otherwise the limitations of commitment seem overwhelmingly repressive.

The Fear of Losing Your Individuality and Your Sense of Self

We have all seen women who spent their waking lives catering to the needs of others. We are all aware of men who have short-changed their dreams in order to care for families. About these people we say, "They gave up their lives." What we mean is that they are defining themselves by the needs of others and in the process they are giving up their own individuality. While we may applaud the amount of love and care these people are capable of showing, we're not so sure that it's what we want for ourselves. It's too confining, too limiting. There is no room to soar, to take care of one's own creativity, one's own sense of self. This is a reason why some people, particularly those who may have watched a parent, a relative, or a friend suppress individuality, fear that with commitment comes a loss, a loss of self.

As a society we spend a great deal of time talking about the value we place on individualism. Making your own choices, making your own decisions, making up your own mind—all of these speak to the fact that we admire people who take care of themselves and think for themselves. We don't always think about the many small ways in which we express our individualism and our sense of self. But think about it now: Our individuality comes across in how we spend our vacations, where we live, the movies we see, the restaurants we choose, the way we decorate our living space, the way we organize our cabinets, how we spend our money, the time we wake, the time we go to sleep, the dinner parties we give or don't give, the firmness of our mattress, and how much we spoil the dog or cat.

When you're single, these are all things you decide for yourself. When you're part of a couple, you've got to make some adjustments in these areas, not to mention even more complicated matters, such as child rearing and which holidays to spend with which relatives. You have to learn to make shared decisions. Yet for some people *compromise triggers panic.*

It's hard to believe that choosing a restaurant or buying new towels is enough to throw a relationship into crisis. It's hard to believe that deciding on a movie, going on vacation, or going grocery shopping is enough to split up a marriage. But plenty of people with commitment conflicts will admit, though somewhat shamefully, that seemingly insignificant events like these have triggered break-ups.

Relationships require compromise. Everybody knows that. No two people will ever be in agreement all of the time on all of the issues that affect them as a couple. Part of being in a relationship is learning to work through these conflicts.

Making compromises means giving up a certain degree of individuality, and we already know how many of us feel about that. Going from "me" to "us" is a tremendous adjustment for anyone, especially if you've been a "me" for a long time. If you're sensitive about your physical and emotional space, the transition can create an almost immediate feeling of being trapped. Sometimes what you might hate is simply that you are being trapped into a role that feels foreign and uncomfortable.

The Fear of Giving Up Control

One of the reasons that claustrophobic environments are so anxiety provoking is because they make us feel powerless. If you are stuck in a meeting in a room that feels stuffy and tight, you open a window. The act of opening that window gives you a sense that you have the power to control your environment and thus alleviate the discomfort.

Even if we don't give it much thought, we all know that we feel more comfortable, more at ease, in any environment we control. If we have power, we feel better. It's that simple. But in a relationship somebody else is going to have some power over your life. That's scary. And it's a major reason why control looms so large in the minds of those with commitment anxiety.

Do you have strong feelings about having anyone control your life? Do you come from a family in which one parent dominated the other? Did your parents try to control you? Do you have a controlling sibling? Do you hate being with someone who tells you what to do?

Some of us are so sensitive to control issues that we try to dominate every element of our relationships. Others, equally sensitive, simply walk away from anyone who is perceived as trying to establish control.

Fear of being controlled is a major commitment fear. Women often fear that men will try to dominate what they think, what they feel, and what they do in a very direct fashion. Men sometimes state that women try to manipulate them to gain control. Certainly we have all witnessed couples who seem to be in an ongoing battle for control. They tell each other how to drive, how to dress, how to wash dishes, how to walk, how to sleep—in short how to live. This isn't a pleasant sight, and many men and women worry about duplicating that type of relationship in their own lives. And with good reason.

It's important to point out that staying in control isn't always accomplished by bossiness. Some people's moods and emotions are so strong that they seem almost to reach out and grab control of another's psyche. Some examples:

• A thirty-four-year-old man says that he realizes that his parents, especially his mother, made him feel guilty. His mother, who managed to hold down a full-time job while still taking care of the household chores, repeatedly reminded him of how hard she worked. He knows that women often make him feel guilty. He hates that feeling and says he doesn't want it in his adult life.

• A thirty-eight-year-old woman told us that her husband's moods when he loses at tennis control everybody in the house. She said, "When he comes home happy, we're all happy. But when he loses and comes back miserable, it is as though this giant cloud looms over all of us. I feel as though all I want to do is run away. It's totally oppressive."

Money is another way in which someone can assume or lose control. Betty, forty-one, says that she was first married at nineteen to a man who was considerably older and wealthier than she was. Not having her own money made her feel totally controlled. When she got a divorce, she consciously decided that she would never again be involved with anyone who had more money than she did. She says, "So for the next ten years every man I went out with was a totally inappropriate, poverty-stricken deadbeat. It was a clear reaction to my marriage, but I didn't figure it out until I went into therapy."

Claustrophobic reactions to the compromises and limitations of commitment are disconcerting at best. When they are combined with some of the universal fears we all carry with us, they can be devastating.

UNIVERSAL HUMAN COMMITMENT ISSUES

As members of the human race, sometimes we are all too predictable in our responses to certain situations. Commitment carries with it part of the human imperative—to produce and raise children, thus ensuring the continuance of our kind. But it also carries with it some anxieties that we all share. For example:

The Fear of Giving Up the Dream

Walking alongside each of us is a dream of the ideal partner, the soul mate, the karmic connection. This is the partner we are waiting for; this is the partner we are looking for. Sure, this person's description changes from time to time depending upon what is happening in life at that moment. Sometimes this partner is supportive, understanding, and sensitive. Other times this partner provides pure sexual excitement. This partner does everything we need whenever we need it.

For some of us this partner is someone we have never met. For others it is someone we've met who has never expressed any interest in being with us. For still others it is someone with whom we've had a relationship, often one in which we've been rejected.

Whoever this partner is, in our dreams he or she is the Right One. And we worry that if we settle down with someone else, we won't be free if Mr. or Ms. Right shows up. Hanging on to this dream is a way of avoiding commitment in all areas of your life. Let's take a look at how this works:

Maddie, thirty-nine, is very attractive, very smart, very accomplished, very nice, and very lonely. Years of her life have been spent waiting for one man or another to realize that they were meant to be together. Her last relationship was with an admittedly commitmentphobic man. Currently Maddie is waiting patiently for her "beloved" to come to his senses and return to her waiting arms. Maddie lives on her reconciliation fantasies. These are her dreams.

Roger, thirty-three, is convinced that the woman who works in a boutique on his block is the woman of his dreams. He has found out that she is living with someone else, so he is biding his time. He walks into her store every now and then to buy something. He's trying to position himself so that when her relationship breaks up, he will be waiting. In the meantime he thinks about her a lot.

Both Maddie and Roger are invested in dreams. Neither of them ever want to admit that their fantasies won't work out. To give them up has more significance than simply turning their backs on particular relationship choices. In their heads, giving up these dreams is akin to giving up God. Their emotions have transcended the category of mere human male/female and have gone into the realm of the spiritual. They can't give up their belief in the positive outcome of their romantic fantasies without questioning the power of faith and belief.

Some people take this to extremes. They attempt to make deals with God; they honestly tell themselves that if they are good enough, they will be rewarded with human, not divine, love. They become convinced that if they are understanding enough, or loving enough, or wise enough, heaven will send them their destined mate. These men and women, well intentioned though they may be, need to find a more constructive outlet for their spiritual energies and charitable concerns. They need to acknowledge that there are more noble and heaven-sent causes than some man or woman who isn't returning affections or phone calls.

All of this is a way of avoiding a commitment to a real life, real people, and real faith. Part of growing up is giving up this dream.

The Fear of Growing Up and Becoming a Real Adult

Getting married, having children, raising a family—these are the classic signposts of commitment in our culture. Commitment is about love, but it is also about responsibility. It's about compromise. It's about sacrifice. It's about work. In short, commitment is about growing up.

Growing up isn't easy for anyone. It means relinquishing hopes and fantasies. It means a lot more work and a lot less play. It means facing reality. For some of us that's way too much to ask. We want love in our lives, but we're not ready to grow up yet. This shows itself in our inability to form and maintain committed relationships.

Some of us are part of a generation that was told we had it too easy. That we are spoiled, selfish, and self-focused. It is true that many in this generation did not have the hardship of war or economic depression that "forced" previous generations into adulthood. But we may not be convinced that this kind of accelerated development is a good thing. Who needs that much responsibility? Why can't we have love without the commitment? Why can't we just have fun?

If our society is going to continue, some of us are going to have to grow up and take on adult responsibilities. But why do there seem to be fewer and fewer volunteers? Perhaps it's because of the hardship so many of us *have* already endured—hardship that is not always acknowledged.

Sometimes our hardship came in the form of a dysfunctional household. This kind of trauma, like most childhood trauma, arrested our development, as opposed to accelerating it. Instead of having the tools and supports to develop into adults, we were left to develop into a nation of "adult children."

Adult children are not necessarily immature or irresponsible, but they *are* deprived. Adult children have been denied the fundamental joys of childhood. If you never had the childhood you deserved, becoming an adult has little appeal. You don't want to be an adult because it can only be seen as more sacrifice, and you've already sacrificed enough. You still want that childhood, the one that you missed. And until these issues are more satisfactorily resolved—until that child has been taken better care of—you will never feel truly ready for adulthood or for commitment.

While some of us were neglected, many of us were overprotected. We were not encouraged to develop our own autonomy. We were not encouraged to develop the skills and ego strength that would make us more capable of making adult commitments. We were taken care of not wisely, but too well. Chronologically we are adults, but psychologically we feel more like imposters.

Even if we want to grow up and want to make commitments, we are scared. We're not really sure we can grow up. We have so little experience making adult decisions and taking on adult responsibilities that the leap seems enormous and overwhelming. Interestingly even if we're not particularly good at taking care of ourselves, we feel smothered when anyone else tries to take care of us. Why? Probably because it feels as though they are perpetuating our struggle.

Being an adult also makes us think about aging, and that's scary too. Aging conjures up images of illness and other limitations—physical, psychological, economic, and practical—that are a realistic cause for concern. At the same time we are constantly receiving overt and covert messages from a culture that celebrates youth and seems to have little interest in the rewards of aging.

Add all of this up and it's not hard to understand why so many of us are fleeing from adulthood. We're not ready, and we don't want to be.

The Fear of Death

If few of us are ready to face adulthood, even fewer are prepared to face mortality. Let's admit it, all of us are afraid of dying. But what does death have to do with commitment? Think about it. Most of us try to shut out the possibility of our own death. Marriage, with those magic words "till death do us part," reminds us that we are not going to be around forever. And once we have completed the ritual of choosing a mate to whom we may be connected for the rest of our days, we are taking a very important step on the human journey that can't help but end.

Many of us view commitment as giving up options. As we give up options, our lives narrow. For some people every commitment, no matter how large or how small, is a small death because it symbolizes fewer remaining choices and a future that is shrinking. For these men and women, refusing to make the commitment compromises that are necessary in life is a rather complicated way of trying to ward off death.

Many of the people we interviewed told us how alive they felt when they were *not* in a committed relationship. They might be in pain, they might be lonely, they might be unhappy—but that doesn't seem to be the issue. The issue is death, and in a sense, to reject commitment is to reject growing up, to reject aging, and ultimately to reject death.

While everyone is afraid of dying, those of us who are most likely to be afraid are those who don't feel as though we've had enough of a life. Once again it is the adult children who are most likely to feel cheated, and are most likely to be running from any hint of death. You can't talk about death to people who feel they haven't really had a life. And to these people, talking about commitment is tantamount to talking about death.

The Fear of Loving Too Much

There are men and women who hear the phrases "falling in love" and all they respond to is the sensation of falling. It's frightening, and it makes them feel as though they are out of control. That scares them.

Some people have felt themselves fall so far in past relationships that they cling tenaciously to a superficial level of reacting. If you have ever seen yourself "give away the store" or if you have any sense that you might not be able to protect yourself appropriately in a loving relationship, then this fear may strike a deep chord.

The Fear of Dependency

This is a major fear, shared by many. For some the anxiety revolves around being overly dependent on another person and losing the ability to take care of oneself. Others worry about the responsibility of having someone else's welfare and well-being placed in their care. It will come as no surprise to hear that these anxieties seem to be directly connected to stereotypical male-female roles and that women seem still to be more likely to worry about being dependent on a man, whereas men are still very concerned about being expected to "take care" of a woman.

Traditionally femininity and dependency have been closely linked. Many women grew up being told that they were "little" women and that they were expected to depend on "big," strong men to take care of them. Men were told that a mark of their maleness was their ability to shelter and protect "their" dependent women.

Yet many men worry that they don't want to spend their lives "taking care" of dependent women, and just as many women say that they don't want to depend on anyone and they don't even have that much confidence in men's ability to "take care." Dependency: should we encourage it, or allow it, or foster it, or develop it? Even if we don't think about it very much, we all have very strong ideas about dependency, and some of these translate into ideas about commitment.

The Fear of Being "Found Out"

"My family is nuts. If I date anyone normal and she meets any of them—my mother, my brother, or my sister—it's all over."

"It's my stretch marks. If you're living with someone day in and day out, they are going to be noticed."

"I don't make enough money to attract the kind of women I'm attracted to. I'm always living with the fear of being found out."

"I owe thousands on my credit card. I live totally above my means. And I would die if anyone knew."

"I don't think anyone will put up with the way I'm attached to my cats."

"It's the dog. He's not one hundred percent housebroken. Nobody will want to deal with it."

"I'm a neat freak. Really obsessive."

"I'm a slob, but I hide it."

"In truth I work sixteen hours a day most days, and I don't want to change it. But a normal woman would think I'm nuts."

"I don't want to sound like I have no self-esteem, but it's close, and I wouldn't want anyone else to figure it out."

Everyone has at least a few insecurities, a few ways in which we worry that we may be slightly substandard, so to speak. However, we don't want to spread the news about these "imperfections," we prefer keeping these things secret. But committed relationships make it tough to have secrets. When we are with our mates, we are about as exposed as we're going to get. This makes many of us at least a little bit uncomfortable. What are those awful secrets each of us is convinced no one could accept?

All of us have less-than-perfect bodies, less-than-perfect families, less-than-perfect finances, and less-than-perfect idiosyncratic behavior. Instead of seeing our flaws and struggles as part of being human, we see them as a source of tremendous shame. In fact some of us are so ashamed of ourselves and our circumstances that we live in terror of being revealed. This causes us to hide much of our real life from the world. We keep the terrible truth a secret: an alcoholic parent, a troubled sibling, a child's medical problems, our own financial problems, a struggle with substance abuse, a terrible scar, a learning disability, a spotty job history, an eating disorder, an embarrassing relationship history.

Why do some of us need to keep secrets like this? Why is being less than perfect so shameful? Not everyone with a less-than-perfect life tries so hard to cover it up. But some of us can't imagine anyone normal and desirable accepting us if they saw all the skeletons in our closet. The things we keep secret make us feel like damaged goods.

This kind of belief system tends to reflect not only underlying narcissistic conflicts but also powerful fears of abandonment. Psychology tells us that when a little child feels emotionally or physically abandoned by its mother or father, the child's thinking is not sophisticated enough to understand the many factors that could be pulling its parents away. The most common conclusion a small child is likely to reach is this: "I must have done something wrong; I deserve to be abandoned." Given this perception, the child is likely to believe that if it can become perfect, hiding all of its problems and perceived shortcomings from the parents, it won't be abandoned anymore.

The child then carries this "personal fiction" into adulthood and into all of his or her adult relationships. Often these feelings, as we will see, are instrumental in propelling us into very unfortunate relationships.

CIRCUMSTANTIAL COMMITMENT ISSUES

For each of us there may be several reasons to prefer to stay away from committed relationships. When a forty-three-year-old man worries about taking on the responsibilities of adulthood, we are less than sympathetic, but if a twenty-three-year-old expresses the same sentiments, they make perfect sense. Age, economics, remaining educational goals—all of these provide realistic circumstantial reasons why commitment may not yet be a sound choice. But there are other special circumstances that may also keep one from looking for a permanent relationship.

The Fear of Creating More Problems

Consider someone like Maxine, a single mother with an attitude that she perceives, perhaps rightfully, as both temporary and self-protective. Maxine says that she is completely conscious of her efforts to ward off commitment. She explains:

"It's the three children. They have such a close relationship with their father that I know if I get involved with another man, they would resent it deeply. I can see it whenever I go out on a date. I suppose if I had only one child, or if my children were younger, or if my ex-husband were less involved, the chaos that would follow my getting involved with someone would be worth it. But right now, with teenagers, it isn't. I figure once the kids are out of the house, then I can think about finding someone long-term. In the meantime I know what would happen. And my children are too important to me.

"Some of my friends tell me that this is an excuse and that I'm still involved with my ex-husband, but I *know* that's not the case. I've seen what happens when someone with several children re-marries. It happened to my cousin. She married a nice enough guy, but he couldn't adjust to the children, the children couldn't adjust to him, she was torn in half, the children suffered. Now her kids are very resentful, and she has a terrible family problem. That's not for me."

Maxine is very clear that she is making a choice, and for her right now it feels like the right choice.

The Fear of Giving Up a Good Life-style

If you're happy, if your life is working, if you don't feel lonely, and if you feel that you have a satisfying life, you may be afraid of rocking the boat by looking for a commitment. For many people this makes perfect sense. Zoe, forty-six, says:

"For the first time in my life everything is working. I love my work, I love where I live, I love my friends. . . . I love my life. Why would I want to change it now? I'm not going to have chil-dren, and that's okay with me. I'm old enough not to get involved with any jerks. It may change, but right now I'm happy the way I am."

One cannot fault such logic. When your life is working, it's working. As Zoe points out, her attitude may change, but right now she is circumstantially unavailable for commitment.

The Fear of Making Another Mistake

If you have married badly one or more times, you may have a circumstantial fear of making the same mistake all over again. This attitude was repeated to us many times by those who claim to suffer from cirrhosis of the heart. If you've been burned on com-mitment too many times, you may be more than gun-shy about the prospect of yet another attempt at permanent union. They say that after a bad experience or two a little self-protective voice cries out, *Hey, you can't do this to me again.*

The Fear of the Financial Implications of Commitment

Many people have a fair number of fears concerning how their money situation will be affected by a committed relationship. These fears may not seem realistic to you, but try telling that to someone who has been divorced several times and gone through the hassle of dividing or giving up assets. You don't have to go through a divorce to be afraid of the financial implications of commitment. When you're committed, you're responsible. Some people, both men and women, take that responsibility very seriously. They worry about having enough to cover emergencies. They worry that if one person gets sick, the other will bear the burden. Older people marrying for the second time worry how this marriage will affect their children's financial rights. Let's not forget those folks who are a bit squeamish about sharing in general. The idea that someone might actually expect them to be generous can be extremely threatening.

The Fear That There Is No Room in Your Life for Another Person

Working day and night to establish your career; studying day and night to get the degree you think you need; struggling day and night to get your business off the ground—demands like these sometimes make us feel that we have little left to give. We're barely able to relate to the television set and the sickly looking cactus on the windowsill in the kitchen. Who would want to make a commitment to us? We're simply not fit for human companionship at this time in our lives. Maybe someday, but not now.

This is an attitude we hear more and more, particularly from professional, goal-oriented, men and women who say they don't have time to meet appropriate partners.

The Fear of the Realistic Burdens of Marriage and a Family

Many of us carry images in our heads of a successful couple sitting in a large, well-furnished space, a pricey Range Rover in the garage, entertaining exciting friends while their adorable toddlers frolic happily nearby. Not only is the couple committed, they are madly in love, incredibly successful, and overwhelmingly rich. They have romantic vacations, unlimited resources, and superb household support. If we ever get married and think about raising a family, this is what we want for ourselves.

But while these images flitter through our heads, we carry with us another, more realistic, attitude. Sexual stereotyping and life experience may combine to make you afraid of certain types of realistic roles you may think you will be expected to play. Women, for example, may fear getting stuck with an unfair share of household chores and child care. Men may worry about assuming the larger share of financial responsibilities. Statistics tell us that both of these fears are founded in reality. Since most of us know women who are solid breadwinners while they are *also* taking their turns in the carpool, this is also a realistic possibility. Many of us also know men who are trying to earn a living *while* balancing babies on their knees. Do you have a nagging little voice asking if you really want a pabulum-stained suit to be part of your personal image? Does the idea of trying to handle the financial responsibilities of a family on your salary make you tremble? Then you may have some realistic concerns about commitment.

UNDERSTANDABLE FEARS, INAPPROPRIATE CHOICES

If you identified with any of the above fears—and who doesn't? —then the next step is to figure out whether these fears may be playing a critical role in determining your pattern in relationships. Are your fears driving you away from good choices and pushing you toward inappropriate partners? That's what the next chapter is all about.

CHAPTER NINE

Understanding How Your Conflict Works

The fears discussed in the last chapter express only part of the commitment conflict. But there's another part: Most of us still want the love and security of long-term relationships. In short we both want and fear stable, permanent relationships. This can provoke amazingly contradictory feelings and behavior. What this all too often means is that while our desire drives us to keep looking for and form relationships, our fears are dictating our choices and our behavior in these relationships.

COMMITMENT WISH + COMMITMENT FEAR = BAD CHOICE

In this chapter we have set up a system to help you figure out how your conflicts might be driving you away from good choices and leading you toward partnerships that are ultimately unsatisfying or hurtful. To do this, we're going to use a variation of the same list of fears that we discussed in the last chapter. But this time we're going to phrase these fears differently so that they highlight the conflict. For example, *I want a commitment, but I don't want to make a mistake.* Each statement will express two separate thoughts: (a) a wish for a committed relationship ("I want a commitment . . ."); and (b) a fear that reflects a specific reservation ("But I don't want to make a mistake").

A statement like this leads one to believe that both thoughts have equal weight. Yet usually they don't. Here's why:

- Those with **passive conflicts** will almost always be more conscious of the wish. The first part of the statement, "I want a committed relationship," has far greater resonance in their lives.
- Those with **active conflicts,** on the other hand, are far more likely to be aware of their fear. "I don't want to make a mistake" will be a clearer expression of what they feel.

The classic commitmentphobic couple is made up of one partner with active and the other partner with passive conflicts. What often happens, however, is that both partners share the same kinds of fears. In fact it often seems as though the similarity in their fears are points of understanding that bring them together. Yet the degree of intensity with which each partner feels the wish "I want a committed relationship" and the fear "I don't want to make a mistake" is completely different. This discrepancy in needs is what typically splits the relationship up.

With that in mind let's see some of the things that can happen when those of us with commitment conflicts (active or passive) form romantic attachments. Let's see what occurs when you *really* want a committed relationship but you also really have a set of anxiety-based requirements.

NARCISSISTIC COMMITMENT CONFLICTS

Do any of the following statements describe the way you feel? Do you think that these statements might describe the way your partner feels?

- *I want a commitment, but I want to be with a partner who is perfect for me.*
- *I want a commitment, but I want to be with someone who makes me feel as though everything about me is perfect and we have a perfect love.*

- *I want a commitment, but I want it to be with somebody who has the right "résumé" and/or physical appeal.*

If you want a commitment, but only to someone who will activate or reinforce your narcissistic needs, you run the risk of finding only relationships that have so many other problems that commitment is hardly a possibility. You may always get involved with people who have major narcissistic issues of their own.

A woman with passive narcissistic commitment conflicts, for example, may feel that she doesn't have a sense of real value unless a man finds her lovable. She may be too easily swept off her feet by someone with the right M.O. This is the perfect setup for getting involved in a series of relationships with the kind of man who runs from partner to partner in order to reinforce his own sense of self. A man or woman with active conflicts may get image reinforcement by going from one partner to another.

Because men and women with narcissistic issues tend to be "picky," one can't help but wonder why they so often fail to be picky about the right things. Here are some of the ways in which narcissistic conflicts can keep you from finding the loving relationship you want:

The Difference Between the Narcissistic Quest for Perfection and Reasonable Judgment

All too often what are triggered at the beginning of a commitmentphobic relationship are all of the narcissistic vulnerabilities. What each person notices about the other depends entirely upon what that person regards as perfection—at that stage of the relationship.

For one person it may be physical beauty. But for someone else it may be wealth. For someone else it may be charm. For many people it is none of these. People whose idea of perfection includes emotional or intellectual depth, for example, may have an entire presentation that revolves around displaying their poetic souls. There are those who respond primarily to the promise of a perfect fantasy scenario. For one person it can be the perfect adventure or the perfect one-night stand. For another it can be just the perfect romance. For some people passion isn't perfect unless it's filled with separation, longing, and despair; the words that resonate for them will be those that spell out challenge and potential pain.

How Image Issues Control Judgment

Not everyone acts out narcissistic impulses in the same fashion. Active avoiders usually have a pattern different from passive avoiders. And, this is one of those instances when men and women may be conditioned to think and behave differently.

Active avoiders, particularly men, may act out their narcissistic impulses by becoming immediately captivated by total strangers. It can be the sparkle in a woman's eyes, the way she walks through a room, the way she looks in a miniskirt. It can be her accent, her intellectual credentials, or her family connections. Whatever the external image may be, what the active avoider typically feels is this: *This is the kind of special woman I deserve.* Somehow this woman satisfies some primal need and offers a sense of completion—and power. You feel good because you are projecting a successful image to the world. Passive avoiders may respond to those who "come on strong" or who make them feel that they will reinforce their worth to the outside world.

Those with narcissistic issues, both male and female, can be held spellbound by those who promise the completion of their special fantasies. As long as the spell lasts—typically until the person has been won over—reasonable judgment is suspended. Any quality that reinforces one's image needs can cast such a spell—status, power, money, and physical appearance are all likely candidates to be the driving force in a narcissistic attraction.

As in most commitmentphobic relationships, once the active avoider has managed to win his or her partner over, all the old commitment anxieties surface, and the narcissistic faultfinding tendencies begin to dominate. Once again reasonable judgment is overcome by narcissistic impulses.

Finding Fault with All the Wrong Things

Because there is always a pull toward perfection, those with image issues act out their commitment anxieties by finding fault with their partners or their relationships. Reason goes out the window, and what replaces it is sometimes so ludicrous that it seems to be a joke. In fact often their partners don't believe what they are hearing. For example:

- After five years of dating, Wayne, five foot eleven, tells his girlfriend, five foot three, that they can never marry because she is too short and he is afraid of having short children.
- After two years of living together, Keisha tells her partner that she is moving out because he has "rotten taste" and looking at his ugly wardrobe makes her sick to her stomach.
- After six months of round-the-clock pursuit, Louis tells his girlfriend that it's over because she doesn't ski well enough to keep up on the slopes.
- Deirdre told Ian that she loved him, but that the relationship couldn't last for two reasons: (1) Although he made three times as much money as she did, she felt that he didn't make enough. (2) Although he had three times as many friends as she did, he didn't have enough friends. She said that someday she wanted to make more money and have more friends, and he didn't *look* successful enough.
- Don has rejected every woman he has ever been out with because they weren't pretty enough. He always feels he can do better.

It's interesting to note that active avoiders with narcissistic impulses frequently reject their partners because of qualities that the avoider was aware of from the very beginning. It's also interesting how rarely one hears these people say they are ending a relationship because their partners are unkind or thoughtless or uncaring.

Narcissistic Fears for the Future

One of the most distressing actions someone with active narcissistic conflicts may take is to dynamite a really good, solid relationship because of some vague worry about the future. Just about everybody who is trying to decide whether or not to make a permanent commitment to another human being has a set of fears that we call the *what if's*. For example:

"What if she gets fat like her mother?"
"What if he gets paunchy like his father?"
"What if she gets wrinkles?"
"What if he goes bald?"
"What if childbirth changes her body?"
"What if he loses his money?"
"What if I meet a woman later who is really perfect?"
"What if my friends think he looks funny?"

We could go on with this list of *what if's* indefinitely. What they all boil down to is the following worry: Suppose I make a commitment to someone who is less than perfect and then I feel stuck?

Women and Narcissistic Image Issues

When a woman's good sense goes out the window in relationships, image issues are often implicated. But women, particularly those with passive commitment issues, find it difficult to relate to the notion of narcissistic faultfinding. They quickly point out that they don't demand perfection. Typically they feel that in relationships they are, if anything, too accepting. While this is probably an accurate assessment, what they fail to notice is how their behavior is influenced by image issues. Too often too much of their sense of value is dependent upon what is happening externally. We understand that a lot of this is a cultural setup; but it can also have at least a part of its roots in narcissism.

Let's take an all-too-common relationship scenario:

Naome, a social worker in a large urban hospital, has been having an affair for fifteen years with a doctor associated with a medical center in another town. The affair consists of two or three dates a year. She says:

"I feel like a total fool. I've been going out with a married man for fifteen years. He never calls, he never writes. He never does anything, but a few times each year he drives through town and we spend the night together. Each time he calls, I get all excited. I feel wanted, and it thrills me. This is stupid because when I'm with him, I don't even have a nice time. The next day I always feel terrible, so why do I have this knee-jerk response when the phone rings and it's him?"

From the time a woman first starts dating, when the phone rings and a man asks her out, she finds reinforcement of her worth. Think about the average teenage girl waiting to be chosen at the school dance. As she gets older, things don't necessarily change. Society has told this young woman that she should have a date for the prom, a man at her side, a husband to give her life meaning. Projecting this kind of image can assume monumental importance. She is told that women who count have these things and that women who don't are objects of pity.

Often her family reinforces these feelings. Think about a single woman coping with relatives who are questioning why she has yet to "get" a husband. When someone sees her with a man, it means that someone wants her and that she has value. And if she doesn't have a date, doesn't have a man, doesn't have a husband, because of all the messages she has received she may well find that *she* is questioning herself. She may need this sense that a man finds her attractive in order to reinforce her sense of worth. And if he is an attractive man with good credentials, so much the better for her image.

Naome, the social worker who is dating the doctor, is a case in point. When she met him fifteen years ago, she was still in school, and he was a guest lecturer and already considered very important in his field. When he singled out Naome for his attentions, she was flattered. She was impressed by the way people treated him and she gave more weight to that than she did to the fact that he was married and living in another town. That's why she allowed this intrinsically unsatisfying relationship to develop.

Looking at this relationship closely, one can see how it triggers both sides of the narcissistic coin. On the one hand, when this man phones Naome and pays attention to her, he makes her feel desirable and worthwhile. Because he talks to her about psychiatry, he makes her feel as though she is smart and interesting. In short he validates her. But being with him on abbreviated dates that revolve around a sexual connection makes Naome feel undervalued and used.

If you are a woman, you should think about Naome's story and then think about the times in your life when getting attention from a man has made you feel like more of a person. Think about the times you have gotten into questionable relationships—often knowing full well that they were fraught with problems—simply because having a man in your life made you feel more desirable. Think about the times you may have gone out with men you didn't particularly like simply because you were thrilled to be seen with a man. Think about the instant image hit you get when a man finds you desirable and attractive. Think about how you feel when you tell your friends some story about a man who is pursuing you.

Then think about how you may have felt when a man didn't complete your fantasy scenario about a relationship. Think about how your sense of self-worth can be threatened by a man's failure to make you feel special. Also think about the amount of energy you may have expended trying to prove to the men in your life that you were indeed a perfect woman.

Like it or not, these are all connected to narcissistic issues. On some level it may all seem harmless enough. After all, what's wrong with feeling good because someone thinks you're nifty? Obviously nothing. The problem occurs when you are so taken with the feeling that you allow good sense to vanish and when your own sense of self-esteem is so shaky that it can be inflated or destroyed by a man's attentions.

This can leave a woman vulnerable to the most inappropriate and unavailable men. Let's consider what can happen when a worst-case commitmentphobic man, one whose M.O. revolves around pursuit/panic, chooses such a woman. Her responses to the heavy pursuit are more extreme, more total, than those of the woman who is centered and sure of herself. He tells her that she is wonderful, and she believes him because his words make her feel wonderful. Then he panics and pulls away, and she is left reeling, with no firm center of her own.

Noticing What Your Narcissistic Little Voice Notices

Allow your narcissistic impulses to outweigh your good judgment and there are so many different ways in which you can choose the wrong partners and reject the right ones that it's almost impossible to categorize. Have you ever been involved in any of the following situations?

• When Al meets a woman, he starts out by telling her all the ways in which *he* is special. He tries to impress her by showing her his nice car, his good apartment. He talks about his interesting job, his interesting hobbies, his interesting neuroses. Once he has proven that he is special, he then turns around and tells her that she is special. Instead of taking her time and evaluating the situation and the man over time, she buys into his pitch. She thinks, *Gosh, he's special and he thinks I'm special. Then I guess I am special.* She doesn't look below his surface presentation, which is often pure hogwash, but she won't find that out until later.

• When Cynthia first meets a man, she manages to let him know about all the men who have found her attractive. She tells him how beautiful she is and how lovable she is and how "picky" she is. He listens to this, and he thinks, *I guess she's pretty desirable, and if I'm with her, people will notice that I'm with a woman that every man wants.* The fact that she is difficult, demanding, and spoiled will not occur to him for a long time.

• Bruce and Elaine have been going together for three years. Bruce loves Elaine. She is wonderful to him—kind, thoughtful, caring, supportive, but he's not sure about this marriage business. Maybe if she were a little bit different. She's pretty enough, but knowing her as well as he does, he knows how she shaves her legs and how she gets a little bit of acne on her back every month. Let's face it, she's not one hundred percent perfect, and he worries she may get fat someday. He meets another woman. She's younger and thinner. He breaks up with Elaine—whom he acknowledges he probably still loves—and leaps into this new relationship, all the while worrying that it may be the biggest mistake of his life. But he can't help himself.

217

- Didi is in a very obsessive relationship with a man who is unfaithful and difficult. When Didi and Doug met, he made her feel that she was desirable and completely loved. When his behavior changed, she immediately felt unattractive and unloved. She feels as though without him, she doesn't exist.

- Bobbie's husband is a good man. He's thoughtful and decent and hardworking and smart, and he loves her. He doesn't make as much money as some of the other husbands in the neighborhood. And he's losing some of his hair. She knows she shouldn't be so critical, but she thinks that people look at her and feel sorry for her because she didn't get a richer husband with more hair.

These stories are illustrative of some of the ways in which narcissistic impulses cause us to maintain distance in our relationships, pursue unrealistic fantasies, and walk away from what is real. In the process we may be destroying our chances for long-term love.

What to Watch Out For

If you have narcissistic conflicts, remember that you are particularly vulnerable to:

- *People who appeal to your narcissistic ideals.* Your narcissistic ideals are those things that reflect the image you want to present to the world. They can predispose you to falling in love with résumés, not people. If someone has the right degree, the right clothes, the right friends, the right car, the right apartment, the right look, the right background —you run the risk of buying the package without examining what's inside.
- *People who are supreme narcissists.* If you have narcissistic issues, you are easily attracted to those whose presentation of themselves is often smooth, appealing, and "perfect." Supreme narcissists frequently have a great deal of charisma and charm. It's all facade, but they know how to use it.
- *People who say that you're the greatest thing since sliced bread and*

tell you what you want to hear—before they really know you. If you were clear about your value, you wouldn't be so susceptible to someone who comes on like gangbusters. Remember that if you have narcissistic issues, you have two little voices in your head—one telling you that you're the greatest and the other picking you apart and tearing you down. Someone who gets to you by flattering your grandiose voice may also carry the power to flatten you by activating your crushed voice.

- *People whom you always try to please or people who make you feel as though you have to prove yourself.* The need to please and prove yourself worthy is frequently connected to low self-esteem, which, in turn, can be connected to narcissistic impulses. Because you want to be perfect, you are always vulnerable to someone who withholds approval. So watch out!

- *People who activate your fantasies.* Because narcissistic issues keep you running between two extremes of "I'm the best, I'm the worst," it's easy to get hooked on fantasies that keep you running between two extremes—very good and very bad. Remember that reality is somewhere in the center, and that's where you want to be.

CLAUSTROPHOBIC COMMITMENT CONFLICTS

If you have a visceral sense of being uncomfortable when someone "crowds" you, then you may be drawn only to people and situations that give you a feeling of space and distance. If this is the case, without realizing it you may consistently turn away from partners who are genuinely looking for a commitment and you may end up with too much "distance" built into all your relationships. Typically your relationships break up because either you or your partners are made uncomfortable by intimacy and commitment. Let's go through the list of claustrophobic conflicts and see how they might play out:

I WANT A COMMITMENT, BUT I WANT TO RETAIN MY FREEDOM TO DO WHATEVER I WANT WHEN I WANT.

What are some of the negative things that can happen when you are primarily attracted to people who appear unlikely to threaten your need for freedom? This conflict tends to play out differently depending on whether you have passive or active conflicts. For example:

If you have active conflicts:

You probably try to stay away from partners who have too many expectations of traditional, conventional behavior. Even so, you may choose partners who want more commitment and less freedom than you do. That's why you may so often find yourself in relationships where you feel as though someone is trying to pin you down. Some questions to ask yourself:

- Do I give out mixed messages, articulating my need for commitment while I act out my need for freedom?
- Do I have a history of unreliability with my partners?
- Am I drawn to partners who represent stability and then wonder why they are trying to get me to settle down?
- Have I ever taken advantage of a partner's caretaker instincts?
- Do I sometimes say the kinds of things that would encourage a partner to have expectations and then wonder how it happened?
- Do I have unreasonable resentments concerning expectations, requests, or demands that might encroach on my time or emotional availability, even within the context of an ongoing relationship?

If you have passive conflicts:

You may be most attracted to those who convey a sense of being free. Often you hope people such as this will help you also experience a sense of freedom. Perhaps you have a dream about forming a relationship in which you and your partner can go off and be "free birds" together. You run into trouble by forgetting that freedom means different things to different people. The person you recognize as your "soul mate" may want to fly off in the opposite direction . . . alone.

You also have to keep in mind that those who convey a sense of freedom are sometimes unsettled and unstable. While your idea of freedom may be a drive through the countryside in a convertible or a mildly unconventional life-style, you might find yourself attached to someone to whom *freedom* means the freedom to be excessive in any way—the freedom to drink to excess, spend to excess, and philander to excess are some examples. In such a relationship you may find yourself always trying to bring someone else down to earth. Or you might always be trying to get an elusive partner to settle down and make a commitment. Here are some questions to ask yourself:

- Do I have a tendency to form relationships in which my partner gets to behave like an irresponsible child and I become the annoyed parent?
- Do I form uneven relationships in which I become the ballast, and my partner becomes the free spirit?
- Do I have a history of forming relationships with people who keep me unsettled and off balance?

I WANT A COMMITMENT, BUT I DON'T WANT TO LOSE MY SEXUAL FREEDOM.

What can go wrong in a relationship when you want commitment, but you want to retain your right to have sex with others? Everything. The list is endless. In our society monogamy goes hand in hand with trust, love, and commitment. Try to separate them and the equation is destroyed, as well as the relationship, which will often disintegrate under the tremendous undercurrents of jealousy, anger, resentment, and insecurity. It's fairly obvious that wanting sexual freedom within a committed relationship is a setup for disaster.

If you have active conflicts: The first question to ask yourself is why you choose partners who will be faithful to you and then take advantage of this quality. Most of the time what you are doing is inflicting tremendous pain on your partner. This is far from loving behavior, and it will be remembered accordingly. Sometimes, however, it can backfire on you in other ways. For example, you say that you need to "reserve the right to have sex" with someone else, and your partner goes out and has sex with someone else before you finish your sentence. Suddenly the roles are reversed.

If you have passive conflicts: Typically while you may understand the impulses pulling your partner toward sexual freedom, you want no part of it for yourself. You are hoping that this is simply a phase your partner is going through and that love will conquer all. Typically it doesn't.

I WANT A COMMITMENT, BUT I DON'T EVER WANT TO BE BORED.

There is a big difference between wanting to lead an interesting life and being scared of boredom. Sometimes people who say they want a commitment really want a roller-coaster ride with all the accompanying highs and lows. Unless they are experiencing an intense feeling at all times, they think something is wrong.

Those who need partners to provide them with a sense of being alive may not know how to appreciate a comfortable, constructive, reasonable relationship between two adults with their own interests. They may always be too busy dealing with dramatic situations to notice potential partners who are kind, well intentioned, and nice, but who lack the hypnotic skills necessary to capture their immediate attention.

A fear of being bored can sometimes lead to particularly destructive relationships. It's easy to make sure you'll never be bored and always be excited. Live with gamblers or drug dealers or people who can't tell you what they do for a living. Hang out with race-car drivers or gun runners or people who live on the edge—alcoholics, drug abusers, sex addicts. Make sure jealousy—either yours or your partner's—is a major component in all your relationships; that's guaranteed to provide a few sleepless nights. In short find someone with problems. Or make your own!

If you're more worried about being bored than you are about anything else, you can almost be guaranteed to find—or create—relationships that are very interesting and very problematic. As one of our interviewees told us about one of her more "exciting" choices, "I saw ten times more emergency rooms, courtrooms, and crisis centers in six months than I had ever seen in my whole life—and that includes the ones I saw on TV shows."

If you have active conflicts: At the first sign of "normalcy" in a relationship, you may panic and start creating problems. Instead of directing your efforts toward your career or the outside world, you may constantly be stirring the relationship to keep it full of chaos. You may try to add spice to your life by seeing a variety of people simultaneously or by creating jealous rifts and scenes. Or you may drum up excitement by fighting and faultfinding. You may walk away from loving, supportive partners whenever things get calm and easy.

If you have passive conflicts: You may fail to be adequately self-protective and may respond most to people who are so "interesting" that it takes up most of your waking hours trying to figure out what they are doing. You may tend to place a great deal of value on those whose deep psychological, albeit interesting, problems don't make realistic commitment a realistic possibility. Even so, you may become obsessed with trying to get such a person to settle down. You may also stir up your relationships by creating scenes and looking for drama. Or you may too soon become bored if a relationship develops gradually, and you may precipitate a crisis by stepping up the pressure for more intensity, more passion, and more commitment.

I WANT A COMMITMENT, BUT I WORRY ABOUT CHANGING MY MIND AND BEING STUCK.

What happens when you vacillate between your desire for permanent love and your fear of never walking out alive? This conflict raises the classic claustrophobic fear of "forever after," and it creates behavior that is equally "classic." Those with this conflict—specifically worried about staying with someone for the long haul—almost always tend to choose relationships in which distance is a given. Sometimes as intimacy increases, they sabotage the relationship in order to create more distance.

If you have active conflicts: Although you may begin a relationship with a great deal of flourish and involvement, you start to have claustrophobic sensations of being stuck as soon as it appears that your partner is open and available for commitment. You are usually aware of your conflict and tend to leave yourself with an escape route in everything you do. You may choose partners who are so "wrong" or difficult that you always have a built-in excuse for leaving the relationship. This means that you always have a hidden agenda that includes a variety of ways in which you can exit the relationship. In your head, no matter how long-term or short-term the relationship is, you always have one foot out the door. Incidentally this can also be true of someone who has been married for years.

Typically the better or more settled the relationship becomes, the more likely you are to feel this conflict. It is this active conflict that often drives someone to walk out of a marriage the day before (or after) buying a new house, shortly before (or after) the birth of a child, or immediately before (or after) the wedding. This conflict almost always creates a plethora of mixed messages and a long string of "I love you, but . . ." messages, both spoken and unspoken.

Often this conflict combines with others to give you the ammunition necessary to leave a relationship or sabotage its development.

If you have passive conflicts: This is the classic setup for choosing relationships that by definition can't work out long-term. You tend to be drawn to relationships in which distance is a given or to partners who are circumstantially or emotionally unavailable. Often they are so actively commitmentphobic that it is blatantly apparent, even to you. They do nothing to activate your own commitmentphobic anxiety, and this frees you to feel nothing but love. Frequently you are completely focused on getting a commitment from someone who is completely incapable of making one.

Because you are so rarely in relationships in which commitment is a possibility, you're not likely to be aware of this conflict until some twist of fate disrupts your pattern. We have, for example, interviewed a great many women who, after a series of disastrous relationships, settle into a marriage and for the first time, much to their amazement, experience what it means to feel trapped and anxious.

For passives, perhaps the most telling sign that this conflict exists is your ability to understand and sympathize with the conflicted behavior of your profoundly uncommitted and commitmentphobic partners.

I WANT A COMMITMENT, BUT I DON'T EVER WANT TO FEEL LIMITED OR RESTRAINED BY THE COMPROMISES AND OBLIGATIONS OF COMMITMENT.

This conflict presents one of the clearest contradictions. Everyone knows that relationships are full of obligations and require compromise. Yet there are vast numbers of people who struggle with this fact. How do they act this out?

If your fears are directly related to a belief that couples exist as one unit and have no boundaries between them, what better way to make certain that you are never limited by a relationship than to limit the relationship itself? Set up your own boundaries and rules of behavior—usually involving an unreasonable degree of spontaneity.

If you have active conflicts: You tend to make it clear in a myriad of ways that you don't want demands, restraints, or obligations. The most typical:

- You set up boundaries, boundaries, boundaries to keep the relationship contained and to assure yourself that your partner has few expectations. Some people start out the relationship by firmly establishing boundaries; others wait until they feel their freedom threatened.
- You insist upon spontaneity, spontaneity, spontaneity. This can't help but keep your partner off balance.

If you have passive conflicts: Because you have a need to keep a relationship loose and nonrestrictive, you tend to make few demands. Unfortunately this often attracts people who recognize this quality in you and take advantage of it. For example, perhaps you are a woman with an ideal of a balanced relationship in which everything "flows" naturally between partners and no demands need be made. Understanding a desire for spontaneity, you may initially make few demands—until your partner has taken such liberty in acting out conflicts that you are completely off balance.

Perhaps you are a woman who thinks of herself as strong and independent with her own life and her own interests. You're looking for a loving peer, a best friend—not a meal ticket. Why do you, of all women, keep meeting men who can't even fulfill the handful of reasonable expectations that you have? Or perhaps you're a man who thinks of himself as liberated in terms of women's needs. You're prepared to be supportive of a woman's career and her life. Why do you, of all men, keep meeting women who believe a request for a steady Saturday night date is destroying the spontaneity of the relationship?

Think about it this way. Perhaps you are attracting primarily those who would immediately run away from someone with more traditional expectations. Often you are so understanding about issues such as boundaries and spontaneity that by the time you are prepared to call somebody on his/her attitude, you are in too deep to be able to walk away. Perhaps you have so many of your own boundaries that you are immediately put off by anyone who looks as though he/she would want a very traditional family structure with a great deal of "togetherness."

I WANT A COMMITMENT, BUT I DON'T WANT TO GIVE UP MY
INDIVIDUALITY AND MY SENSE OF SELF.

What happens when you want a committed relationship but believe that once in such a relationship you will be asked to give up your individuality and your sense of self? A very common reaction is to start guarding everything that you believe makes you special. This can make you vigilant about protecting everything you do, think, and own.

One's territory is frequently viewed as an extension of self. That's why this conflict often makes us think, *I need more room.* What we mean is we need room to be ourselves, room to grow, room to move about as we wish. Our need for space, whether it be emotional or physical, is very much tied to our need for individuality and for a sharply defined sense of self.

"Let me do it my way, get out of my way." "I'll think what I want to think, get out of my head." "I'll be who I want to be, leave me alone." All of these are battle cries in domestic disagreements, whether they be between two partners or a parent and child. This is the conflict that is most closely tied to one's need for emotional space. The difficult thing about this is that not all of us are conscious of how threatened we feel. All we know is that we can barely breathe.

One frequently voiced desire is to always retain a space of one's own. This wish may be particularly true of women who have a fear (shaped by historical fact) of being asked to give up too much of themselves in return for a commitment.

If you have active conflicts: Although you may be pulled by an urge to merge, you tend to announce your need for individuality in a variety of ways. These mixed messages confuse and upset your partners. When you announce your need for space, for example, they typically become insecure.

Sometimes instead of looking for partners who are equals, you choose those who are overly passive and easily dominated. Perhaps they may give you a sense that they will provide a "cheerleader" role in your life; that way you can assert your individuality without having to compromise or make shared decisions. Ultimately you may find their passivity suffocating and may reject them for the very reasons that you found them attractive.

If you have passive conflicts: You may be attracted to those with a highly defined sense of individuality for two reasons: (1) You respect this kind of personality; and (2) You may believe that they will, in turn, respect your need for individuality and perhaps even help you develop a stronger sense of self. Ultimately the reverse may turn out to be the case, and you may find yourself being overwhelmed by someone else's agenda.

Because you are made insecure by a partner who announces a need for even more space than you require, you tend to get clutchy. This of course gives your partner the sense that his/her individuality or space is being threatened.

I WANT A COMMITMENT, BUT I DON'T WANT TO BE CONTROLLED.

I WANT A COMMITMENT, BUT I DON'T WANT TO GIVE UP CONTROL.

These particular conflicts, which speak to just about everyone, are direct offshoots of the previous one. To get a sense of how control issues influence a commitment conflict, you have to ask yourself what pushes your control buttons. Are you sensitive to others' moods? Are you easily controlled by anger? Are you easily controlled by guilt? Are you controlled by money? Are you controlled by fear? Are you controlled by love? What is it that makes you feel that someone is controlling you and your behavior? Which "spaces" in your life do you need to control? Do you allow anyone else to share your "space"? Do you have "rules"?

There are so many different ways in which someone with controlling tendencies can make rules. They can be about anything from the use of the kitchen sink to the way to spend a vacation. When you combine commitment issues with controlling behavior, the control usually involves ways in which one's space can or cannot be shared.

If you have active conflicts: You will tend to try to stay in control of everything that's going on in a relationship. The boundaries and "rules" that you establish will often serve effectively to make certain that no one ever controls you. Your relationships are often centered around your needs, and you choose partners who will go along with this. Often you have a "*my* life," "*my* house," "*my* rules" attitude. Sometimes this makes you feel guilty, and then you feel controlled by guilt; this may make you respond with resentment and anger. If you care for someone, the intensity of your feelings may make you feel that someone else has the power to control you. This, too, can make you angry and resentful.

If you have passive conflicts: Although you are probably very much aware of your antipathy toward people who try to control you, you may be so afraid of "rocking the boat" that you rarely confront control issues within your relationships—until after marriage.

Nonetheless your partner's insistence on controlling everything can leave you feeling as though you are powerless and out of control. Because you have inadequate power, you feel driven to get more control. This is often a motivating factor in your persistence in maintaining destructive relationships. Your inability to tolerate the feeling of having no control, understandable though it may be, can be a large part of what makes you almost desperate in your attempts to get resolution and closure.

Incidentally people with major commitment issues rarely engage in small domestic squabbles before marriage, and sometimes even after. They are usually so busy dealing with large concerns that they may never get around to arguing about the details of living—how high or low to keep the thermostat, for example. Instead they are usually fighting about much bigger issues such as whether to get or stay married.

If you have conflicts around the issue of control, here are some things to watch out for:

- If you think control is directly associated with money, you may always choose partners whose financial status reflects your concerns. You may, for example, gravitate toward those who have less money than you do.
- If you fear being controlled by anger, you may always choose partners who can't express their feelings.
- If you worry about being controlled by guilt, you may choose partners who are so impossible that there is no way that you could ever feel guilty.

UNIVERSAL COMMITMENT CONFLICTS

Some conflicts touch all of us to one degree or another. They appear to be part of the price of being human in this contemporary global society. For example:

I WANT A COMMITMENT, BUT ONLY IF IT'S MAGIC AND IT'S WITH MY INTENDED SOUL MATE.

We've all been to the same kinds of movies. We all want to "hear bells" and "feel the earth move." But some of us are so invested in finding perfect romance that we have to guard against a tendency to be more interested in magic than we are in commitment.

What does it mean to want a realistic commitment, but only with someone who meets all your fantasy "soul mate" requirements? If you feel this way, you run the risk of spending large chunks of your adult life either absorbed in obsessive relationships or with no relationship at all. Typically you are often feeling lonely and fantasizing about what might have been in relationships that didn't work out, what should be happening in existing relationships, or what might happen in relationships that have yet to take place.

If you have active conflicts: You tend to pursue partners who look as though they will fulfill a personal fantasy and then reject them when it is clear that they are mere earthlings. In your dreams about what it means to be part of a couple, you always feel a romantic high. When that high fades in your real life, you become convinced that you are making a mistake. You have to guard against walking away from solid relationships in favor of unrealistic dreams.

If you have passive conflicts: Your dreams have such power in your life that you tend to superimpose them on all of your relationships; therefore it's almost impossible for you to deal with the concept of limited relationships. Once someone activates your responses, you want to jump right in, bringing your whole dream with you. Although you find this difficult to believe, you are typically as committed to a dream as you are to a partner. For example, no matter how good, bad, or indifferent your partners may be, you often imbue them with all the qualities of your dream.

Often your responses in relationships aren't based on what's really happening. For example: In your dreams you have a very clear sense of what you should feel and how you should behave. You try to behave accordingly—*even when the relationship is giving you no reason to do so.* A belief in your dreams, even when reality is screaming otherwise, makes it very difficult for you to recover from relationships once they are over. If this sounds like you, it's important to learn to keep your dreams in check so that you won't use your fantasies to leap forward in relationships before it's appropriate—or use them to hang on to feelings about relationships that have ended.

I WANT A COMMITMENT, BUT I DON'T WANT THAT TO MEAN THAT
I'M GOING TO HAVE TO GIVE UP MY YOUTHFUL WAYS.

If a part of you still wants to be a kid, it's going to influence
whom you choose as a partner and how you treat this person.
This conflict is not always as obvious as it appears, because there
are so many different ways in which one can try to stay firmly
entrenched in adolescence. Here is a list of the kinds of partners
who might make you feel that you are warding off adulthood. You
might be attracted to:

- Someone who is chronologically younger
- Someone with a childlike personality
- Someone with fewer career responsibilities
- Someone who is less realized as a person, but whom you
  perceive as having great potential
- Someone who isn't settled and doesn't present an estab-
  lished or stable persona
- Someone who is still struggling with issues that are associ-
  ated with growing up—what to do, where to live, what to
  feel
- Someone with adolescent attitudes
- Someone who fulfills the role of parent
- Someone who makes you feel as though you are a charm-
  ing child
- Someone who tolerates an adolescent attitude
- Someone who assumes all the responsibilities of the rela-
  tionship

The fear of stepping forward and becoming part of the adult
world is directly connected to accepting one's mortality. That in
turn is tied to the next universal conflict.

I WANT A COMMITMENT, BUT I DON'T WANT TO FEEL THAT MY LIFE
IS OVER IN ANY WAY BECAUSE OF IT.

Do you believe that making a commitment means that you will
experience less of life? Are you putting off getting married because you feel that you have too much "left to do" before you
settle down? If you have even the slightest sense that marriage
represents a closing of doors rather than an opening up of new
options, you're going to be affected by this conflict.

Men and women with both active and passive commitment conflicts feel these anxieties equally. The difference: Actives typically
feel it before making a commitment; passives may not feel it until
after the commitment has been made.

How might you respond if you sense that doors are closing
around you? "Anxious and angry," "confined and cramped,"
"frightened and furious," "stifled and stuck" are some of the reactions we've heard. How might you behave? Usually by trying to
kick down the doors of the commitment that is closing in on you.
Sometimes this is done very directly in one bold act—this level of
anxiety and fear can lead directly to the divorce courts or to infidelity. Other times it leads to subtle relationship sabotage—picking quarrels and faultfinding. Here are some common reactions
that indicate that this conflict is at work:

- You still love your partner, but you wish that you could put
  this person "on hold" for a period of time until you get to
  live more and do what you have to do.
- For reasons you can't explain, ever since the possibility of
  commitment became real, you are fighting off an anxiety
  attack that seems directly connected to a fear that life is
  over or that death is around the corner.
- You are suddenly struck by an inability to fantasize or
  dream about the future because you no longer feel as
  though you have a future.
- You've spent so much time dreaming about marriage and
  commitment that now that it is actually happening, you feel
  strangely sad, as though you have no dreams left to dream.
- Your partner makes you so anxious that you want to dis-

tance yourself, and yet you know that this person is not directly responsible for what you are feeling.

Often when men and women have this conflict, they want the best of both worlds: They wish that their partners would function as undemanding security centers, giving love and support, while allowing them to continue to wander off, fulfilling adventures.

This conflict, which is as old as time, is probably best represented by the story of Ulysses. Everyone remembers Ulysses. After the Trojan War, he put off returning home to his wife and family. Instead he continued to sail around the Aegean seeking adventure, some romance, and a fair amount of danger. When Ulysses finally returned to his wife, the patient Penelope, it symbolized his willingness to stop running and come to terms with who he was and where he belonged. At that point the story of Ulysses ends, but the life of Ulysses begins. We have no idea what happens in the marriage when Penelope gets fed up with hearing his tales and watching his travel slides. What we can assume is that they raised their family, bought another dog, and took their place in the human continuum.

What Ulysses the hero learned is that life does not happen on a sailing ship, nor on a jetliner. In short, life doesn't happen when you are in motion; it happens when you stop and dig in. You can fill your life with the most extraordinary adventures and moments, but you run the risk of looking up and discovering that you have many souvenirs but you don't have a life. So long as he was chasing fantasies around the Aegean, Ulysses wasn't truly connecting to his world. He returned home because he discovered that the only way to have a life is to show up for it.

Commitment begins the day the fantasy ends and we accept another real, live human being as our real-life mate. This means accepting our place in the cosmos, accepting our humanity, and thus acknowledging our own mortality. Of course this is frightening, but it's a fundamental part of being human.

And a special note for all those women with passive commitment conflicts who believe that if they are patient enough, their personal Ulysses archetypes will also return. Remember, Ulysses didn't show up until Penelope had announced her engagement to another man. She wasn't kidding this time, and she was planning to go through with it. Ulysses came home on the eve of the wedding.

I WANT A COMMITMENT, BUT I DON'T WANT TO LOVE ANYBODY SO MUCH THAT I LOSE A PIECE OF MYSELF.

Look at the great love stories and you can't help but notice that many of the lovers end up dead by the end of the story. It's as if the feelings generated are so powerful that the lovers can't survive. It's very scary to think that a merger with another human being can be intense enough to threaten one's very sense of self. We want to feel the passion, yet we don't want to be overcome and engulfed by the emotions. Yet, to many people, to be fully committed means being fully vulnerable in this way.

Those with **active conflicts** are most likely to compensate for the fears this generates by establishing walls to keep others out. Those with **passive conflicts** recognize that they have problems maintaining boundaries when they love.

Finding ways to feel and accept appropriate levels of intimacy is often the motivating reason for going into therapy or seeking some form of counseling. We all need to learn to love and be loved without losing ourselves, and dealing with the deep struggles that this conflict can present should be a priority for all of us.

I WANT A COMMITMENT, BUT I'M AFRAID THAT ONCE ALL THE THINGS ABOUT ME THAT I'M ASHAMED OF ARE REVEALED, I'LL BE REJECTED.

Everyone has some feelings of inadequacy. Most of us have areas in our lives about which we feel some degree of shame; we worry about exposing this to someone else. In a committed relationship we are exposed to the intimate stares of our mates. Soon enough they will discover all our secrets. They'll find out about Uncle Fred, and black-sheep Cousin Beauford. They'll get to meet "eccentric" Aunt Dot, and they'll hear about the foolish and embarrassing things we did as children. They can't help but learn about the unwanted hairs that grow in various secret places on our bodies and the dimples of fat that form on our hips. All of our unvarnished truths will be there, hanging out, for our mates to see. Does this scare you just a little?

How do you handle wanting a committed relationship when there are things about you—your past and/or your present—that make you feel inadequate, things you believe are so shameful that you worry about exposing them to your mate?

If you have active conflicts, you tend to choose partners who you *know* will put up with what you perceive as your shortcomings. If you have passive conflicts, you tend to get involved with partners who you *hope* will help you overcome your feelings of inadequacy. Here's how this works:

If you have active conflicts: You are very conscious of what you perceive as your inadequacies. In fact you often bring them up within the first date or two, sometimes using them almost as a lure to draw someone into your sphere. If you drink, for example, you may quickly involve new partners in your struggle. If you have a difficult childhood or a dysfunctional family, you may talk about it on your first date. That's how you screen new partners to make *absolutely certain* that they know and accept the "ghosts" in your life. It sometimes may appear as though you use the problems in your life as a way of increasing your partner's sensitivity and commitment to you.

Typically you take this one step farther. Instead of allowing anyone to reject you because of your perceived shortcomings, you yourself use them as part of your excuse for rejecting others: For example:

When John met Mary, he told her just about everything about his lonely childhood, his hurtful mother, and his feelings of pain. For two years the relationship revolved around John's sensitivity and his moods and his needs. Finally John rejected Mary saying that she should have understood that he had "demons" from his past that kept him from making a commitment.

When Jane met Dick, she told him about her problems with food and how bad she feels about herself whenever she gains weight. As the relationship progressed and they got closer, Jane started eating more and gaining more weight. Dick feels that the better the relationship becomes, the more weight Jane puts on.

He feels it is her way of avoiding intimacy. However, he also feels that he can't say anything because to do so makes Jane feel bad.

John and Jane have very intricate defense systems and are engaged in a very subtle way of keeping their partners at a distance. This includes encouraging partners to become involved with their problems and then using these problems as built-in ways out of relationships.

If you have passive conflicts: For some of us the struggle with "less than perfect" takes on a new dimension when we start looking for romantic relationships. Instead of seeking someone appropriate—someone who has what we want and deserve in a partner—we gravitate toward people who we think are less likely to judge us critically and reject us. Typically this means people who have bigger problems than we have. Initially these people feel "safe," but that can be *extremely* deceptive.

It is our experience, and the experience of our interviewees, that any attempt to compensate for what you perceive as your own shortcomings can lead to making disastrous relationship choices. If you fear situations where your imperfections might be revealed, you are likely to find partners who are so dysfunctional that the relationships are bound to maim you. Sandi, thirty-three, is one individual who has subjected herself to a never-ending pummeling by poisonous relationships. Her story is classic:

Sandi has one child, a ten-year-old boy, who has presented her with a series of parenting challenges. Todd, who is very bright, is a hyperactive child with a learning disability. Todd has been very hostile and angry at every man that Sandy has tried to get involved with. To compound Sandi's problems, she has a difficult ex-husband who has a way of appearing on her doorstep.

Sandi is an extremely devoted mother and has a very traditional idea of how relationships should develop. If you question her carefully, you discover that she doesn't really believe that any reasonable man would be willing to cope with the day-to-day demands that are placed on her by her child and her ex-husband. In fact when she meets a nice, attractive, appropriate man, she often has an internal dialogue in which she says something like this: *He would never understand the kind of stress you are under. . . . He would never understand the kind of life you live. . . . He would never understand you.*

On the other hand when Sandi meets someone with a thousand and one problems, she thinks, *There's somebody who could understand me and the difficulties I face. I don't have to worry about having too many problems—he has even more.* The result has been one nightmare after the next.

I WANT A COMMITMENT, BUT I DON'T WANT TO BE DEPENDENT ON ANYBODY.

I WANT A COMMITMENT, BUT I'M NOT READY TO HAVE ANYBODY BE DEPENDENT ON ME.

Both of these conflicts—associated with a fear of stereotypical gender roles—can be directly connected to how your parents were with each other or how they were with you when you were growing up.

Unfortunately when we have these fears, we may be equally stereotypical when we choose partners. Men, for example, may jump to conclusions about how dependent or independent a woman is by what she wears or what she does for a living. Women may be so terrified of being dependent on another person that, without realizing what they are doing, they choose men who can't make a living or who are completely inept. They may seek out men who are dependent financially or emotionally. Sometimes they later feel resentful about this.

Which side of the dependency issue you fall often has to do with what you want your financial role within a relationship to be. This obviously can be tremendously complicated and needs to be thought out carefully.

Conflicts that revolve around dependency can also involve feelings about trust. You may be asking yourself whether or not you can trust this other person enough to feel dependent. Sometimes what this brings into question is one's ability to trust in general. Issues of trust, like issues of intimacy, sometimes need professional guidance in getting sorted out.

CIRCUMSTANTIAL COMMITMENT CONFLICTS

I WANT A COMMITMENT, BUT I DON'T WANT ANOTHER MISTAKE IN MY LIFE.

I WANT A COMMITMENT, BUT I DON'T WANT TO COMPLICATE MY LIFE.

I WANT A COMMITMENT, BUT I LIKE MY LIFE JUST THE WAY IT IS RIGHT NOW.

I WANT A COMMITMENT, BUT THAT DOESN'T MEAN THAT I WANT TO SHARE MY MONEY.

I WANT A COMMITMENT, BUT THERE IS NO ROOM IN MY LIFE FOR A REAL PARTNER RIGHT NOW.

These are some of the most common circumstantial reasons men and women have for postponing or avoiding a committed relationship. And they can all be valid. At different times in your life there will be different circumstances that need to be addressed. Some of them are realistic; others are excuses. It goes without saying that often we use circumstances to reinforce and support underlying fears that are always present, no matter what is going on in our lives. It's up to you to examine your fears to decide those that are clearly grounded in reality and those that are directly connected to unresolved issues that you are carrying in your head.

What you need to keep in mind is: If you have **active conflicts,** you have the capacity to take any circumstance and enlarge its significance so that it provides an argument against making a commitment. If you have **passive conflicts,** you tend to minimize the importance of any circumstance or piece of information that makes it apparent that a commitment will not work out.

CHAPTER TEN

Making Commitments That Count

In the preceding chapters we have talked a great deal about commitment problems. We've talked about your feelings, we've talked about your behavior, we've talked about your choices, and we've talked about your fears. Most of all we've talked about conflict. There is one thing we haven't yet talked about, and that is how to go about establishing and sustaining a genuinely committed relationship.

That's what we want to do here. We would like to start out by saying that we don't believe it's simple. We haven't found it simple in our lives, and we don't expect you to find it simple in yours. However, if you're tired of always sitting on the edge of the pool, envying those who have had the courage to dive in and lead committed lives, there is a way to learn to take the plunge and swim in this intimidating body of water.

THE FIRST STEP: ACKNOWLEDGE YOUR CONFLICTS AND MAKE A COMMITMENT TO MANAGING THEM

Before you can do anything else, you have to stop kidding yourself and stop trying to kid everyone else. Stop looking for excuses —either for yourself or for your partners. Whether you are always ambivalent or you always find yourself in relationships with am-

239

bivalent partners, recognize that you have issues that need to be resolved.

In life, there are always reasons why commitments haven't been made or shouldn't be made. For example if someone is twenty-two and has only dated a few people, it's appropriate to be unsure. But at a certain point you need to acknowledge those rationalizations that keep you stuck. When you start facing the ways in which commitment fears control what you do, you begin to reduce the power these fears have over you.

You may never feel one hundred percent certain about any *realistic* and appropriate choices, romantic or otherwise. There is only one solution to this dilemma: Instead of trying to find a relationship in which you have no ambivalence, commit yourself to managing it and constructing your life in such a way that you control this ambivalence, rather than letting it control you.

KNOW YOUR PATTERN

Know yourself and recognize how you behave. For example:

- Know whether you have an active or a passive pattern
- Know the ways in which you make inappropriate or unrealistic commitments
- Know the point in any relationship at which you are most likely to panic and run
- Know the ways in which you scare yourself by moving ahead too quickly
- Know the ways in which you set up expectations that will ultimately make you want to bolt and run away
- Know your commitment fantasies
- Know the ways in which you respond to someone else's fantasies
- Know the ways in which your response is so immediate and so intense that it might make a potential mate feel trapped
- Know the ways in which you distance partners by constructing boundaries
- Know the ways in which you fail to erect reasonable boundaries

- Know the ways in which your ambivalence is acted out in the nonromantic areas of your life

RECOGNIZE YOUR FEARS AND KNOW HOW YOU ACT WHEN YOU ARE AFRAID

Commitmentphobia is about fear. Fear of being stuck, trapped, or tied down; fear of losing options; fear of losing freedom; fear of losing control; fear of dependency; fear of being bored; fear of leading an ordinary life; fear of making a mistake or repeating mistakes (yours or someone else's). You need to be very specific in examining precisely what it is you don't want in a relationship and then look at how these fears can cause you to choose badly or behave badly.

Here's a good way to do this: Starting with parents and other relatives, think about all the people you know in long-term relationships. Make a list of what it is about these relationships that makes you uncomfortable and that you don't want to duplicate in your own life. Then think about all the people you know who have lives or jobs that you consider settled but dreary. Make a list of everything you consider negative or stultifying about their lives. Then think about how these "fears" might be determining your patterns and behavior. Have any of your less-fortunate choices been extreme reactions to some of your fears?

We realize that there are many more complicated issues that can be reinforcing commitment conflicts, including fundamental fears of abandonment and intimacy that have their source in early childhood. These are obviously best managed with the help and support of a professional in a therapeutic situation. Be prepared to take those steps if necessary.

LOOK AT THE NARCISSISTIC ELEMENTS OF ALL YOUR CHOICES

All too often the narcissistic voices in our heads lead us to make choices that reflect fantasy images of ourselves, but not who we really are. We live in homes we can't afford, buy cars we can't maintain, and choose careers that are not truly fulfilling. Worst of all, we find partners who make us look good but are not necessarily good for us.

If there is a strong narcissistic voice in your head, you are walking on eggshells all the time. Prisoners of the need to be perfect are always searching for the perfect passion, the perfect career, the perfect car, the perfect VCR, and the perfect dog. If you are relentlessly judging, criticizing, labeling, and typing, you may assume that everyone is doing the same to you. Always anticipating being scrutinized by the world, you give these feelings top priority. Your real needs are lost. You can't make choices just for you.

If you want to liberate yourself from the prison of perfection, you must find the origin of the judgmental voices inside your head and start replacing them with self-acceptance. Try to become comfortable with the concept of "good enough." You need to see yourself as good enough right now, and you need to see your choices as good enough. There is no such thing as perfect; it's a word we can all learn to live without.

MAKE A COMMITMENT TO YOURSELF AND YOUR OWN LIFE

Many people believe that once they meet the "right" person, all of the elements of their lives will fall into place. We believe that you should behave as though the exact opposite is true and start by putting all the nonromantic areas of your life in order. It sounds simplistic to state that everything needs a foundation, but it's a fact nonetheless. Before you build a house, you lay the foundation. Without that base the house can't stand. It's the same with commitment. Before you can make and sustain a satisfying committed relationship, you need to have a solid foundation of commitment to building a real life for yourself, partner or no partner.

When we interviewed people, we noticed a very interesting pattern: While it is apparent that those with active conflicts have a terrible time making even the smallest commitments, those with a passive pattern typically appear to have a more committed life. They seem more stable, less fearful, and more connected to their world. This can be very deceptive, however. Time and time again we've seen how those with a passive pattern are willing to give up

242

their lives—friends, interests, and home—when a new relationship beckons. If you are ready and able to walk away from a life that you've constructed in order to accommodate a new partner, we have to question the degree to which you've been committed to your life and to your previous choices.

Whether you are a passive or an active runner, the path to a satisfying, committed relationship is exactly the same. First you need to construct true and lasting commitments in every area of your life. That requires that you construct a meaningful, integrated, rooted life. Not a rich fantasy life and not a life that you would give up tomorrow for the "right" person, but a life that an appropriate partner could easily enter and share.

COMMITMENT BEGINS AT HOME

Being grounded and committed to the place you call home is one of the most crucial first steps in being able to make a commitment to another person. Some people have to start with basics such as finally getting around to unpacking the books and buying a bed. Others have to take personal responsibility for their environment as opposed to hiring someone to buy the furniture and make all the decorating choices.

The idea is to create a living space that reflects as much of the important aspects of you as possible. You don't want to feel as though you are living in a hotel or motel and that you are never fully unpacked. You don't want to distance yourself from your external environment. Quite the contrary, you want to feel as connected as possible.

GIVE UP THE NOTION OF TEMPORARY

Some people only make commitments when they perceive their choices as being temporary. That's how many of us end up with closets and cupboards and garages overflowing with stuff that we don't really want. Instead of purchasing the one sweater we love, we end up buying three that probably cost just as much, telling ourselves that these are "temporary" choices that will do until we can afford what we really want.

When you have commitment conflicts, this kind of logic can extend into everything you do. Instead of taking the time to find and commit yourself to living in an apartment you like, you end up living in a space that you regard as temporary. Instead of buying the sofa you want, you buy one that you plan to discard. Instead of making firm appointments that you know absolutely you plan to keep, your internal schedule is filled with plans that you've agreed to but that you tell yourself you can always get out of. If your secret way out of every experience and every choice is an internal reliance on the belief that it is temporary, you don't need us to tell you that you're not living your life fully.

MAKE A COMMITMENT TO LIVING YOUR LIFE TO THE FULLEST

What are the ingredients that make up a full life? Work, friends, home, community, love, creativity, personal interests. Since those with commitment conflicts often resist being defined by their choices, the result can be a life of no choices and no real connections to one's world.

If you're going to resolve your conflicts, you have to come to terms with these feelings and start making appropriate investments of your time, psyche, and energy into all of the elements in your life. That involves identifying with your work, identifying with your community, and identifying with your own interests.

LEARN HOW TO MAKE SMALL COMMITMENTS AND SMALL CHOICES

What are the nonromantic choices in your life that paralyze you? Making firm appointments? Deciding what to wear? What to eat? Which organizations, if any, to join? Which interests to pursue? Which movie to see? What type of computer to purchase? Which car? When to take a vacation?

Start with the commitments that you perceive to be less intimidating and begin to take small steps in overcoming your conflicts. Perhaps that means finally getting business cards printed with your current address. Perhaps it means buying a plant for your kitchen or hanging a picture on your living-room wall. Perhaps it means making an appointment two weeks in advance and keeping it.

Praise yourself for every success, no matter how small. If you fall short of your goals, try again. If you've always been unable to make wholehearted commitments, there is no reason to believe you will suddenly be able to take on the whole world. If your small choices overwhelm you with anxiety, back up and try something smaller. As your successes accumulate over time, challenge yourself to take on *slightly* more ambitious commitments. Don't torture yourself with unnecessary pressure, but keep building slowly.

LEARN TO SAY NO

Commitment isn't just about saying yes and accepting another person, situation, or thing. It's also about saying no and being able to walk away, understanding that you might lose the option to return.

None of us want to lose options if we don't have to. Giving up anything is painful. However, always keeping your options open can be monumentally unfair to people who are counting on you. Not only does it keep others from getting on with their lives, it keeps you from moving forward with your own.

RECOGNIZE THAT JUST BECAUSE YOU'RE ANXIOUS DOESN'T MEAN YOU IMMEDIATELY HAVE TO DO SOMETHING ABOUT IT

As you start making commitments, no matter how small, you will discover something that many already know: Many people get a case of the jitters after making any kind of commitment. The bigger the commitment, the greater the jitters. When you buy a house, buy a car, get a dog, rent an apartment, get engaged, get married, or have a baby, you may get nervous. This doesn't mean that it's the wrong house, car, dog, apartment, mate, or child.

Also keep in mind that the same reactions can occur when you decide to say no and walk away from something in your life, whether it's quitting your job, selling the house, or leaving your spouse. The problem is that often we interpret our apprehension as a sign that what is going on is terribly wrong. So if you are anxious about having said yes or no, wait an appropriate period of time to see how you feel before you start acting on all your impulses.

STOP ACTING OUT YOUR CONFLICTS BY RUNNING AWAY

When we are unhappy or dissatisfied with a situation, a person, or a decision, sometimes it seems as though the only way out is to run away or to do something similarly outrageous. As humans we have been gifted with the ability to communicate with one another. Use that gift.

DON'T SCARE YOURSELF BY THINKING TOO FAR AHEAD

People would never be able to make commitments if they thought about the possible ramifications, implications, complications, and permutations that a decision can bring over the course of a lifetime. If you project everything you do into the future, you're bound to be overwhelmed. None of us can be sure of what will happen tomorrow, so it's senseless to think ahead to the year 2012. The best we can do is to keep our intentions good and make the best decisions possible moment by moment, hour by hour, day by day, and pray for the best.

MAKE A COMMITMENT TO BEING PRESENT IN ALL OF YOUR RELATIONSHIPS

Sometimes it's a lot easier to maintain distance in our relationships. Even with our closest friends, we may be more comfortable holding back what we feel, what we think, who we are. Perhaps we play roles. Perhaps with some friends we are always the adult, with others we are always the child, with still others we are affectionate clowns or elegant sophisticates. While all these roles may represent aspects of who we are, they don't represent the complete picture. By keeping little parts of ourselves hidden from others, we are creating distance and putting limitations on our capacity to connect and experience intimacy.

MAKE A COMMITMENT TO BEING FULLY ACCOUNTABLE IN ALL YOUR RELATIONSHIPS

If you say you are going to call, call. If you make a lunch date, keep it. If you promise to visit, do so. With everyone you know, become totally reliable. Don't always give yourself a hundred and one ways out of every situation, no matter how trivial.

Obviously sometimes conflicts arise, and even the most important plans sometimes need to be changed. But this should be an exception in your life, not the norm.

STOP FALLING IN LOVE WITH POTENTIAL

If your model for love and commitment is based on longing and inaccessibility, you have to start thinking about what it is you are doing and what it is you really want.

We think all of us need to be especially aware of a tendency to commit to situations that could be perfect, someday, if only. . . . For too many people, the primary method of avoiding commitment is to become enmeshed in commitment fantasies that get played out in relationships that never, ever become settled, steady, and even. You may have convinced yourself that if you could just get your partner's attitude to change even a little bit, the relationship would become the one you dream of. It's painful to come to terms with the ways your behavior may be self-defeating. But if you want change, you have to work on yourself, not your partner.

247

GIVE UP THE MYTH OF THE RIGHT PERSON AND THE PERFECT RELATIONSHIP

Those of us with unresolved commitment conflicts often meet people we think could be "perfect." These right choices are almost always notable because they are fantasy choices—people themselves unwilling or unable to commit and therefore posing no real threat.

One of the great myths of our culture is that if a relationship is right, it will be easy to make and sustain a commitment to it. Yes, even though we've never met them, there may be some fortunate couples for whom everything is always magical, but for most of us mere mortals, that's not the case. No matter how perfectly suited any two people are to each other, it's not easy. Instead of trying to find the perfect relationship, work at making your relationship the best it can be.

DON'T GIVE AWAY THE THINGS YOU REALLY NEED

It's one thing to be picky. It's another to compromise on your true values or true needs. These are important issues that will come back to haunt you. Don't, for example, play into roles, traditional or otherwise, unless that's who you really are. Trying to be anything you are not, whether it be a Madonna sex symbol or a Ward Cleaver husband, distances you from yourself and from your partner. It's important that you maintain your own authenticity. Be clear about who you are before you negotiate any partnership. If you betray your sense of self, you will only end up filled with resentment.

STAY AWAY FROM UNAVAILABLE PARTNERS AND UNSATISFYING RELATIONSHIPS

Getting involved with the wrong partners is the single most effective way of avoiding commitment. Everyone knows that, right? Well, if everyone knows it, how come so many of us have wasted so much time in this kind of fruitless effort?

There are three ways in which someone can be unavailable for commitment—emotionally, circumstantially, and geographically. Falling in love with someone who is unavailable is very easy to do. It keeps you fully absorbed, makes your senses tingle, and fires up all of your romantic fantasies. The best clue to recognizing an unavailable partner: He or she is always a little bit out of reach.

In the interest of saving you endless hours of pain and confusion, let's take one last look at some of the most common types of unavailable partners and the ways in which these relationships play out.

The Classic Commitmentphobic

Let's start with the obvious. Men and women with serious commitment conflicts are unavailable. No matter how sensitive they may appear, no matter how seductive and loving they may sometimes be, no matter how interesting, no matter how deep, and no matter how much they may need to be loved, they have commitment problems. And people with commitment problems tend to advertise them up front. Depending upon age, the classic commitmentphobic typically will have a romantic history littered with ex-lovers who have been embraced and then pushed aside.

Often classic commitmentphobics will make a point of saying that they have problems with "love," "commitment," or "trust." They may talk about needing space, hating to feel pressure, wanting to keep things spontaneous and unpressured. They may explain that they hate expectations, they may warn you not to fall in love, they may even hint that you will never be "the one." While doing this, however, they will also be involving you in their lives, in their hopes, and in their most inner world. This is very gripping material. It's the stuff of psychodrama, not to mention soap opera. It's romantic, it's passionate, it's frequently obsessive. However, it is not committed.

How do you know a commitmentphobic when you meet one? Simple. You pay attention. For example:

- *How many relationships has he or she ended and why?* The classic commitmentphobic has typically walked away from love several times. A person's history is the single most important determinant in how he or she will behave with you. If the underlying conflict that ended past relationships revolves around the issue of commitment, there is no concrete evidence to say that it will be different with you. So be warned and be wary.

- *Does this person openly discuss commitment ambivalence?* The rule: When someone tells you that he/she is aware of personal commitment conflicts—no matter what kind of language is used—believe the words you hear. These attitudes and feelings are not going to disappear overnight. No matter how adorable, desirable, supportive, or intellectually stimulating you may be, it is highly unlikely that you will have the wherewithal to transform another person.

- *Does this person have an unrealistic attitude toward relationships?* At the beginning of a relationship commitmentphobics are often too quickly involved, too responsive, too interested. This kind of behavior may be an indication that you are dealing with someone who is fantasy driven. Fantasy and commitment are not compatible. This does not mean that "love at first sight" never happens. It does not mean that romance is dead. What it does mean is that someone who is serious about finding a committed love recognizes that it takes time to develop, and he or she behaves accordingly.

- *Is your attitude toward this person overly romanticized and unrealistic?* If you find that you are spending more time fantasizing about this relationship than living it, be aware that you are being pulled into a commitmentphobic relationship.

- *Does this person have unreasonable boundaries?* Does he/she exclude you from areas of his/her life? Is he/she able to share interests and friends? Are there inappropriate limitations placed on the relationship and its growth?

- *Does this person appear to have problems with commitment in other areas of life?* Commitmentphobics don't like to be pinned down in general. They often need a great deal of space and may be unreliable.

- *Does this person tend to be unfaithful?* Commitmentphobic men and women are often experts in seeking out or moving on to a new love while still involved elsewhere.

Married or Living with Someone Else

A simple fact: Men and women who are living with others are not available because they have primary relationships elsewhere. Even if the participants in these primary relationships hate each other's guts, live independent lives, or live in separate wings of the house, when two people are sharing the same space, it is a primary relationship. Even if they are together only for the children, for the real estate, for the convenience, or to keep up appearances, it is a primary relationship. Until that situation ends, this is someone who is very unavailable for a commitment.

If we sound a bit harsh here, it's only because we know how many people have spent years of their lives tied into this kind of convoluted dynamic. So many women, for example, have experienced being used as a crowbar by a man who is separating from his wife, only to be left in the driveway when the job is done. Waiting for someone to leave a spouse is like waiting for Godot. And even if it does ultimately happen, there is no guarantee that your relationship is going to move forward.

Falling in love or getting involved with someone who is living with or married to someone else is a time-tested method for avoiding commitment. It's also almost always guaranteed to be a painful experience.

Great Unrequited Love

Maintaining fantasies about someone who doesn't respond in kind is another surefire way of acting out commitment conflicts. From the people we talk to it would appear that both men and women are equally capable of becoming absorbed with these kinds of fantasies. Sometimes the love objects are people with whom one comes into daily contact; other times feelings can be directed toward celebrities or even strangers on a bus. When the one you love is totally remote, it's an artificial experience. It may be romantic, but it's not a relationship.

Off-Again, On-Again Love

He loves you, he loves you not. She's there, she's not there. He cares, he doesn't care. She needs you, she wants her freedom. He loves you, he's not ready. She loves you, she's not sure. He misses you, he forgets to call. She wants you, she wants to be alone. This can make anyone slightly crazy. Your becoming this way is not only a reflection of someone else's inner chaos, it's also a statement about your own ambivalence.

B. F. Skinner used pigeons to prove that nothing is more magnetic, more hypnotic, and more involving than intermittent reinforcement. But you probably don't need to see his research. You may well be living proof of its power. If your lover's giving was consistent, it wouldn't have the same magical powers. It's the inconsistency that keeps you stuck like Krazy Glue.

Nonetheless the off-again, on-again lover is completely unavailable.

Mr. or Ms. Elusive

It's clear that "Elusive" likes you. It's just never clear how much. "Elusive" phones a lot, but not regularly. Sometimes the two of you talk for hours; other times "Elusive" cuts it off after just a few minutes. When you see each other, you have a great time, but then "Elusive" can disappear for weeks or even months. It all seems secretive and romantic. It gives you food for your fantasies and your dreams. You wonder why the relationship never moves forward, but you never get comfortable enough to ask. "Elusive" is always just a little too hard to reach, too hard to find, too hard to keep around, too hard to pin down. In short—too hard to have a relationship with. But, boy, is "Elusive" attractive.

If you haven't slept together, it feels as if you could at any moment. In fact it feels as though a whole bunch of things could happen at any moment. But they never do.

Perhaps you fantasize that there are good reasons for this peculiar behavior. Perhaps "Elusive" has a dark secret, a shameful past. Perhaps "Elusive" is involved with someone else—someone unloving and cold. The possibilities are endlessly intriguing, but none is likely to be true. Chances are that "Elusive" is just terrified of intimacy and this behavior ensures that intimacy will never happen, no matter how intoxicating the chemistry.

Great Challenges

To change and redeem another human being and in so doing to save yourself—that's what it means to be attracted to partners who provide interesting challenges. There are so many ways in which someone can do this, all of them guaranteed to sidestep realistic commitments. Some of the most common:

The Substance Abuser

You don't really believe it's a serious problem. You're sure that with enough understanding and support you can convince your partner to attend a twelve-step program. Maybe you believe that if you are perfectly loving, perfectly understanding, perfectly exciting, the problem will disappear by itself once the relationship is strong enough.

The Womanizer

You ask him if he's a man who can't love. He says, "That's not my problem. I love too much." He has a wife and a girlfriend, or two girlfriends or three. No matter how many women he's seeing, he swears he loves them all. Although he talks about the joys of commitment, he is a full-time juggler—womanizer of the year. Your challenge: Make him monogamous and get him committed.

The Full-time Flirt

She goes out with a lot of guys and she's having a terrific time. Although she talks vaguely about babies and a house in the country, right now she is packing her bags for Spain. She's cute, she's adorable, and she loves her freedom. Your challenge: Make her into a stay-at-home wife.

The Tortured Soul

He's a brilliant novelist, she's an angry poet, he's a depressed painter, she's an angst-ridden environmentalist. The torment in his or her head is the stuff of great foreign films. Ever catch yourself thinking, *Is this person ever* not *miserable and unhappy?* Ever feel guilty for not being deep enough, or global enough, or caring enough? Well, enough's enough. Whatever the cause that gives "Tortured" so much distress, the emotional connection these people have to their discomfort makes them unavailable to their partners.

MR. OR MS. INDECISIVE

One voice tells him you're the one, but another keeps whispering that he should keep looking. She loves you, but she really cares about him too. Can't you please be patient and understand?

Whether your beloved is torn between two loves or two lifestyles, he or she seems to be in the throes of a struggle with demons you can't understand. But you stay. In fact you participate in the contest. You may almost feel as though you are fighting for someone's soul, and you're convinced that your rivals are inferior, so you do whatever you can to prove that you are the worthier love. And it goes on and on.

Caught between two needs, "Indecisive" has discovered a perfect way to avoid a real, live human relationship while still getting a whole lot of real, live human attention. It may feel chaotic, but it's an exquisite kind of chaos. It must feel pretty good for "Indecisive" to know there are so many options available.

THE CRITIC

You say tomato, she insists it's tomahto. You say potato, he says you're eating too many carbohydrates. Something is always wrong with what you're doing, what you're wearing, what you're thinking, what you're feeling. Something is always wrong with who you're with, where you live, what you like, what you need. It's never right, it's never enough. Something is always wrong.

If you are with someone like this, it feels like you'll go to your grave trying to get your partner to tell you how wonderful you are. You could clearly spend the rest of your life struggling to win his or her approval. What a challenge!

What's going on? If you can't win, if you never feel totally accepted, you'll never feel a true sense of commitment. And maybe a part of you wants it that way. Yes, your partner is impossible. But don't let that hide the fact that you're willing to put up with it . . . whatever your reasons are.

THE IRRECONCILABLE DIFFERENCE

Some people have a pattern of setting up relationships in which there is already a great deal of distance between the partners. It seems apparent to everyone that this spells trouble for the long term. For example, your values are so different that you can't have a conversation without an explosion. You genuinely believe that you could never marry because it would kill your parents. It's against the teachings of your faith. Your cultures, attitudes, backgrounds, politics, and ideas are worlds apart. It would be unfair to your children. You don't speak the same language, literally or figuratively. The age difference is crazy. Whatever the explanation, the translation is the same. This person is not appropriate for a close relationship, except in your fantasies. There, in your head, everything gets resolved. Your parents calm down. One of you changes religion, political affiliation, or ethnicity. Your children grow up.

If you've got commitment conflicts, there is something truly wonderful about being with a completely inappropriate partner. You can have a deep, loving relationship and feel totally committed while still knowing on some level either that ultimately it has to end or that this person is so different, it will never be genuinely close or intimate.

The problem with this kind of relationship is that it never seems to work out smoothly. Chances are that one of you will get deeply involved and ultimately come to see the obstacles between you as challenges worth overcoming. Unfortunately it's unlikely that you'll both feel that way at the same time. Typically at least one of you couldn't have gotten involved if those obstacles weren't in place.

START LOOKING FOR REAL PEOPLE

A large part of resolving your commitment conflicts is bringing different kinds of people into your life. If you want a long-term relationship, you need to concentrate on meeting potential partners who are capable of relating. We know that people like this exist. It's up to you to start allowing yourself to seek out and respond to a different type than you are accustomed to. In order of importance make a list of real qualities that you want in a mate. Keep it concrete and attainable. Your list, for example, may look something like this: Loving, honest, dependable, humorous, accepting, communicative, attractive, intelligent, down to earth, emotionally available, etc. When you meet someone new, make sure that person has qualities that match those you consider most important. If you are continually attracted to people whose qualities don't even come close to matching the ones on your list, put on the brakes and think about what you are doing. If, for example, you say you want someone who is practical and honest, with traditional family values, yet you are always trying to reform pathological liars and sex addicts, you have to come to terms with the ways in which you are sabotaging your own life.

FACE YOUR CONTROL ISSUES

Commitment means compromise. That means learning how to live with and make equal decisions with another person. If one partner controls a relationship, financially, emotionally, or otherwise, the partnership is unequal. So try to understand the obvious and hidden ways in which you attempt to control your relationships and the ways in which you allow yourself to be controlled. If control plays a large part in your life, you might want to consider exploring its possible psychological origins. You may need professional help in protecting yourself from controlling partners, or you may need guidance in learning how to manage your own impulses to control.

GIVE UP UNWORKABLE FANTASIES AND STOP RUNNING AWAY FROM YOUR REAL LIFE

Everyone has dreams and everyone has fantasies. It's normal and it's healthy. But instead of inspiring us, sometimes our fantasies get in our way and hold us back from having a real life. If your pursuit of elusive dreams has veered you away from satisfying, reasonable partnerships with reasonable men and women and drawn you straight into damaging relationships with extraordinary jerks, then your fantasies aren't serving you well.

If you want to help yourself, you should try to understand how your fantasies got constructed and how much you have vested in them. Fantasies that take us away from reality are sometimes seized upon as a solution to pain we couldn't or didn't want to deal with. We fantasize about "special" partners because they make us feel more special, something we don't seem always to be able to do for ourselves. But there comes a time when we need to come to terms with who we are right now, not who we could be if our fantasies came true. There comes a time when we must find more power within ourselves so that our fantasies don't have such a powerful grip on us. We fully understand that often the real world is nowhere near as exciting or involving as an active fantasy. But ultimately it's much more fulfilling.

MAKE A COMMITMENT TO BEING PART OF THE WORLD

Perhaps the final stumbling block to commitment is the largest one of all because it means accepting your place in the human continuum. We feel this point was best expressed by the writer Anatole Broyard in an article we read several years ago. He wrote, "Commitment means agreeing to have not only an honest relationship with another human being, but with the human condition itself. You have to take them together, because one means nothing without the other."

As we see it, in order to have a real life, you have to be prepared to make a commitment to society, to community, to your values, and to your spirituality. You have to see yourself as part of something much larger than yourself or the couple. You have to be prepared to take your place in the continuum of human history.

This is a very difficult step because it means accepting your limitations and accepting your mortality. But so long as any of us needs to see our individual path in life as separate from and above the human experience, we will struggle with our attempts to make commitments.

Making real commitments means abandoning a self-centered point of view and finding a broader, more comprehensive perspective. It means surrendering to the realities of the world as they exist right now. It means integrating yourself into the world through your work, your love, your caring, your participation, your humor, and your presence. It means accepting the humanness of our common experience. In essence for each of us, this means becoming part of the larger picture, going from me to "us" in the biggest sense.

APPENDIX

Managing Your Conflicts and Changing Your Relationships— A Guide for You and Your Partner

---

We have included this Appendix for anyone who is currently caught in a destructive relationship dynamic, as well as for any reader who is eager to avoid this kind of trap in the future. We realize that the following material, read in its entirety, is repetitive. Please understand that our effort to account for all points of view—passive and active, male and female—made this unavoidable.

Learning to Behave Differently
Despite Your Conflicts

How do you act when you meet someone new? What do you worry about? What do you say? What don't you say? In the very beginning of a commitmentphobic relationship the groundwork is established for what may follow. Time and time again the active partner starts out by shaping and establishing the kind of interaction that he or she will later come to fear and resent. Time and time again the passive partner commits to a fantasy of a relationship that doesn't exist and goes along with a questionable scenario. Is it possible to change these patterns?

Following the publication of *Men Who Can't Love* and *What Smart Women Know*, reader response prompted us to start facilitating nonprofit recovery-support groups for those who needed more understanding and information about making and keeping appropriate romantic commitments.

The following section, which reflects some of the most common issues raised in those groups, is meant to help you redesign your relationships and provides a series of guidelines to help you manage your conflict and behave appropriately and responsibly. We hope it helps you protect yourself from destructive and self-destructive behavior.

CHANGE THE SETUP

If you want your relationships to be different, you have to be different from day one. If the setup is always the same, despite your best intentions what follows will be the same. Change is necessary because if you act the way you have always acted and send the signals you have always sent, the odds are your relationships will always be the same.

In the best of all possible worlds you have come to this book just as you are beginning a new relationship. Successful management of commitment conflict requires a great deal of groundwork, and this is most easily accomplished at the beginning. But regardless of whether you are in the beginning, middle, or end of a relationship, or currently not in any relationship at all, here's your chance to make a commitment to start changing and becoming more responsible to yourself and others in relationships.

The following material is broken into two sections. One is for those with active conflicts, the other for those with passive conflicts. We recommend that you read both sections to get a better understanding not only of your own behavior and feelings but of your partner's as well.

Managing Your Relationships: A Guide for Those with Active Conflicts

THE BEGINNING—THE SETUP FOR A LETDOWN

As the active partner you will actively choreograph the "pursuit portion" of your relationships. This means you construct the setup, and you select the "operating system" from which all future "programs" in this relationship will run. You determine the intensity, you choose the style, and you set the pace. Typically you set it up so that you will have control and power. Regardless of how good your intentions are, the potential to abuse this power is enormous.

In the beginning your goal is seduction, be it emotional or physical, and everything you say and do is a means of accomplishing that goal. Typically you place emphasis on information that will get a positive response and withhold or downplay information that might serve as a warning. You want to be with this new person, and you aren't considering any ambivalence that might follow. In addition your seduction will be fueled by your fantasies; all of your hopes and dreams are going to be expressed through your words and your actions—with no thought to the expectations these may provoke. Given these feelings, how can you act responsibly? How can you be certain to attend to both sides of your conflict in a way that is fair to both your new partner and yourself? We urge you to follow these guidelines:

Don't Rush In

You know that when you get yourself in too deep too fast, this level of involvement makes you panic when the fantasy lifts. You have to keep reminding yourself of how badly you react when relationships start to get real. You also need to think more about how your behavior is making the other person feel. Your breakneck pace sets up a whirlwind. If it doesn't scare your love interest away, it's so compelling, it can only provide the basis for an enormous fall.

There is one very simple way out of this: SLOW DOWN. Take your time. Let the intimacy develop gradually. Think before you leap. Avoid breakneck courtships and start evaluating a relationship step by step as it's developing. What you need most are constant doses of reality. It's easy to get so caught up in the tension of the chase that you lose track of whom you are chasing. How is he or she reacting to your behavior? If your own insecurities keep kicking you into fast forward, that's something you may want to examine.

Don't Give Partners Unrealistic Expectations

You have to understand the weight of your words. Phrases such as "I've never met anyone like you before," "I'm never this attracted to anyone," and "I can't wait for you to meet my sister—the two of you will really get along," are incredibly seductive.

They evoke a feeling of specialness that encourages your partner to have high expectations as well as placing heavy pressure on you to come through with a commitment. Sure, romance is fun. But to many people romance means love, and love means marriage.

Watch your words. If you use words that convey caring and the promise of a future, the other person may respond accordingly. Certain phrases can cause even a first date's attitude toward you to change totally—sometimes from casual to "overboard" in a single evening.

Your words can make you sound as though you're planning to be together for a long time—very long. But the reality is that you aren't ready to plan a future together. You haven't known each other long enough, and you don't know each other well enough. That takes a lot of time. Until you've had that time, don't act as though you're certain "This is it." Better to save your words until you're ready to back it up with something real.

Don't Misrepresent Your Romantic History or Your Romantic Attitude

Don't make it sound as though your previous relationships ended because your ex-partners were somehow lacking. It's important that you accept responsibility for your participation and learn as much as you can from it.

Blaming your exes can also deceive your new partner. Someone who likes you is going to want to accept what you say at face value. If you tell someone, "You're different," he/she wants to believe you. If you say, "I want this relationship to be different," or, "I think this relationship can be different," he/she wants to share that hope.

Don't convey attitudes without thinking about what you are saying. For example, if you mean "We don't know each other well enough to have sex," don't say, "I would never go to bed with anyone unless I was certain the relationship is going to work out." Otherwise the moment you go to bed, your partner is going to assume it means a long-term commitment.

Keep in mind that at this stage you have no idea how the relationship will work out. You may want it to be different, but wanting is not enough. Until you are totally sure, avoid implying anything that can confuse your partner about your past or your intentions for the present—or the future.

Don't Knock Yourself Out Trying to Impress a Potential Partner

When you pull out all the stops to make an impression, your actions are saying, "This relationship is very important to me; I want to make it work." That may be true right now, but how will you feel in six weeks or six months? Today you are overwhelmingly interested; tomorrow you may just feel overwhelmed.

Everyone has a different method of impressing dates. What are yours? Do you share the most intimate details of your life right away? If you do, your partner can't help but think you are already clear about your intentions for developing a very sharing and exclusive relationship. Do you spend excessively on restaurants, gifts, or trips? Do you cook wonderful meals or bring elegant gifts? All of this makes it appear that you're taking the relationship *very* seriously, and it puts a lot of pressure on you to keep delivering.

The reality is that you can't possibly be ready for something this serious this soon. Your behavior needs to reflect this fact. If you have a history of eventually being haunted by everything you gave in the beginning, it's time to become comfortable with giving less. No one who is interested in you is going to walk away because you didn't tell them your deepest, darkest secrets during your first phone call or take them to Paris on your first date.

Don't Mess with Someone's Kids; Don't Mess with Someone's Life

What most impresses a struggling single parent? Someone who cares about the kids. It shows that you are sensitive, caring, and well intentioned. So you try to include them in your plans. Bring them along. Bring them gifts. Why not? You probably like them—you're not faking it. It seems harmless enough. But it's not.

Getting someone's children involved in the courtship is a powerful sales technique, but it isn't fair to the kids and it isn't fair to the parent. Involving children suggests that you must be thinking long-term. The kids start to count on you, and your partner starts to count on you. But you're not ready to think long-term. Right now you need to be working on this relationship one day at a time. Besides, you know how this kind of pressure makes you feel: trapped. If you're not absolutely certain that you will be there for these kids way down the road, this level of involvement is totally inappropriate right now. You're not a parent or stepparent and you're not their best friend. Later perhaps. But not now. What these children need is someone who is sensitive to their emotional needs and boundaries. That means you need to keep your distance.

The same kinds of rules apply when it comes to another's life. Respect this new person's reality, and don't mess it up. Don't encourage someone to change jobs, pull up stakes, or abandon an ongoing life-style to fulfill some momentary fantasy. Think before you do or say anything that has long-range consequences.

We know that getting someone else involved in your long-term fantasies is a very efficient screening process. If your new partner goes along with what you are saying, you have the advantage of knowing that this person is serious. But this isn't fair if you aren't fully committed to these joint plans.

Stop Talking About How Important It Is for You to Have a Committed Relationship, a "Normal" Life, or a Settled Pattern

When you tell someone you are looking for a committed relationship, it seems as though you are ready for and capable of handling one. If you speak about wanting children, needing a family, or trying to develop a normal, settled life-style, it's natural to believe that you have thought these feelings through. Even if this new partner wasn't thinking about commitment before, he/she is going to start thinking about it now. Your words may be music to someone's ears . . . until the music suddenly stops.

There is no need to introduce the concept of commitment so soon. By talking about it right away you only put additional pressure on yourself. It's pressure you may not handle well and don't need.

Don't Confuse New Partners by Immediately Including Them in Everything You Do and Think

This behavior gives the impression that you will *always* want this person to be included in your life; it makes someone feel needed. For example, if you have an appointment with your doctor, you make this person part of the experience. If you have an important exam, you ask him/her to help you study. If you have a problem at work, you tell him/her all about it and ask for advice. Once again the underlying message is "*I need you* to be part of everything I do and think."

This behavior is giving your partner expectations. These expectations can easily make you feel pressured and resentful, but when you start acting on those feelings, your partner will be stunned by the change.

Starting a relationship with someone who really excites you is exhilarating. You want to be together all the time . . . at least until the deal has been clinched. But you can't upend your life for someone now if you're going to resent it or take it away later. Sure, you're feeling nervous and vulnerable, but what about the other person's feelings and the other person's vulnerability? Let the relationship evolve at a reasonable pace.

Don't Call All the Time

Here's why: All this attention is going to make the person on the other end of the line feel like a priority in your life. He/she is also going to start counting on those phone calls. Sooner or later you're going to resent this.

It's easy to understand why you keep reaching for the phone. You're on a romantic high, and you have so much to say. You could talk for hours and hours. Your mind is running wild. Of course you want to call again and again. The problem is that it sets up a false intimacy before the relationship can handle it. You need to stop working the phones.

Don't Act Like the Perfect Partner If You Can't Sustain It

You're going out of your way to do everything you can for this new person because you're trying to sell yourself. If you're not always going to be this way, you shouldn't be acting this way now.

Look at what you're doing. You've only known this person for a few days, weeks, or even hours, and in a wide variety of ways you're indicating that you want to be the perfect helpmate. You certainly don't look like someone who is afraid of a committed relationship.

But you *are* afraid of a committed relationship. And that means you need to keep your distance in the beginning. Sure, you're enjoying it, but if it's an act, you're not going to enjoy it for long. The more you lead your partner to expect it, the more you're going to resent it. You don't need to do things like this to be liked.

Skip All Future Talk

It's fun to fantasize about the future, but it's another thing to share those fantasies with someone you've just met. Using words such as *us* and *we* imply a real future, not a fantasy. Talking about the things you'll do together next month, the family wedding in the spring, and the trip to Europe next year suggest your readiness for long-term commitment. But you don't know what you can deliver next week, let alone next month or next year.

You need to stick to the current reality and let the future unravel in its own time. Today, tomorrow, this weekend—let those be your limits. Keep the fantasies to yourself and spare your partner from future shock.

Don't Put Others Down for Unfaithful or Insensitive Behavior

We all know people who are insensitive, unfaithful, abusive, calculating or opportunistic. Pointing out the frailties of your fellow humans makes you feel better about your own track record, *and* it also gives you a good way to hide it. But when you turn these people into targets, it makes your partners think that you are different and you will always be different.

Maybe your commitmentphobic behavior isn't as severe as the

behavior of others you've seen, but it is damaging. The problem is that when you point a finger at others, it suggests that you have never and could never hurt anyone. And that's not true. Best to keep these judgments to yourself. If you must comment on others' behavior, it's a lot more honest and fair to acknowledge your own transgressions as well.

Don't Push for Trust

You're doing everything you can to earn this person's trust. Why? Is it because you deserve to be trusted, or because you need to alleviate your own anxiety? When people give you their trust, they don't believe you will ever hurt them. If you're not so sure this is true, stop pushing so hard.

Don't Act as If Sex Is Going to Cement the Relationship

Sexual intimacy is serious business. Some actives, often men, press for physical closeness and use it to get a foothold into their partners' hearts. Others, often women, hold back from having sex, indicating that once they do, the relationship will be written in cement. Whether it's meant that way or not, it can be deceptive.

People are very vulnerable when a relationship becomes sexually intimate. Overwhelming desire, however it's expressed, can easily be misinterpreted as a statement of your profound interest in a committed relationship.

Don't Push for a Commitment of Any Kind from Your Partner

Maybe you will be ready for a commitment down the road. Maybe not. But it's way too soon right now even to mention the word. Too soon for you and too soon for your partner. There are different kinds of commitment you might be asking for. Perhaps you are asking for exclusivity; perhaps you are asking to move in together; perhaps you are actually suggesting marriage. You may simply be sounding out how this new partner feels. And you may be asking for nothing more than a commitment to start a sexual relationship or take a vacation together.

Be certain that whatever kind of commitment you might want is appropriate for your particular relationship stage. If you've known someone for two days, don't insist that he/she come with you to Aruba for three weeks, no matter how appealing that might be. If you've known someone two weeks, don't suggest getting an apartment together. Certainly don't start talking about marriage until a reasonable time has passed.

There's something else to keep in mind. If you ask for too much too soon, your partner will probably interpret this as a sign of your commitment. This will only encourage someone to get more serious about you.

THE MIDDLE—WHEN YOUR AMBIVALENCE TRANSLATES INTO ACTION

How does someone with active conflicts know that the relationship has entered a different stage? The middle begins when the first sensations of panic set in. In the beginning it was one hundred percent full speed ahead. But now the mood has changed, and you are expected to deliver on your words and promises. Suddenly you're beginning to have doubts and regrets. If you pushed really hard in the beginning, you may be in a complete panic right now.

Whether you realize it or not, typically you reach this stage because your partner has given you some form of assurance or commitment that you've asked for. You've won. Your fantasy is becoming a reality. Problem is, you're not ready. And your ambivalence is demanding action.

What you need to know at this point is that many of the actions you are contemplating will not help you resolve your conflict. Many of the things that are intended to create distance and give you "breathing" room will have the opposite effect. Your sudden change of heart is going to push all of your partner's most vulnerable buttons. It will make him/her insecure, confused, frightened, clingy, needy, and nuts. In this kind of emotional state your partner is going to want more from you, not less. Your partner will try to narrow the space between you for reassurance. But being supportive of your partner is the last thing you can handle right now.

Don't use your partner to work out your ambivalence. If you

are feeling overwhelmed by your conflict, it's your responsibility. We urge you to consider the following suggestions:

Don't Assume Anything

You're constructing worst-case scenarios in your mind. "If we spend this Christmas together, we'll have to spend every Christmas together from now on." "If we go on one more date, there's no way out." "If we sleep together one more time, we'll have to get married." Maybe that's how you expect your partner to interpret your interaction, but the only person who really knows how your partner feels is your partner. You can't assume anything. Your partner may be taking this one day at a time while you're jumping ahead and seeing it as a life sentence.

Don't Break Dates; Don't Change Plans; Don't Break Promises

If you make a commitment to do something or be somewhere, honor it. If you can't keep promises, don't make the commitment. Recognize that it's not the date or the plan that you're afraid of, it's the expectations surrounding the event. You need to deal with these expectations separately. Unreliable behavior is confusing and crazy-making for your partner. Keep in mind that sudden, erratic behavior can make your partner worry about you. That concern may cause him or her to behave in a way that you interpret as smothering.

Don't Create Unreasonable Boundaries

If you're making passionate love every night you're together, refusing to have dinner with someone's family doesn't serve to make it clear what the limitations of your relationship are. These kinds of boundaries are confusing and hurtful. Nonverbal mixed messages are even more confusing than the ones you articulate. Keep in mind that your partner, who is struggling to hear the hopeful message, isn't sure how to respond to all the differences in your behavior. If you want to back away, do it in a more forthright fashion.

271

Don't Ruin Special Occasions

Special events such as parties or theater tickets and special occasions such as holidays and birthdays can fill you with dread. You see them as powerful symbols of commitment. So to compensate, you sabotage the event, thereby keeping these special occasions from feeling so special. But this is painful for your partner. You need to deal with the feelings and fantasies that these occasions stir in you in a more constructive fashion. Your interpretation of these events may be way out of line. Ditto, your behavior.

Don't Pick Your Partner Apart in Order to Justify Your Need to Find a Way to Exit

At this time terror at the prospect of commitment may make you picky and unreasonable. This is mean, it's hurtful, and it's inappropriate. Everyone has flaws, including you. Your partner's "flaws" didn't bother you in the beginning. The only reason they bother you now is because you're frightened. You need to turn inward and face your fear instead of turning outward. Your ambivalence is your issue; it isn't about the ways your partner deviates from perfection.

Don't Use the Phone to Maximize Distance

You're not ready to end it, but you need to minimize contact, so instead of seeing your partner, you use the telephone to keep the connection alive—but at a distance. You have no idea what your phone calls are doing to your partner. Chances are your telephone behavior has your partner strung out on the other end of the line waiting for a clearer signal. These mixed signals can be making your partner feel paralyzed by confusion.

Don't Use Sex to Regulate Closeness

Are you withholding sex right now? Are you feeling turned off? Distant? Mechanical? It's easy for your ambivalence to surface in the bedroom. Are you discussing this honestly, or are you allowing your partner to jump to all kinds of conclusions? The thinking is, if we're not as intimate sexually, I can get out of this more easily. But this thinking is flawed. Sexual withholding is going to make your partner more insecure. And that may make your partner crave intimacy even more.

Don't Use Infidelity to Get Distance

Infidelity is the ultimate cop-out and the ultimate hurtful act. You are having a claustrophobic reaction to a relationship and you see an affair as your "open window." Well, jumping out this window is certainly one way of escaping from a relationship, but it is a cruel way. This behavior is motivated by fear, not desire, but your partner doesn't know that. All your partner knows is that you are trying to destroy the relationship. Chances are, your partner is assuming too much responsibility and feeling less desirable and somehow to blame. Your partner deserves more than this. And you're not doing the third member of this triangle any favors either.

Don't Cry in Your Partner's Arms

You may well feel torn apart by your ambivalence. One moment you want the relationship, the next moment you want to run away. You're in terrible pain, and you're causing your partner terrible pain. It makes you want to cry.

Don't throw your emotions out there for someone else to sort out. You may need to cry, but you don't need to cry in your partner's presence. You think that crying will show how much you care. Perhaps you're hoping it will buy you some time to get clearer on whether or not you need to leave. Perhaps you're not even sure why you're crying. The problem is that the crying is easily misinterpreted to mean "We'll work it out." This kind of drama can only draw your partner closer to you, and that's probably the last thing you want right now. Cry at home.

Don't Say You Need More Time If You Don't Know What You Need

If your behavior changes drastically, sooner or later your partner will ask for an explanation. You are completely confused by your feelings. You can't move forward and you can't move back. You don't know what you need, but you imply or actually say that what you need is more time.

Perhaps you make something up to justify what's going on—you blame work or family or money or moodiness. You may allude to mysterious psychological distress. You say, "It's not you; it's me." When you say this, you look soulful and worried. It makes your partner feel sympathetic and concerned. The bottom line is you're not being honest.

Your partner is prepared to believe any plausible explanation you offer. So, if you talk about time, your partner takes you literally. In fact your partner will probably accept whatever you say. Don't say, "It's nothing," if it's something. Don't say, "It's not you," if you think it is. Don't say, "I'm just not ready," if you think you never will be. Your partner can't be self-protective right now, unless you tell the truth.

Don't Make Promises You Can't Keep

Often at this point the passive partner threatens to end the relationship. But even though you are ambivalent, you don't want to end the relationship. You still have too many feelings, and you're not prepared to let go. So you promise you'll change. You promise you'll stop being so hurtful . . . you promise you'll make a commitment . . . you promise whatever it takes to get your partner back. Your partner will probably accept what you say. But that's not fair. You may want to change, but you have no idea whether or not you can.

If you want to make a promise, promise yourself you'll get more insight into your behavior.

Don't Act Out Your Ambivalence by Moving Back and Forth As Your Emotional State Dictates

You're like a rubber band, and it's making your partner crazy. It also makes your partner frightened and wanting to move closer. You need to start managing your commitmentphobia reflex. Stop acting on impulse and start talking yourself through these moments of discomfort.

Don't Praise Those Things About Your Partner That Make You Feel More Trapped

When she cooks dinner for you, it makes you feel trapped. When he sends flowers, it makes you feel smothered. When your partner reflects solid values such as fidelity, home, and family, it makes you feel tied down. Yet you praise these things. And that only encourages your partner to do more of the same.

You know you should appreciate these things, and you do. Obviously this is a good person who cares for you a great deal, and you are trying to acknowledge that. But at the same time it's causing a form of claustrophobic anxiety, and that may well make you angry. If there are two voices in your head, it isn't fair to present only one and then blame your partner for acting on it.

Don't Take Away Everything You Gave at the Beginning

In the beginning you made the relationship seem so special. But now you're not so sure. You're feeling trapped by that specialness. So you start taking things away. You give less time, less emotion, less sex, less everything. You're trying to make the relationship seem less important through subtraction. There's one problem: The less you give, the more your partner wants. Your attempts to pull away only draw him or her closer to you. Once again, your attempts to get distance are backfiring. And it's hurting your partner in the process.

Don't Turn Your Partner into Your Therapist

The more you feel torn apart by your conflict, the more you feel as though your partner is the only person you can talk to about it. But this kind of conversation is incredibly intimate. You may be trying to express your conflict, but all your partner hears is the intimacy. And that makes the relationship feel closer, not more distant. It gets your partner more involved in your life, not less. Your partner is not supposed to take care of you. Don't encourage it.

Don't Talk About Problems Unless You Want to Work on Them

Because you want to create distance, you start looking for problems in the relationship—big things, small things, whatever you can find. You know that these are just excuses and rationalizations to get away. You know that you don't really want any of these problems to be resolved. But your partner doesn't know this. If you present this person with a list of problems, it seems you are pointing out these problems because you want to work them out. Your partner may start trying to make changes. And that makes you feel more trapped and more resentful. If there are issues you want to resolve, talk about them. But you need to keep the non-issues to yourself.

Do Get Help

At this point in the relationship you have two options: You can hurt someone else, or you can help yourself. You may need someone to help you sort things out. No one says you have to struggle by yourself. There are many people who are trained to help, and counseling can make a critical difference at this point in your life and your relationship.

Do Get Honest

If you know, in your heart of hearts, that this relationship isn't going to work out, it's time you shared that information honestly with your partner. If you are completely torn by ambivalence, it's time you shared that information—without placing blame or responsibility on your partner. We realize that your partner doesn't want to have this conversation, but telling the truth—without any mixed or confusing messages—will make it easier for your partner to adjust.

THE END—SCARED AND RUNNING

We hope you don't reach this point in your relationships, but we know that for many of those who are unable to manage their conflicts, there ultimately comes a time when the pressure becomes too great. Perhaps the passive partner is pushing for more of a commitment or is insisting on more accountability. Whatever the reason, you, as the active partner, may feel as though you are gasping for air or experiencing a full-blown phobic attack. All you can think about is reducing the discomfort, and to you that means getting away. However, even at this stage you're probably unsure because you still have so many feelings for your partner.

Remember, this level of conflict can be directly attributed to the depth and closeness of the relationship. Despite your ambivalence you and your partner may share an intense emotional involvement. When we interview people about their commitmentphobic relationships, we always ask them to describe the ending. An amazingly large number of people describe almost identical scenes: The active partner, the partner responsible for the breakup, is sobbing and talking about how much love he or she feels for the person who is being rejected. In other words, even though the relationship is about to be finalized, the conflict hasn't diminished.

If you have active commitment conflicts, your relationships tend to end in one or a combination of the following three ways:

1. Your behavior (often infidelity) and your ambivalence push your partner into provoking a final argument.
2. You construct so many barriers, allow so little intimacy, and introduce so much distance that the relationship dies slowly—and painfully—of attrition.
3. You end it so abruptly that you seem almost to disappear.

Often you immediately establish another relationship that serves as a barrier between you and the partner you have left behind.

All of these options are hurtful, and none are honest. If you have reached what you believe to be the end of a commitmentphobic relationship, before you do anything, we would like to ask you to consider the following suggestions:

Spend Some Time Trying to Figure Out Precisely What You Are Running From and Why

You need to think seriously about whether your behavior will accomplish what you want. You may think you're escaping from your partner, but you may actually be running away from your expectations, from your projections, from your fears, and from yourself.

Maybe ending this relationship is the answer. But there is a chance that it's not. You need more information, and you need it immediately. If you're going to run anywhere right now, we firmly believe that the first place you need to run is to a place where you can get help with your conflict. Ideally this means finding an understanding therapist.

This is not the time to jump to conclusions. Once you have engaged yourself in the process of self-exploration, you may see a way of working with this relationship that you couldn't see before. Or you may truly understand why this relationship could never work and you may learn how to establish better relationships in the future. Whatever the outcome, at least you won't be swinging wildly in the dark.

We can't make you go for help. That is of course your decision. But we can ask you to minimize the kind of hurtful behavior that typifies these endings.

Don't Provoke Your Partner Into Ending Your Relationship

We realize that you may be feeling much too guilty to want to face ending your relationship honestly and directly. Under these conditions it's very tempting to drive your partner into doing the dirty work. If you propel your partner into drawing a line in the sand, you can pin at least part of the blame on someone else. No guilt, no responsibility—it becomes the perfect scenario. Right? Wrong.

Your partner doesn't want to end the relationship, you do. Pushed to the wall, your partner may end it, but that's clearly not what this person wants. It's what you want. Later, when you're feeling relief, your partner will be feeling horrified and thoroughly confused by what has happened. Your partner will be filled with doubts and regrets wondering whether he/she may have jumped to conclusions or not been understanding enough. Your partner may even feel guilty.

Here are some dos and don'ts:

- Don't hurt and demoralize your partner by leaving "evidence" of another romantic interest lying around for him or her to find.
- Don't indulge in provocative behavior such as breaking dates or not phoning when you say you will.
- Don't pick fights or become unrealistically faultfinding.
- Don't become childishly uncooperative.
- Don't ruin special occasions.
- Do maintain a sense of respect for your partner and the relationship you have shared.
- Do understand that your partner wants to be with you and is bending over backward trying to adjust to and accommodate your needs.
- Do understand that any faultfinding you indulge in will make it even harder for your partner to recover a sense of self-esteem and get on with life.
- Do understand that announcing infidelity (real or planned) by leaving evidence lying around will create tremendous confusion for your partner who doesn't know whether to believe what is seen or what you say.
- Do assume responsibility for your feelings and for what is happening and act accordingly.

When Leaving, Walk Out the Front Door So That Your Partner Can See You Going

Don't make the mistake of thinking that if you back away gradually, over time, it won't be noticed. You want the relationship to slowly fade to zero for two reasons: (1) It may hurt less to withdraw slowly; and (2) you won't have to take responsibility for ending it.

You think if you give less and less while building bigger and better barriers, you can reduce the relationship to dust without ever having to say you want out. You think that by doing it piecemeal you will spare yourself the intense pain of total separation. But that's not fair. When you take a relationship away piece by piece, it chips away at a partner's self-esteem. Sometimes the worse you make a partner feel, the more he or she will want you to come back and make it better.

In the meantime, as you back away, your words and your actions are probably totally out of sync. For example, you tell your partner that the two of you are still together, even though you rarely see each other. Or you may take a different approach: You say that you want less of a relationship and then spend several days making passionate love.

Your partner doesn't want to think the relationship is over, so if either your words or your actions deny that it's over, your partner is going to listen to that message. Your partner will probably accept your excuses, your explanations, your impossible boundaries, and your behavior. Even when the relationship isn't even a blip on the radar screen, your partner may still be there, trying to be loving and to do the right thing.

It's not enough to say that you have "demons." You owe it to your partner to describe those demons. It isn't fair to keep one foot in the relationship while you're busy removing every other piece of your body. You think your partner will "get the message" from your actions. We're here to tell you that it won't happen. Your partner will just keep staring at that foot. As long as you keep denying that it's over, he or she may keep waiting and hoping.

A few specific dos and don'ts:

- Don't use the "I need more time" excuse.
- Don't continue to involve your partner in your emotional *sturm und drang*.
- Do encourage your partner to find more of a life, independent of you.
- Do keep your words and your actions in sync.
- Do state the facts.
- Do be honest.

Don't End a Relationship Without Saying Good-bye and Explaining Yourself

We know why you want to disappear. You're in so deep, you truly believe it's the only way out. But you have no idea what this will do to your partner. You said a great many things you wish you hadn't said, and you made emotional promises you can't keep. Now you want to forget all this and pretend it didn't happen. Before you leave the state, disconnect your telephone, or move in with—and thus hide behind—some stranger or ex-lover, you need to stop for a moment.

To disappear from a relationship at the height of its intensity is like ripping out a piece of your partner's insides. For your partner it's a perfect setup for a painful obsession. For you it's a setup for guilt, remorse, and possibly your own obsessive thoughts.

As difficult as it may be, you have to accept responsibility for what happened in this relationship. If you don't do this, it is almost as if you are denying that the relationship ever existed, and that means denying a part of yourself.

We realize that your partner may be refusing to let go. We recognize how difficult that makes it for you. But if you are clear about your decision to move on, then you should be able to have an appropriate and necessary, albeit uncomfortable, conversation. Many people find it helpful to go into counseling together for a few sessions in an attempt to work out a way of ending things that is more satisfactory and less painful.

Ask yourself whether or not your reluctance to formally close doors is a reflection of your continued ambivalence and unresolved issues.

Some dos and don'ts:

- Don't stop calling completely.
- Don't refuse to take your partner's phone calls.
- Don't indulge in a Houdini-like escape and disappear from view.
- Do behave responsibly.
- Do get immediate professional help if you feel overwhelmed by guilt or a hopeless feeling that you can't do anything right.
- Do try to come to your own understanding of what happened.
- Do help your partner understand what happened.

Managing Your Relationships:
A Guide for Those with Passive Conflicts

THE BEGINNING

If you are the passive partner, you are responding to someone with demonstrable ambivalence about permanent relationships. Although you may start out with serious reservations about this new partner, you typically ignore them. For example:

- Even when this person presents sufficient evidence, either through words, deeds, or history, that he/she is commitmentphobic or otherwise unavailable, you are likely to hold nothing back.
- Even when you recognize—or others tell you—that this person is not emotionally reliable, your fantasies and hopes become focused on cementing a permanent relationship.

Sometimes it seems as though you respond almost as if you are being tested on your ability to respond. Perhaps because you sense that your partner is not fully capable of commitment, you are inappropriately frightened of losing this fledgling relationship. For reasons that are illusory, you quickly become overly committed to what you perceive as the relationship's potential.

This attitude leaves you vulnerable and exposed. But instead of attending to this condition, you may take pride in being able to achieve this high degree of involvement and responsiveness. You may tell yourself that your ability to trust, before trust is earned, is proof of your capacity for love and sharing.

Although it is hard to accuse you of being irresponsible to others, you are probably not being responsible to yourself. Your tendency to cooperate with an agenda designed by someone you barely know leaves you open for disappointment and confusion. You need to be more self-protective and to behave more wisely. Here are suggestions for changing the course of your relationships:

Keep Your Fantasies Under Control

You know by now that you have a very active fantasy life and that at the beginning of a relationship you immediately adjust your fantasies to include this new person. This can't help but influence both your behavior and your expectations.

For example, you're meeting someone for coffee, and in your fantasies you're thinking about words of love and commitment. You have a date for the movies, and in your fantasies you're planning a wedding. You go out to dinner, and in your fantasies you're on your honeymoon. Even your sexual fantasies tend to be committed. The only problem with this is that it makes you too invested in a relationship that hasn't gotten off the ground and too committed to a person who has done little or nothing to earn it.

You should always try to keep your fantasies under control. Otherwise your responses may be more influenced by your dreams than by the real flesh-and-blood human being with human failings.

Maintain Appropriate Responses

If you give too much too soon, you put too much pressure on the relationship. You have a responsibility to maintain appropriate boundaries. Enjoy the pursuit, but don't get totally caught up in it.

Don't treat the beginning of a relationship as though it's already the most important relationship you'll ever have. You don't know what's going to happen. If this new person's interest is as reliable as you think it is, it's not going to disappear overnight. We've said it before, and we'll say it again: If this is the romance of your lifetime, you'll have a lifetime to enjoy it. So slow down.

Always remember, when new partners tell you they have commitment conflicts, no matter how attentive or loving they may be, listen to their words, believe them, and adjust your expectations accordingly.

Don't Allow Yourself Unrealistic Expectations

If you allow your expectations to soar early in a relationship, it leaves you vulnerable for a terrible disappointment. Keep your expectations realistic and don't jump to commitment conclusions about what is said, no matter what your new partner says or promises.

Always keep in mind that those with active commitment conflicts frequently use romantic phrases they mean only for the moment. They are capable of making plans they will never follow through on. The words raise your expectations because they gibe with your fantasies of what a new romance should feel like. But words can't always be trusted, particularly in a new relationship.

We're not telling you to be cold or rejective. We're saying you have to be careful and self-protective. We're telling you to pay attention to the subtext. Until the relationship has passed the test of time, don't start weaving fantasies and planning a whole life around a new partner who has done nothing real to deserve what you are prepared to give.

Get a New Partner's Romantic History and Pay Attention to What You Hear

If this person has a rocky history with others, don't expect it to be different with you. Yes, we know that you are special. That doesn't mean that you will be able to drastically change someone's pattern. Heed what you hear and be forewarned.

You don't have to prepare a test and sharpen all your number-two pencils in order to find out what you need to know from a new partner. Typically people like to share information. And even if someone is trying to conceal information, no one hides emotional garbage very well. Your job is to wake up and smell the garbage.

Don't Be Too Easily Won Over

There are a million and one different ways to impress or "win" someone over. Perhaps your new love is buying you gifts or being kind to your grandparents. Perhaps what impresses you most is his wit, or her sensitivity or emotional depth. He or she is telling you about childhood incidents, adolescent trauma, and adult pain. This is very winning and seductive. Listen and take it all in. Perhaps you *are* establishing an intimate, connected relationship. But you may also be with someone who bares his or her soul regularly.

Always give the relationship some time before you decide that it's the right one.

Protect Your Children, Your Work, and Your Life

Lovers can come and lovers can go, but your children, your work, and the rest of your life are going to be with you for a long time. Don't start rearranging your life until you are sure you are with someone who is kind, supportive, caring, involved, and committed.

We don't mean to be dogmatic about this, and we don't mean to be cynical, but we have heard too many horror stories from people—mostly women—who have upended their lives and careers because someone asked them to do so within the first few months of a new relationship. So don't move in with someone too quickly; don't allow someone to move in with you too quickly; don't involve someone with your children; don't move to another state or city; don't give up your house, your apartment, your dog, your cat, your job, or your friends. If you turn your whole life around for a new romance and then that romance ends, you will have a much tougher time.

Yes, we know that sometimes people have to take risks, but

don't put any of the essential elements of *your life* at risk until you are operating on more than a romantic promise. Allow someone into your life slowly one step at a time—over a period of time. Keep in mind that committing oneself too soon is as indicative of a commitment conflict as not being able to commit at all. It shows an unrealistic attitude toward love and romance.

Often those with passive conflicts are anxious at the beginning of a relationship and feel a need to cement everything immediately. Otherwise they are sure this new love will disappear. You may feel that you are following your instincts, or being true to your real self, but more than likely you are being driven by your insecurities.

You may be right in thinking that someone is going to vanish, or you may be wrong. Either way there is every advantage in waiting to be sure. If your partner has conflicts, your need to have a more committed relationship will almost always create more anxiety and ambivalence. If you are with a sincere partner who is totally smitten, this person is not going to go away because you are being realistic. We're not saying that you should be rejective here —we're saying be realistic and self-protective.

Keep in mind that the best way to protect yourself from disastrous relationships is to make sure that you always have a full life of your own, partner or no partner.

Don't Start Trying to Be the Perfect Partner

You are trying to sell yourself by giving your new partner everything you can. He looks a little thin, you start filling his refrigerator with goodies. She says she's sorry she never finished college, you offer to give her the money to go back to school. He mentions a painful childhood incident, you become an expert on the effect of trauma in childhood development. She breaks her leg, you set yourself up on the couch as round-the-clock nurse. He mentions that he would like to get away for the summer, you borrow the money so that you can rent a beach house in his favorite community.

There are three reasons why you shouldn't engage in this kind of behavior: (1) It is appropriate behavior for a devoted spouse in a long-term relationship; it is not appropriate behavior at the beginning of a relationship. (2) Your partner is apt to regard all attempts to endear yourself in this way as suffocating, smothering, entrapping. The harder you try, the more terrifying it becomes. (3) Placing your energy, your income, your time at another person's disposal is taking away from your own development. Trying to be perfect for someone else will usually keep you from being the best you can be for yourself.

Don't Be on Call

You can't take care of your own life if you are prepared to drop everything at a moment's notice to take care of somebody else's life. We know what all those intimate phone calls between lovers are like, but they can set up a bad pattern.

As the passive partner you may assume that the person who is pursuing you has an ultimate goal of catching you and starting a committed life. This is often wrong. You need to know more about this person before you can jump to such a conclusion.

Those with passive commitment conflicts sometimes worry that if they are not home, sitting by the phone, their partners may not call again. They get frightened and anxious. Total availability can be a very bad message to convey. Your partner may come to resent your availability because it feels like a silent demand for more attention.

Recognize That Great Sex Does Not Automatically Translate into "Forever After"

Just because someone seems completely connected in the bedroom doesn't mean they want to be connected for life. You may have a different set of boundaries than your partner. You may assume that because someone is totally passionate, loving, intense, and connected during sex, this person is going to be that way when the two of you leave the bedroom. Not necessarily the case. Those with active commitment conflicts sometimes have no boundaries in the bedroom and nothing but boundaries outside of the bedroom.

To you passion, intimacy, love, and commitment may seem to fit together, but not everybody feels the same way. So, for the record, even when someone appears to be totally absorbed in your body, this doesn't automatically translate into "I want to share my life with you."

Don't Give a Commitment of Any Kind Until You Know It's Mutual

What spells commitment to you? What does commitment mean to your partner? When do you start feeling committed? At what moment do you begin to believe that a promise has been made? Do you believe that people who seem connected on a good first date owe it to each other to have a second date or to explore the relationship to its fullest potential? How about after the first time you have sex? Does that make you feel committed?

Is time the operative element in your commitment scenarios? Perhaps you don't begin to feel committed until after you've been together six months—or a year. Maybe you don't feel committed until after you've moved in with someone, or until the exact moment you say, "I do."

To save yourself grief, know the point at which you typically start to get those "feelings" that you both owe each other more. Try to get a sense of what your partner views as commitment and don't give more than you're getting.

Don't be afraid to say no. Don't think that if you hold back on anything, be it sex or marriage, you will immediately lose the most important relationship of your life. If you are sincere about building a relationship, an equally sincere person who cares about you will respect your need for more time.

As someone with passive commitment conflicts, you need to be a little more cautious about pledging your heart and soul. You need to think more about what it means to make a promise about tomorrow.

THE MIDDLE—WHEN YOUR PARTNER PANICS

For the passive partner the middle of a commitmentphobic relationship begins at the moment your partner starts announcing ambivalence by backing away or behaving differently. Usually this ambivalence seems directly connected to your deepening commitment and caring. It may result from some event that your partner perceives as a commitment point of no return. Something has happened to move the relationship too far along, and your partner is scared and is announcing it in a variety of ways.

This change in behavior reflects a change in attitude, although you find it hard to believe that this could be the case. Your partner may have a thousand and one excuses as to why he or she is behaving different, and because you love this person, you believe the excuses.

You have two major enemies right now: (1) denial, which keeps you from facing the facts about the ways your relationship is eroding; and (2) fear of losing the relationship, which can create a paralyzing state of mind.

If your relationship has progressed this far, you have to focus your energy on facing the facts and protecting yourself. This may not be easy. The sense of losing power and control in the relationship can be sending you into a tailspin, making you feel insecure and unsure. Make sure that you don't respond by losing sight of who you are and what you deserve.

Important rules to remember: Don't focus your energies on the possibilities of your partner seeing someone else. Don't focus your energies on proving your worthiness and the value of the relationship. Both of these responses aren't ultimately self-protective, and they may place more pressure on your partner, increasing his or her phobic responses.

Once again you need to maintain appropriate responses. If your partner is giving less, it is not appropriate to give more. You need to pull back and reassess what is going on. Spend more time protecting yourself than you do in proving yourself. To help you do this, we have the following suggestions:

Recognize and Accept Your Partner's Conflict

It's a big mistake to hear only the messages you want to hear—the words of love, the assurances, and the excuses. These can drown out the reality of the other set of messages. Your partner's fears are not going to disappear because you pretend they don't exist. Often we don't want to hear our partners telling us that the relationship may not work out. Instead we keep reassuring ourselves by remembering those things we want to remember.

If your partner is ambivalent, you need to know in order to protect yourself.

Don't Accept Intolerable Behavior

Don't reward unacceptable behavior by becoming more loving, more giving, and more accepting. If you are being treated badly, if your partner is breaking dates, breaking promises, and changing plans, it's time to start backing away from the relationship.

This is not the time to be supportive and understanding. It will not make your partner appreciate you. In fact it may make your partner feel more threatened. We know it is difficult to walk away from someone you love. We know that you care about this person and that you want to help resolve his/her conflicts—but being more accepting of this kind of hurtful behavior is not going to help anyone.

Explain to your partner that his ambivalent behavior is making you unhappy, and if you see no *real* attempt to change or work things out, you have no choice but to back away. If your partner is treating you badly, you're not losing very much.

Don't Try to Prove Your Worthiness

When the one you love is ambivalent, it may seem perfectly normal to do everything you can to prove that you are the right choice, the perfect choice. Don't. Don't try to show that you are more sexual, smarter, wiser, kinder, more generous, more giving or more worthy than any other potential partner. Your partner's conflict has nothing to do with your value as a human being or a mate.

Maintain Your Own Boundaries and Work on Building Your Own Life

If your partner starts withholding by erecting boundaries to closeness, there is a tremendous temptation to try to break these barriers down with arguments, tears, logic, or love. This response typically creates more anxiety. Instead of thinking about what your partner is withholding, concentrate on finding other interests and other ways of enjoying life.

You have to construct a full life that provides an emotional safety net for you if this relationship doesn't work out. Maintain your own boundaries and work at building a life without this person. For some people this means starting to date. Many women, however, say they're not ready or they don't have the opportunity to meet potential new partners immediately and that this is not an option for them. We recognize the difficulties involved, particularly when you're in love with someone. Nonetheless you can start doing what is necessary to get yourself into a different frame of mind and different social arena. You have to start somewhere, so start.

Don't Let Your Self-esteem Suffer from Your Partner's Ambivalence

Your partner may be finding fault with you. Your partner may be less attentive, phoning less often, seeing you less often. You may get the sense that your partner is thinking about someone else. This kind of behavior can have a serious effect on your self-esteem.

Recognize that your partner's behavior is typical of someone with commitment conflicts and don't allow yourself to be brought down by it. Surround yourself with supportive friends and situations and think about why you want to be with someone who isn't placing the value on you that you deserve. Start getting away and getting ready to find someone who will give you more.

Do Work on Your Own Life, Not on Your Partner's

You think that you are strong enough to deal with your partner's conflicts and that you can work it out together. You encourage your partner to talk to you, to share feelings. You spend much of your time focusing on your partner's problems. It would be nice to be rewarded for this effort by getting what you need. But we doubt it will work out that way. In fact your partner may feel smothered from all your good efforts.

A much better way of handling this is to focus on your own life. You have to back away and let go. Yes, this is frightening: you may lose the relationship. But if that's the case, the ending would have come about sooner or later. For your sake, even if you don't believe this, it might be better if it happens sooner. It has been our experience that backing away at times like this is far more likely to strengthen your position than to jeopardize it.

Here are some dos and don'ts:

- Don't become your partner's therapist.
- Don't make your partner your first priority.
- Don't focus all your energy and thoughts on your partner's conflicts.
- Do think about seeing a professional therapist or counselor to help you cope during this period.
- Do focus all your energy and thoughts on ways to get strong and independent without your partner.

THE END

Your biggest task at this time is to come to terms with the end of a relationship. Your partner, who is still ambivalent, is not making this any easier for you. No matter how much active partners may want to get away, they may be unable to disconnect emotionally unless they are absolutely convinced that you will always "be there" should they ever have a change of heart. So while they are backing off, they are also trying to confirm your dedication and love. You have to be resolute about not going along with these mood shifts and determined to take care of yourself.

Some hints on how to do this:

- Don't be understanding like a parent.
- Don't be loving like a spouse.
- Don't be accepting like a best friend.
- Don't wait by the phone.
- Don't use the phone to check up on your partner.
- Don't make your relationship the topic of all your conversations.

- Do get involved in as many activities as possible.
- Do keep your calendar full.
- Don't rearrange your life to fit into your partner's erratic scheduling.
- Do find support.
- Don't excuse your partner's behavior.
- Don't get hooked on fantasies about what the relationship was.
- Don't cooperate with your partner's commitmentphobic agenda.
- Do resist the incredible pull to try to move closer.
- Do make every effort to start building a life that is separate.
- Do take a vacation if you can.
- Don't be accountable to your partner if your partner is not accountable to you.
- Do maintain some reserve and distance when you get together.
- *Do back away as far as you can comfortably go.*

Don't Get Stuck in the Jealousy Trap

Jealousy is a powerful emotion that activates all of your insecurities and doubts about yourself. If your partner is pulling back, your mind almost automatically jumps to the possibility that there is somebody else. Why else would something that seemed so good suddenly be turning so bad? Why else would your partner start behaving differently?

Yes, it's possible that there is somebody else. But it's also possible that there isn't. The truth is, that as far as you are concerned—although we realize that this is almost impossible to accept—it doesn't matter.

Your partner is behaving this way because of commitment conflicts. This behavior has nothing to do with your desirability, your value, how good the relationship is, or how you stack up against any competition.

Under these conditions many men and women with active conflicts are always unfaithful. This is a time-honored method of creating trouble and distance within a relationship.

There is another surrealistic element to the jealousy problem in commitmentphobic relationships. Often the sex, passion, and emotional connection are so intense that to the passive partner it seems inconceivable that a "rival" could enter the picture. These feelings create even more confusion because the passive partner ends up feeling as though he/she is dealing with two separate sets of information that don't go together. The passive partner doesn't know what to believe, what to think, what to feel, or how to act. Is this simply some last-ditch case of premarital jitters? Does a partner's infidelity deny the truth of the passion that existed? Instinctively you may feel as though you should "fight" for your partner and fend off this new rival, who can't possibly be as much in love as you are. What to do?

Well, here are a few things not to do. Remember that when your jealousy gets activated, you may act in hundreds of ways that even you have trouble believing. Not only do you want to try twice as hard to prove that you are better than the competition, you may find yourself acting out your jealousy. You need to be very careful now. So don't start going through your partner's pockets, checking telephone bills, sitting outside doorsteps waiting for your partner to come home, or making thousands of "check-up" phone calls.

What you need to be more worried about than your partner's fidelity, or lack of it, is whether you are falling into an obsessive, jealous trap. Jealousy heightens your emotions and draws out your competitive spirit. It brings up all unresolved childhood rivalries, and it fans any feelings you may have about abandonment and unworthiness.

You have to start controlling your jealous knee-jerk responses. You need to know how to manage these feelings. You need to take care of yourself. And most important you need to be thinking about how emotionally to turn your partner into your ex-partner.

Don't Do Anything That Borders on Obsessive Behavior

Don't call your partner's parents, friends, or fellow workers. Don't spend all your waking time talking with friends about what's going on. Don't start visiting psychics, astrologers, or trance mediums, insisting on hearing good news. All of this can keep you stuck.

- Do get counseling if your feelings are getting out of control.
- Do keep yourself as busy as possible and surrounded by as many supportive people as possible.
- Do recognize that if your jealousy is warranted, your partner is probably incapable of the relationship you want—with anyone!

Do Move Back and Maintain Your Own Boundaries

We know that your instincts are telling you to move forward and to try harder. In these circumstances, following these instincts will probably make matters worse. Your partner doesn't need to be assured that you are there. Your partner knows you are there. That is a major part of the problem.

Moving closer may be much more threatening to the relationship than moving away. We understand that you want to move closer because you are frightened, and we know how difficult it is to keep away when you're worried about losing someone you love.

Be clear that we're not suggesting that you start playing games. All we're saying is that you should make a point of taking better care of yourself and maintaining your own boundaries and distance.

Understanding the Ending of Your Relationship

Let's now talk about the three major ways in which active commitmentphobics orchestrate the endings of their relationships, and the major ways in which those with passive conflicts respond:

1. *Your partner's behavior provoked you into ending it.* Don't think that if you had just tried a little longer, worked a little harder, this relationship would have had a different ending. Not true. We are willing to give one-hundred-to-one odds that if you had hung on longer, your partner would have become even more provocative. So know that you did absolutely the right thing. Don't feel guilty. And get on with the healing process.

2. *Your relationship is going through a slow erosion, and your part-*

ner is taking things away one at a time. You are being conditioned to expect less and less. In the process don't make the mistake of believing that if you gave more and more, things would eventually get back on an even keel. Backing off in stages is your partner's way of being self-protective. You have to go about protecting yourself. Stop going along with your partner's agenda. Don't be available on your partner's schedule. Set up a schedule of your own, and keep to it. Get busy with your own life, vow never to let this kind of relationship occur again, and get on with the healing process.

3. *Your partner ends the relationship by disappearing, either physically or emotionally.* This is the nightmare that we call the classic Houdini syndrome. Suddenly your partner, the one who you thought loved you and cared about you, is not available to you. Perhaps he/she has literally gone away. Perhaps he/she is simply refusing to speak to you ever again. And you're not even sure why. You don't know what happened. Is it someone else? Was it something you did? Was it something you didn't do?

When things have progressed to this kind of ending, you are in the worst-case commitmentphobic scenario. You have to accept that and behave accordingly. Your partner may well be back for another round, but even so you have to move on and heal.

Finding Support

Since so many people at this point make the sensible decision to get professional support to see them through the trauma of a sudden breakup, we'd like to offer a few suggestions, based upon the many interviews we've conducted.

Right now you are tremendously vulnerable and emotionally needy. You need to find somebody who understands your position and has helped others in similar situations to get on with their lives. Your best bet in finding such a person is to get recommendations. You want someone who has a track record in working people through recovery and getting them back into life. We have spoken to many women who went to a therapist for help, wound up transferring all their need onto the therapist, and then got stuck in the process. It's essential that you find a therapist who has strong, clear boundaries and who establishes clear goals that help you move forward. We think it's important to be wary of establishing therapeutic situations with someone to whom you are blatantly attracted or who seems attracted to you.

We believe very strongly in the value of good therapy, but we know that not all therapists are appropriate for this kind of help. Don't be afraid to interview potential therapists and ask them about the work they do. Ask them if they've worked with people like you before. Ask them what kind of time frame has existed for other people like you.

Curtain Calls

In our fairy tales and romantic stories lovers are often separated and then brought back together. There is pain and longing, but eventually the lovers are reunited. Perhaps there was a terrible misunderstanding. Perhaps it was all a mistake. Perhaps it was timing, and distance made hearts grow fonder. Both members of the couple matured, and finally they walk off into the sunset together. The end.

We want to warn you against placing all your hopes on this kind of reunion scenario. Your partner may well return, but unless major changes are made, you will simply replay the same old relationship. True, there often comes a time where the active partner, having tasted freedom, begins to have second thoughts about what has happened. If your partner wants to see you again, it is our opinion that you should only do so in a controlled environment—the office of a truly understanding and helpful couple's counselor or the office of a clergyperson who has been trained in couple's counseling. You cannot jump back in willy-nilly until you have some concrete assurance that things will be different.

Recovering from a
Commitmentphobic Relationship

Because many people come to a book such as this just as a relationship is ending, we felt that we had to say something about recovery. Many fine books have been written dealing with recovery in more depth, but we want to talk here about some of the special circumstances that affect men and women in relationships in which commitmentphobia is the underlying theme.

You will notice that the emphasis in the following pages is different depending on whether you have active or passive commitment conflicts. Those with passive conflicts typically have to learn to move through their loss and on with their lives. Those with active conflicts need to be certain that they spend enough time thinking about what they are doing and what they are losing.

We both know what it means to recover from a commitmentphobic relationship. Not only have we talked to countless men and women in the various stages of recovery, but we've also experienced this process on a deeply personal level. We have both had our own losses and conflicts to work through. It is our hope that the insights we gained, as well as the insights our interviewees provided, will be helpful to you as you move through your own process. We know all too well that there are no easy answers or simple formulas for getting over the loss of a love, but we also know for certain that you can heal, and you can change your pattern.

RECOVERY FOR THE ACTIVE PARTNER

If you were the active partner, the time leading up to the breakup was undoubtedly one of tremendous conflict for you. Only you know the depth of your conflict. Only you know the kind and quality of the conversations that led you to decide whether or not to let go. Only you know how many times a day you asked yourself what to do and whether you did the right thing.

Well, it's over. Now what? Even if you are the one who wanted out, the loss of a relationship with a person you cared about is going to stir up all kinds of uncomfortable and unexpected feelings. If you are like most people with active commitment conflicts, you are going to try to spend as little time as possible dealing with these feelings. You are going to want to get away from them, much as you wanted to get away from the relationship that provoked them. We believe very strongly that if you want to be able to change your pattern in the future, all of these feelings need to be acknowledged and attended to.

We think it's important that you be prepared to experience all of the following:

- Expect to feel very ambivalent
- Expect to feel relieved one moment, scared and lonely the next
- Expect to be confused and overwhelmed
- Expect to feel sad and sentimental
- Expect to feel guilty
- Expect to think about your ex-partner a lot
- Expect to want to blot out all thoughts about your ex-partner
- Expect to question seriously whether or not you made a mistake
- Expect to entertain thoughts of trying again
- Expect to fantasize about reunion scenarios
- Expect to want immediately to jump into a new relationship

300

We think any action you are likely to take right now, whether with your ex-partner or someone new, will not be appropriate. You want to feel better and get rid of all those unpleasant and confusing feelings. We understand that. But now is the time to sit with those feelings and try to understand what happened and why. It's not the time to do anything that can cause even more confusion and chaos.

You need to see this ending as a new beginning. Not necessarily as a second chance to make your relationship work or as a chance to find someone new, but as a chance to come to terms with your ambivalence in a way that will no longer hurt your partners and hurt yourself. And that's going to require real work, not just good intentions and wishful thinking.

Recovery Means Cleaning House

If you are the active partner, the challenges you face at the end of your relationship depend a great deal on how you orchestrated that ending. Once again we need to look at the three most likely possibilities:

• *Did you provoke your partner into ending the relationship by starting a huge argument or engaging in some type of outrageous behavior that you know your partner would be unable to tolerate?*

If you provoked your partner into ending the relationship, it's very easy for you to play the role of victim right now. Your partner was the one who ended it, so you can lay all kinds of blame. Your ex-partner was "too jealous," "too crazy," "too needy," "too possessive," and so on and so forth. But all this does is help you avoid the truth and thus keep you stuck.

You have a choice right here. On the one hand you could let your former partner accept the blame. But doing this is not going to help you resolve your conflicts, and it's also incredibly unfair.

Your other choice is the truth. Part of you knows just how much you wanted this relationship to end. Part of you knows how cleverly you brought this relationship to the point of no return. If you want your life to be different, you need to start facing your refusal to work on the relationship. Your ex-partner deserves this for his or her peace of mind, and you need it for your own recovery.

You need to honestly face how much you participated in pushing your ex-partner over the top. You need to take responsibility for your part in this, and you need to do so now.

If you constructed a triangle with a third person to fuel the fire, you had better face that too. Dealing with both partners honestly and appropriately is also an important part of your recovery.

• *Did you construct such enormous boundaries (emotional or physical), withdraw so thoroughly, or create so much distance between you and your partner that the relationship died of attrition?*

If you took the back door out of this relationship, your first order of business is dealing with the expectations you left behind. Your ex-partner may be holding on to some powerful fantasies that the relationship may one day be revived. Maybe you think you are being kind by letting your ex-partner believe there is hope for the future. Well, you're not. You need to release your ex-partner so that he or she can get on with life. It's only fair.

You also need to release *yourself* so you can get on with *your* life. That means thinking about how you behaved and the mixed signals you gave. You probably have your own fantasies that you're not ready to give up. You may sense that if you changed your mind one day, you could take the boundaries down and bring the relationship back to life. It may feel reassuring to have a contingency plan, even if you doubt you'll ever use it, but keeping this plan alive in your brain is a tremendous obstacle to accepting responsibility for your behavior and the end of the relationship. If you want to be with this person, you have to figure that out and work on it. If you want the relationship to be over, you have to come to terms with your loss and grieve it. It's the only way to recovery.

You need to let go, and so does your partner. Confronting your partner with the truth is going to hurt both of you a lot, but it is also liberating and healing in a way that none of your convoluted explanations could ever be. The hurt, the anger, and the sadness that follow are appropriate and ultimately manageable. What is not appropriate and not manageable is the desperation and confusion that come from trying to hold on to the shadows that were once a relationship.

If you back out of a relationship slowly and never offer an honest explanation, nothing changes. But if you face what you have done and cop to your problem, the opportunity for real recovery, real growth, and real change begins.

• *Did you up and disappear, perhaps finding a second partner to hide behind?*

If you leave a relationship without an appropriate explanation, your partner is not going to be the only one who suffers. The sudden ending is going to take its toll on you too, and your abrupt exit may come back to haunt you very quickly with feelings of guilt.

Before you move to another state or join the Peace Corps just to get out of this relationship, you need to stop for a moment. There is nothing more healing for you and for your partner than the truth. Yes, it may provoke incredible anger. Yes, it may generate tremendous hurt. Yes, it may trigger incredible disgust. Yes, it may bring about enormous sadness and guilt. But all of these feelings may be appropriate and ultimately manageable.

Don't run away and pretend the relationship never existed. To do so is tremendously cruel to your ex-partner, but it's also unfair to you because when you wipe out what you shared, you're also wiping out a part of yourself.

Curtain Calls—When You Have Second Thoughts

Once you are "free," even if you are seeing someone new, you may find yourself thinking a lot about your ex. You may even start obsessing. You may question your decision. You may wonder if you've lost the best thing you ever had.

Before you "reappear" on your ex-partner's doorstep, swearing your true love and promising to change, think about this. Right now you have not done anything that will enable you to back up these words. Maybe at this very moment you're not feeling frightened at the thought of making a commitment, but that doesn't mean that you don't have a commitment problem. It's easy to want a commitment when you don't have one. It's something else entirely to make and keep a commitment when a real opportunity presents itself.

If you're going to contact your ex-partner, it should be to present an explanation, not a plea for reconciliation (a letter would be just fine—a personal visit is not necessary and not recommended). Part of your recovery involves facing the fact that the conflict doesn't go away just because you've gone away. If you want a second chance, you need to earn that second chance. And the only way you're going to do that is through a lot of hard work, preferably in the office of a competent therapist.

Learning to Grieve

Men and women with active conflicts rarely take the time they need to evaluate their past relationships and grieve their losses. Take the time. We know you're not sure if you did the right thing. We know you're not sure of what to do now. Here are some ideas to help you get more clarity:

1. Try to resist the impulse to rush into another relationship.

   Jumping from one relationship into another isn't appropriate, and it's very confusing. It's almost impossible to know what you are really feeling. This is difficult for everyone, and you are apt to act out the same old scenario. It's your pattern. Or you may do something that looks different but turns out to be very similar. Whatever you do, do not triangle this new person into your old drama. If you don't know who you want to be with or what you want right now, you probably need to be alone for a while.

   Try to show some respect for your feelings, for the feelings of your ex-partner, and for the feelings of any person you might meet. Take some time to grieve one relationship before getting into another.

2. Don't use the person you left behind to work out your conflicts.

   When you aren't sure whether you've done the right thing, and if you still have a great many feelings, there is a tendency to hurry back to your ex-partner to reassure yourself that you can go back if you want. Then you may change your mind again. In fact you can go back and forth this way many times.

This is unfair because you're not fully considering what this is doing to someone else. If you can't control your ambivalence, consider some form of therapy to help you through this period. If you truly want to resume your relationship, it might also be wisest to do so with the help of a trained couple's counselor who can help both of you establish new ways of being together.

3. Take time to reevaluate your relationship pattern.

This is your time to think about what your conflicted behavior does to others. Recognize the ways that your fear is dictating behavior. Now is the time to sit with the consequences of your pattern and not blame others for what has gone on in your relationships.

4. Don't get ex-partners or new partners involved in your quest to "find yourself."

This is a job for you. It may not be your fault that you attract people who too quickly become involved with your psyche and your emotional destiny. It is your responsibility to be aware of this and not use the people around you in this fashion.

5. Evaluate your reasons for leaving this relationship.

Here are some questions to ask yourself:

- Were your reasons for wanting the relationship to end valid?
- Did you honestly give this relationship your best efforts?
- Why were you holding back?
- Did you engage in unrealistic faultfinding?
- Are you still searching for somebody who may not exist?
- Did you start running away emotionally as soon as it was apparent that your partner was available for a commitment?

6. Don't maintain the fantasy that you can always have this person back in your life.

Holding on to this belief is what allows you to continue to deny the depth of your feelings. We don't know whether giving up this relationship is a wise move or the biggest mistake of your life. We do know that you will never have a clear answer if you refuse to investigate the truth about what you are feeling.

WALKING AWAY: A GUIDE FOR THE PASSIVE PARTNER

As the passive partner you are the one who is most in touch with your pain. Whether your ex-partner left or your ex-partner's behavior provoked you into ending it, you are the one who wanted to work on the relationship. You probably haven't yet given up hope that things will eventually work out, and you may be in so much pain that you feel numb.

Traditionally the passive role has been the woman's role, and women often seem to have a tougher time getting over the loss of a love. They often feel they have fewer ways in which they can meet new partners, for example; this can keep them stuck in a "pining" or "longing" mode for an extended period of time. But many men, even though they have greater opportunities to initiate new romances, also get stuck in the recovery process.

Male or female, you can recover from the way you feel no matter how distressed you are, and when you do, you will probably look back and wonder what you were so upset about. You might even look back and laugh. We have talked to many people who were completely devastated by their actively commitmentphobic partners; and we can tell you with a good degree of certainty that there is definitely life beyond this person. There are even other partners—better partners. It's up to you.

The First Obstacle to Walking Away: Wanting to Understand
Everything That Happened at the Price of Your Own Well-being

We believe people should have as much understanding about their lives as is possible, but this is not the time to focus on understanding. This is the time to focus on getting out with all your "faculties intact." Many men and women in pain from a failed love say that they have to "understand" what really happened. Often this is another way of saying, "I have to continue to have feelings for this person who hurt me." Understanding is translated into "understanding what the other person is doing, feeling, and experiencing." This is a definite roadblock to your own happiness.

Think about it this way. You have been on a ship that is about to sink. You are over the side, and you can see the shore. Do you hang around and exhaust yourself by treading water, trying to figure out why the disaster occurred? No, the sensible thing is to save yourself and try to get to shore. And don't make the mistake of thinking that your partner, the one who sank the ship, is your personal life raft.

Be self-protective. Focus on taking care of you. You can get understanding along the way, but you shouldn't dedicate yourself to trying to understand your partner's psychology—no matter how interesting it may be. We agree you should try to understand everything that went on, but it can be done from a safe distance and with more perspective. The emphasis should be on understanding your reactions and your behavior so that your future relationships will be better.

More Obstacles to Walking Away: Believing That Your
Relationship Is Different, Believing That Your Ex-partner
Is Different

Commitmentphobic relationships are very compelling. They seem so complex and feel so special, it's almost impossible to believe that anyone else could really understand what happened between you and your ex-partner. It feels almost as if you were predestined to play out these peculiar roles with each other. You may feel that this person is your soul mate and your destiny. You may feel that no two people have ever loved this deeply or have been so totally bonded.

You may feel it is your karma to work this situation out. You may believe that your loved one is so wonderfully talented, intelligent, sensitive, troubled, confused, or generally messed up, that your situation is special and requires special care. If someone tells you that your reactions are typical, you don't want to hear it. If someone tells you that you're not being smart or self-protective, you don't want to hear it. If someone tells you that your partner's convoluted, conflicted, or outrageous behavior is typical, you don't want to hear it.

You are going to resist and resent any friend, relative, counselor, or theory that tries to neatly package and label what is happening in your life. We know that your relationship is unique. But we have also seen this enough times to know that the underlying mechanisms dictating your partner's behavior and your responses are not unique. You have been with someone who has a serious commitment problem. No matter how special or unique you or your partner may be, the dynamic is not.

Another Obstacle to Walking Away: Believing What Went Wrong in the Relationship Was Your Fault

Often the beginning of commitmentphobic relationships are totally electric and magical. Therefore when they don't move forward from that spot, the passive partner tends to believe that if he/she had behaved differently, everything would have been different. We would like you also to feel certain that you are not responsible for your partner's behavior.

If you think you were not nurturing enough, sexual enough, demanding enough, loving enough, smart enough, tall enough, or thin enough, get rid of the thought.

Frequently when someone with an active commitment conflict is running away from a relationship, his or her behavior seems so odd and out of control that the passive partner feels that something can be done or said to change the course of events. This is not the case. Anything you might do to try to stop it, no matter how loving, will be interpreted as a kind of entrapment. It does not make things better.

Write this on your mirror: *A real relationship and a real love requires two real people.* One person can end a relationship, but it takes two to make it work.

Another Obstacle to Walking Away: Believing That You Are Responsible for Your Ex-partner's Fate

By the time a commitmentphobic relationship ends, the passive partner may be totally invested in the active runner's life. Active commitmentphobics, who are particularly skillful at leaving bits and pieces of their psyches and their souls scattered about for others to deal with, often encourage their partners to get involved in coping with all the "demons" and conflicts that seem to be at work. This is very seductive and speaks to a very deep place in many of us. We want to be perfect helpmates, and we want to make a difference. But forget it. This is not an appropriate place to put your charitable energies.

Turn the following statements into your own personal mantras. There is nothing you can do to solve this other person's problems. There is nothing you can do to change this person's problems. There is nothing you can do to make this person work on his or her problems. You are not responsible for this person's ultimate salvation. It is not your fault, and it is not your responsibility. All you can and must do is take care of yourself and resolve your own issues.

We realize this kind of advice is given so often that it becomes tiresome. We also realize it's not what you want to hear. You want to hear about the little tricks that will make your partner's conflicts manageable, or about the extraordinary epiphany that will make him or her change. We believe in miracles as much as anyone else. But unless your partner wants to change and wants a miracle, nothing is going to change. You have to work on your own change and your own miracle. The fact that you are reading this makes it a real possibility.

The Most Important Rule: Get the Support You Need

Often the shame of losing "the love of a lifetime" stops us from reaching out for help. We are afraid to tell our friends, family, and others how we are hurting. Sometimes we feel so deeply that we don't know how to express it. Other times we feel foolish and are afraid of being seen by others as failures. While the loss may be terrifying, reaching out to others can be terrifying also. Yet not reaching out can lead to painful isolation.

There is another reason why you may be isolating yourself. The relationship probably felt so special, and the loss so devastating, you can't imagine that anyone else could comprehend what you are feeling right now. Your plight feels so unique that you are convinced it is yours alone. We know that your pain is enormous. But it is our experience that there are many people who do understand and many who can help.

Right now you need all the support you can get. You are not supposed to be able to manage this by yourself and you don't have to. We encourage you to consider all of the following:

• *Turn to others.* For some people, getting support means turning to their most loving friends or family members and letting them know how intense the pain is.

• *Get professional help.* For many others, getting support means finding professional help—a therapist or counselor who has experience with this kind of loss. This is something we strongly recommend, with the understanding that therapy will focus on getting you out of pain and back into life, not on understanding your partner.

• *Find a support group.* Support groups that focus on codependency or love addiction can be lifesavers. These groups exist in most cities and towns. If you can't find groups where you live, contact your local hospital or your local chapter of Alcoholics Anonymous. If that fails, talk to local clergy for referrals. Or start your own group. All it takes is a small personal ad in the local paper. You would be amazed to know how many people are wrestling with these very same issues. Over and over again, we have seen the extraordinary value of sharing your struggle with others and listening to others share their struggle with you.

Here's the bottom line: there is no such thing as too much support at a time like this. Do whatever it takes, but do it.

What Are You Grieving?: A Relationship Lost, a Future Lost

Commitmentphobic relationships are usually filled with magical
promises, expressed or implied: promises about next week, next
month, next year, and forever. It's what helps make these relationships feel so unique and so powerful.

Promises create the feeling of potential, and the commitmentphobic relationship is almost always a relationship that seemed
full of potential. A relationship with this much potential is going to
feel incredibly special. There is so much to look forward to, it is
truly captivating. How could this relationship not be "the one"?

Given all of the promises and all of the potential, the loss of a
relationship such as this seems cataclysmic. It's not just a person
that you are losing. You are also losing all of the hopes and
dreams and plans that this person represented and you believed
in.

In essence you have lost a dream and you have lost a future.
This future may have been a fantasy, but it's a powerful fantasy. If
you are going to heal, you need to grieve the loss of this fantasy
every bit as fully as you need to grieve the loss of what you really
had. While grieving the lost relationship is bound to be painful,
grieving the lost potential—the future you envisioned for yourself
—can be overwhelming. It helps to have a clear perspective about
what you are mourning.

Clarifying Your Perspective: A Reality Check

Promises and potential can be so powerful that they can easily
blind you from seeing your ex-partner with any objectivity or clarity. Do you know what you really had in this relationship? Do you
know what you really lost? Before you try to answer these questions, consider the following information.

In a typical commitmentphobic relationship the active partner
begins withdrawing or pulling away from the relationship just as
the "fantasy" ("everything's perfect") phase of the relationship is
ending and the "reality" ("I love this person and I want to make a

commitment to work on what we have") phase is beginning. This means that the passive partner rarely gets a chance to clearly experience a not-so-perfect here-and-now relationship with a fully accountable and present partner. Also, because the active partner starts pulling away when things are going well, it tends to leave the partner full of questions and confusion.

Because you are always focused on "tomorrow," you rarely have a chance to fully experience all the areas of disagreement and disappointment that can occur between two equal partners in a committed relationship. On some level you are always waiting for the real relationship to begin. Because your partner is always pulling away, even if just a little, you never get to experience this person as a normal human being, complete with quirks and flaws. All you really know is the initial fantasy.

It's like going to a play and having to leave after a brilliant first act. Your assumption is that it will continue to be brilliant. But as any theatergoer well knows, the second and third acts could prove to be a tremendous disappointment. The problem is, you'll never know.

There is one thing we can say here with great certainty that may help you through this process: You probably already got the best this person had to offer. Here's why:

In the beginning active runners give one thousand percent. It's full-throttle fantasy, no holds barred. No matter how sincere this may all seem, the active runner knows that bliss like this can't last. This person knows that the long-term reality can't be anything like the fantasy that has been created. This person knows that he/she can't deliver on all of the promises. This person knows that this first act—the fantasy act—was the best act. The problem is, you don't. That's why he has to sneak out the stage door before Act Two. It leaves you always trying to recapture the magic of that first act. But you are alone in the theater, reeling from such an unexpected ending.

What You Can Expect to Feel: The Many Stages of Grieving

When we lose someone we love through death, the stages of grief are fairly predictable and linear. These stages have been written about extensively and eloquently in books such as *On*

312

Death and Dying by Elisabeth Kübler-Ross. But when we lose a relationship, there is no "corpse" to make it clear that the loss is irreversible. In fact the "corpse" may still be calling, may still work in your building, may still have the keys to your apartment, and so on.

Because of these complications the stages of grieving a commitmentphobic relationship are not always so clear, nor is the progression. At some point, however, you are likely to experience all of the following:

- There is the initial *shock*, even if a part of you knew the end was inevitable.
- There is the *denial* ("It's not over," "This can't be happening to me," "Things will change," "My partner will come back," "I can get her back").
- There are the feelings of *shame, embarrassment,* and the accompanying *isolation.*
- There is the *anger* ("How could he/she have done this to me?").
- There is the *bargaining.* We may try to bargain with our "higher power" ("Please, God, I'll give anything to have him back in my life"); we may also try to bargain with our partner, begging to be taken back even if it means making enormous compromises and unhealthy adjustments ("You don't have to see me every week," "We don't have to be monogamous," and so on).
- There is the *depression.* As despair grows, periodic attempts to deny the loss are common.
- Ultimately, if we let these stages proceed, there is the final stage: *acceptance* of the loss.

Because one never feels completely certain that the relationship is over, there is not likely to be any orderly progression of these stages. Instead we tend to bounce back and forth. One moment we are angry, the next we are depressed; one moment we are denying that it's over, the next we are trying to negotiate or strategize our way back in with the support of friends, therapists, family, psychics, astrologers, and ouija boards. It's as confusing as it is painful.

On top of all this there is almost always a tremendous amount of self-blame. Every step of the way we wrestle with the voices in our head that tell us that somehow all of this is our fault. "If only I had said something different, done something different, been somehow different." We feel that this ending could have been avoided if we hadn't "blown it." We wonder whether or not we can salvage it now by somehow correcting our errors or shortcomings. We desperately search for a way to rewrite the script so that the ending will be different.

This is a painful, difficult process, but healing will come with acceptance. And that's the goal that we need to be working toward. We are not working to get a partner back. We are not working to find out what we might have done wrong. We are not working to get our partner to understand how we feel. We are working for acceptance so that we can get through this painful stage and get on with life.

The Big Step: Preparing to Cut Your Losses and Walk Away

Right now what you probably want more than anything else is hope. You want to believe that at some future point this person will be back and you'll have another chance to live the relationship you've envisioned. We can't predict your future. But there is one thing we know for sure: Holding on to the relationship at this point in time is an overwhelming obstacle to healing.

Yes, we've heard of people seeing the error of their ways and returning to old relationships, but almost without exception this kind of turnaround comes about *after* the passive partner becomes self-protective enough to walk away from the feelings, the unanswered questions, and the promise of the relationship.

Try to think of your relationship as a failing business, and you are the proprietor. You have given this business (your relationship) your time, your energy, your love, and your devotion. Yet no matter what you do, it isn't paying off. It isn't showing a profit. Sometimes it looks as though it could start to show a profit sometime soon—that's what keeps you hooked in—but the bottom line is that it's not working.

Every business person knows that the time comes when you cut your losses. Sure, the industry could turn around; sure, the mar-

314

ket could change and the economy could pick up. But when a business is draining you, you have to let it go before it becomes an even bigger loss. You have to protect yourself, your resources, and your future. You have to walk away.

The same thing is true of relationships. This is not coldhearted; it's self-protective. You have love to give and you have a life to share. You need to get over this and find someone who can take what you have to give and give what you need to get. But first you have to recover from the pain of this relationship.

Only when you walk away and accept the loss can you truly grieve. It's sad. It's awful. But this feeling will eventually lift. Grieving is painful, but the pain ends. If you keep fantasizing or strategizing reunion scenarios you are holding on to the relationship and holding up the grieving process. This brings more pain not less. It is at a time like this that you have to trust all those who have come before you and believe in the healing power of letting go.

How Can You Walk Away When the Other Person Has Already Done So?

One woman reported to us after dating a twice-divorced thirty-nine-year-old lawyer. Both of his divorces were precipitated when the lawyer started seeing other women. The lawyer told this woman that he had recently broken up with his last girlfriend because she had been pressing for a commitment. When the woman visited his house, the first thing she noticed was a beautiful and very feminine hat sitting on a table in the entry hall. The next time she was there, the hat was still in the same place, so she asked about it. "Oh," he said, "that belonged to my second wife." The woman asked why he kept it out. "Why not?" he said. "No matter what happens, I guess I think she'll always be my wife."

Our friend then asked if he had more things that belonged to other women in his life. Sure enough, his house was filled with intimate apparel—robes, nightgowns, shoes—that each ex-love had left behind and that he was reluctant to return. When questioned why he did this, he said that one never knew what was going to happen. He said that he thought it was entirely possible

315

that he could get back with one of these women sometime in the future.

There is a point to this story, and this point is part of the catch-22 of commitmentphobic relationships. If you have been the passive partner, you know—in your heart—that the other person hasn't truly left the relationship or stopped having feelings. This is true even when an ex-partner has moved in with someone else. This is true even if you never speak to each other. You know your ex-partner still believes that the option to come back into your life at any time exists. You know that this other person wants you to be there waiting, making no demands.

In your mind at least we want you to be clear that you are not going to allow this option to continue. We want you to acknowledge that you're not getting anything in return for your feelings. We want you to be clear that you are walking away from the feelings that keep you hooked in. In short we want you to reject the relationship—even though it may already seem to be over. We want you to do this because we understand that commitmentphobic relationships don't end until the passive partner ends it.

What Does It Mean to "Let Go"?

What does it mean to let go and walk away? Here's what we think:

1. It means making a clear and firm decision to end your involvement.
2. It means taking responsibility for the decision and knowing that it is the right thing to do.
3. It means making a promise to yourself that the relationship is over.
4. It means reinforcing that promise by telling friends and family it's over.
5. It means making it clear to your ex-partner by your actions that it's over.
6. It means sticking by this decision, no matter how painful the process.

316

You Don't Have the Right Attitude If . . .

Walking away may be necessary, but it isn't easy. It could in fact be one of the hardest things you've ever done. If you're trying to let go but you aren't feeling any relief, you need to take an honest look at what you might be doing to keep the connection alive. Are you *really* walking away and letting go? The work you have to do takes place in your head. Keep in mind:

- As long as you keep hoping for your ex-partner to change, you're not walking away
- As long as you fantasize about reunion scenarios, you're not walking away
- As long as you try to manipulate and strategize this person back into your life, you're not walking away
- As long as you allow this person access to you, you're not walking away
- As long as you say, "what if . . ." ("What if I change my behavior?" "What if I wait six months?" "What if I change the way I look?" "What if I try to be more understanding?"), you haven't let go

The bottom line is that as long as you refuse to believe that it's truly over, it will not be over.

Giving Up the Drug

It's easy for us to tell you to let go and move on. It's always easy for others to see what's probably best for your emotional health. But when you're neck deep in a commitmentphobic relationship —and you're the passive partner—the best advice in the world is hard to take.

When two people give a relationship their best efforts and it still doesn't work, letting go is painful, but it occurs in stages, making it more bearable. By the time the breakup occurs, you feel as much a sense of relief as you do of loss. Relationships with active commitmentphobics, on the other hand, do not usually deteriorate in this fashion. These relationships stop working because one partner stops trying. They also tend to take sudden turns for the worse, often when the closeness is at a peak. This abrupt swing is a setup for an incredible crash, and that means an extraordinary amount of pain for the passive partner. At a time like this you feel that the only thing that can stop you from hitting rock bottom is your partner. So of course you don't want to let go. You want this person back in your life.

Getting yourself out of such a relationship is like going cold turkey on an addictive drug. You may not even know how addicted you are until that substance is taken away. But once the pain starts, you'll do anything to get it back. You don't want to hear lectures about what's best for you, you don't want to hear about the dangerous long-term effects, you don't want to hear about how much better you will feel six months from now—all you want is the drug.

A relationship with an active partner is intense, addictive, and living hell to kick. But the bottom line is this: It will never be over until you decide to "kick it," and it's a decision only you can make. It's highly unlikely that the partner who caused this pain is going to help you. This person doesn't want to let go either. This person is much too conflicted. Men and women such as this can go back and forth in their minds for years. Even when they never again speak to their old loves, they are still carrying these conflicts around with them.

You may not feel you have any power left, but that's not true. You have the power to put the relationship to rest and start your healing. The person you care about can't make a commitment, but you must. You must commit to your own recovery, and that begins by making a commitment to becoming self-protective. Instead of thinking about someone else, you need to be taking care of yourself.

One Thousand Questions and No Good Answers

As you wrestle with your decision to let go of this relationship and start the process of recovery, countless questions are likely to be racing through your mind. It is for example not uncommon to be thinking any or all of the following:

Can this person change? Can I do something to make him/her change? Should I be helping this person work through this? What can I do to help even if he/she doesn't want any help? Could a therapist be of help? Could a therapist help me get him/her back? Did this person ever really love me? Should I call? Will he/she call me? Should I take the call? What should I say? Should I play it cool? Should I be confrontive? Should I say how much I hurt? Should I try to see this person again? When will this person realize how much he/she needs me? Does he/she miss me? How do I know for sure it was a commitment problem? What are the odds of this person coming back around? How long will it take? Is he/she having a complete nervous breakdown? Should I call his/her parents and friends and tell them I'm worried? Should I try to be this person's friend? If he/she isn't dating anyone else, does that mean there's still hope for me? If he/she is already involved with someone else, does that mean there was no commitment problem at all? How does someone get to be this way?

There is one thing we know for sure. If someone has a *severe* commitment problem, you have no reason to believe that he or she will ever be able to interact with you in a way that isn't hurtful and destructive. It would not be fair to say it's impossible. But it has been our experience that it isn't likely.

"How Could My Special Love Treat Me This Way?"

There is a category of questions that those with passive issues almost always ask at the end of relationship: "There was so much intimacy and caring between us, how could he/she treat me this way?" "How could he/she betray me?"

This question is actually most likely to come in one of four specific variations:

- "How could this person have left me if he/she really loved me?"
- "How could anyone have turned away from so much feeling?"
- "How could anyone walk away from so much potential?"
- "How could he/she be so insensitive to my feelings?"

Considering the typical progression of a commitmentphobic relationship, it is no wonder this question always arises. These relationships tend to feel unusually close and connected well until the end. In fact it is the intensity of the bonding and the absence of major disagreements that is so seductive. It's what makes you begin to feel this could be "the one." That's why the ending comes as such a shock. It has to make you seriously question just how "connected" you and your partner really were.

The active runners we interviewed consistently made it clear how deeply connected they were to their partners. If what they say is true, then how can they walk away so easily? The explanation is surprisingly simple: Active runners can walk away because they are thoroughly confident that their partners will take them back should they have a change of heart.

Essentially, active runners are not really committed to leaving. They have contingency plans. If they can't make it alone, they believe it will always be possible to return. Sure, it might require a lot of begging and pleading and promising, but it can be done. Your active partner truly believes this option exists, and you are probably the one who made that sense of security possible.

"Why Didn't I Have More Warning?"

The primary reason for your confusion probably stems from the way your ex-partner handled his conflict. Active runners usually confess to having an ongoing dialogue in their heads about the merits and demerits of leaving. Many say they had one foot near the door, if not out the door, from very early on. This may be hard for you to imagine since your partner shared so little of the struggle with you, but it's true. Why didn't your partner tell you? Because you'd think he/she was crazy. Because you'd think he/she was a creep. Because you'd leave. Because you'd be hurt. Because there is too much conflict. Well, that's how active runners explain it.

We could devote a good portion of this book to trying satisfactorily to answer questions about your ex-partner. But without knowing you or your partner, we don't think we could do a very good job. And the truth is that we don't really want to answer these questions. We just believe very strongly that it's time for you to stop focusing on your partner and start focusing on yourself.

Get Angry for a While

Once you have decided that you are the one who has to let go and walk away from an uncommitted relationship, the real work begins. You will feel very sad, you will feel terribly hurt. There may be times when you feel hopeless. What's most important, however, is that you let yourself get angry at this hurtful behavior —*in a constructive way.*

Anger is one emotion few of us are truly comfortable expressing toward anyone but ourselves. We beat ourselves up without mercy, yet we protect others who hurt us. This is particularly true of passives. Passives feel most comfortable thinking it's their fault.

Yet the reality is that if you have been involved with an active runner, you have a great deal to be angry about. Yes, you were a full partner in this nightmare, and you need to accept responsibility for that, but it doesn't excuse the hurtful behavior of your partner.

First and foremost you need to stop blaming yourself for everything. But you also need to stop making excuses for the other person. You need to stop protecting him or her, and you need to stop trying to "understand" his or her psyche. You have to start connecting with how deeply you have been hurt and how angry that makes you feel. Understanding that you are angry is a crucial part of the grieving process. Any attempts to suppress it will only sabotage your own healing.

Please Note: Trashing someone's car, turning him or her in to the IRS, stealing his or her mail, or other acts of vengeance are not appropriate or acceptable ways of dealing with your anger. It is one thing to rage in a safe, controlled therapeutic environment. It is another to take some action in a fit of anger that could have significant negative consequences in your life. So protect yourself by not allowing your anger to become destructive to yourself or anyone else.

Get Clear (Do Some Homework)

Have you ever seen friends or family sanctify a mean and hurtful person who suddenly passed away? Remember how crazy it seemed? So why doesn't it seem crazy to you when you do the same thing with your hurtful ex-partner?

Passive partners have notoriously poor memories. No matter how much you questioned the relationship when you had it, now all you can remember is how wonderful it was. You romanticize and magnify the specialness of the relationship while forgetting or downplaying all of the things that weren't so special. This does not help the grieving process.

At times like this it is important to sit down and make concrete lists of the many aspects of this relationship that were less than perfect. Lists like this have proven to be a powerful healing tool. Here are some suggested topics for your lists:

- Things about this relationship I didn't like
- Needs of mine that weren't getting met
- What I gave away in this relationship
- Wonderful things about me that my ex-partner didn't value
- What I will get in my next relationship that I didn't get this time

Be as comprehensive as possible. Leave nothing out; every little detail helps. Read your lists over and over again. Carry them with you. Every time you find yourself having romantic thoughts about this person, take out the lists and refresh your memory about the things you didn't like. Add to them whenever a thought comes to mind. And hold on to them for however long you need them.

"What Do I Do About the Sexual Longing?"

You were probably deeply bonded to your partner sexually. You have been cut adrift, and you may feel as though you have lost a part of yourself. What do you do with all those feelings that were suddenly trashed? We have another thought about this that may help explain why the sexual feelings in your relationship were so intense.

Because active runners are so often aware of their conflicts, they tend to carry that awareness with them into their sexual behavior. Active runners know the intensity of what they feel for their partners, and yet they also know that they may leave at any time. Because of this each sexual encounter is supercharged. Every time could be the last time. Each time feels like the last romantic interlude between lovers who are being separated. This is one of the reasons why it is so difficult to come to terms with the end of this kind of sexual relationship. You can't help but ask yourself, "If it was always this highly charged, why did it end?"

As you're going through the recovery process, try to force yourself not to use the person who caused you this pain as your sexual fantasy. In fact, as much as possible try not to think about the sexual bond between the two of you. Don't dwell in that place. Don't play the music or read the books that bring back memories. In short, try not to obsess about the sensual aspects of your relationship.

Getting Closure When Your Ex-partner Isn't Making It Any Easier

The need for closure is common for any loss, but the need is particularly acute when there is a sudden, unexpected loss. Because "sudden endings" are a trademark of commitmentphobic relationships, there is almost always a deep cry for some kind of resolution that will bring you a measure of peace.

You want an explanation that makes sense. All the conversations that are haunting you and that you are having in your head you want to have with your ex-partner. You want to explain yourself because you think that if this person only understood, it would change. You believe that if you could only reach him or her for a minute, it would change.

Right now you may be thinking, *If only I had one more chance . . . one more conversation . . . a clearer explanation . . . one more night together, then maybe I could let go.* Maybe you're thinking, *If only I could let him know just how much I've been hurt,* or, *If only I could make her see what we had together.* The problem is that there is a hidden agenda here. Although you say that this is what you need so that you would be able to let go and walk away, part of you believes that this is what you need to get your ex-partner back. As long as you have expectations like this, there can be no true closure.

323

You Have to Get Closure on Your Own

Active runners are extremely skilled at frustrating their partner's attempts to get any closure. Because they aren't sure precisely what they feel, they typically refuse to assume complete responsibility for what they say or what they do. They can't end anything. And that means you will probably never get the kind of closure that you *want*. But that doesn't mean you can't get the kind of closure you *need*. You still have power in this relationship, enough power to give yourself the kind of closure your partner is unwilling to give.

So how do you begin?

• *Clean house.* It helps enormously to "say good-bye" to your relationship memorabilia. We are not saying that you need to cleanse your home of all reminders of this person, but it is *always* advisable to put all significant relationship memorabilia in a place where you don't have to face it every day. Pack it away in boxes or give it to a friend you trust. In time you may feel more able to let most of these things go for good. Don't throw things out that have some value (financial or otherwise) in your life because you may later regret doing so. Just pack them away and forget about them until you can go back and sort it all out.

• *Write a letter.* A technique we highly recommend to help purge the relationship from your system is writing a comprehensive good-bye letter. *But don't mail it.* This letter is for *you*, not for your ex-partner. In it put all the things you want to say, not just the things you want her to hear. The act of writing this letter is immensely therapeutic, but the act of sending it can easily turn into a setup for further hurt. Please take this warning to heart.

• *Read your lists.* The process of making, reading, and re-reading the lists described in the preceding section can be of enormous value. Carry your lists with you and read them whenever you need reinforcement. Revise them whenever new thoughts come to mind.

• *Bury the relationship.* Holding a "mock funeral" for the relationship is another technique that sometimes helps. This may sound a bit extreme, but many interviewees have told us how profoundly helpful this process was. Invite those you feel closest to, the people whose support comforts you most in a time of need. Treat it like any other funeral. Celebrate afterward if that feels appropriate. Just don't turn it into a gag.

• *Commit yourself to a clear set of feelings and try to stick to them.* We know that you are involved with someone with serious conflicts, but don't allow yourself to fall into the trap of equally conflicted responses (angry when he/she is unkind and forgiving when he/she regrets destructive behavior). The fact that you are able to understand so much of your ex-partner's conflict is indicative of your own conflicts. Try to take a position and stick to it. This person has hurt you. Therefore you are upset, angry, annoyed, and self-protective. And you don't want to feel this way again. Stay with the self-protective feelings.

• *Put a time limit on yourself.* We know this is difficult, and you can't force your feelings. But put yourself on a recovery schedule and try to keep yourself from spending too long a period mourning the relationship. Those with passive commitment conflicts can easily settle into the recovery process for an excessive amount of time, so watch out for this tendency. If you are in therapy, we suggest discussing concrete goals with your therapist for getting yourself back into the world within a reasonable timeframe.

Another Major Obstacle to Closure: Refusing to Lose

Some people can't face themselves and say it's over. They can't accept the loss; they can't let go. Some passive women have very strong internal voices urging them to hold on and hope. The waiting role model that they are adhering to doesn't take into account the eternal unavailability of someone with deep conflicts.

Other passives, particularly men, can't let go because their egos can't take the loss. They don't want to "go out as losers." Instead of seeing that there are no winners, they deeply personalize the breakup and keep trying to "win" at it.

If you are hanging on to a relationship because you feel as if your entire ego is on the line, you need to take a careful look at all the voices in your head that are primed to beat you up. Why do you have so much ego vested in the success of this relationship? What does it mean for you to lose? Why are you terrified of telling friends, family members, and/or acquaintances the bad news? What do you imagine they would say or think?

Right now, it may feel like it's your own voice that is beating you up, but that voice is an internalization of many voices you have heard throughout your lifetime. You need to face each of those voices, with the help of a therapist if necessary, if you are going to be able to lose this relationship without losing your sense of self.

Be Wary of the Obstacles to Your Healing

- ### The Obstacle of Friendship

Right now your number-one priority is healing. Healing requires grieving, and it is almost impossible to grieve if you are trying to be friends with "the corpse." No matter how much you care about this person, no matter how much you still want him/ her in your life, and no matter how much he/she says about wanting to stay in contact with you, right now you need to separate.

You also need to ask yourself some questions. Why do you want to be this person's friend? Is it because you think she would be a supportive, loving friend? Is it because he is pushing for this friendship? Is it because you need to keep the connection? What we are trying to get at is this: Is it really a friend that you want or are you holding on to give yourself another chance to revive the relationship down the road? Be honest.

Regardless of your agenda, a friendship cannot work *now*. Maybe in six months or a year, but not now. If you want to start healing, you need to try to sever all ties, at least for the time being. If this person truly cares about being your friend, he/she will understand and will wait. If your ex-partner can't accept your need to take care of yourself right now, he/she is not a good friend.

There is something else that needs to be said here. Maybe you really believe that you can be your ex-partner's friend, no strings attached. Maybe it seems crazy to you to never again speak to someone who has been such a significant part of your life. We understand these kinds of feelings. But we also know that it's hard for an active runner to become a good friend, even with the best of intentions. Beneath the desire for friendship is often a powerful and selfish need to maintain an entrée into your psyche. For this reason any kind of friendship, now or later, needs to be approached with extreme caution.

- *The Obstacle of Getting Caught Up in a Partner's Conflicted Behavior*

"We had been living together for three years and were talking about getting married and having a child as soon as possible. He said we should take it slow because he was scared. That's what I was doing. Then one night he said he had to get away for a while because it was too much pressure. He called me a month later to say that he missed me and that he was marrying someone else. Now he calls once a week; he says he's confused and wants to talk about his feelings."

"She says she doesn't want to see me anymore, but she calls me every time she has a problem—every cold morning when her car won't start, every time she has a situation at work, every time she has an argument with a friend. These problems happen sometimes as much as three or four times a week. I'm supposed to just listen and not say anything. The minute I sound like I'm a real person with real feelings, she tells me that I'm making demands on her and hangs up."

"When he moved out, he left all his clothes. I can't get him to take them. He keeps coming by to get things a little bit at a time. Whenever he does, he acts like he's jealous about anything else I might be doing. It's as though he doesn't want to see me anymore, but he wants to make sure nobody else does either."

"She said that I was closing in on her and she needed to be away from me. Since then she has called every single person I know and said she wants to stay friendly with them. Then she asks them about me. If she wants to be away from me so much, why does she attach herself to my life?"

"He calls me and leaves messages on my machine. If I don't call him back, he keeps leaving messages. When I call him back, when he hears my voice, he sounds annoyed and tells me he's too busy to talk."

Right now you have to be especially concerned with protecting yourself from your ex-partner's conflicted behavior, behavior that can be both bizarre and provocative. Your ex-partner's conflict can wreak havoc on your attempts to grieve.

What you have to understand is that leaving the relationship may have ameliorated your partner's anxiety, but it did not eliminate the conflict. This person is still hearing different voices. When you were together, the loudest voice was the one telling him or her to get free. But no sooner is he or she "free" than another voice is apt to be activated—the voice of longing. This person can now look back on all of the positive aspects of the relationship and appreciate them in ways that were not possible when you were together. Far away from the pressure to deliver, this person can reconnect and start to miss the relationship, but the minute the two of you are together, the anxiety and the need to get free surfaces again.

Here's the rub: Ending a relationship is also a commitment, and your partner may be discovering right now just how difficult it is to make any commitment. This produces new conflict. Let's look at how this gets acted out.

- *The Obstacle of a Partner Who Is Hanging On*

Your ex-partner knows that if you are left alone to grieve and recover, you may be lost for good. That may be too much of a commitment. So, just as you are preparing yourself to believe that it is truly over, suddenly you are the recipient of strange phone calls, peculiar visits, or unexpected mail. He/she wants to be "your friend" and wants to keep in touch. You may find it difficult to get your belongings back, especially your keys. About your ex-partner's belongings: you are told to "hang on to them for a while." The hidden message is "I will return."

All of this can make you feel, and rightly so, that the person who just left you is still hanging on, though you may not understand why. This person seems to be having second thoughts. Once again you are the recipient of mixed messages. These messages encourage you to believe that it's not really over. This can stall your healing process.

When Your Ex-partner Cuts You Off Completely

It's your worst nightmare come true. Suddenly the person who was totally there for you is totally gone. Not only is it over but it feels as though your ex-partner is denying what existed. It's mind-boggling. You can't believe it's the same person.

The worst part is that your ex may have found someone else. They might be talking about getting engaged; they might even be talking about marriage. It's so soon, how could this be possible? Here you sit, in tremendous pain, and the one you love is with someone new, holding hands in your favorite restaurant. The breakup has been painful enough, but this is overwhelming.

Why is this happening? Because the only way your ex can deal with the conflict is to bury it. Your ex-partner can't live with the two loud voices of conflict, so one of them has to be destroyed. The easiest way to turn off the voices and try to eradicate the conflict is to find someone new.

The fact that someone can jump from one intense relationship to another is proof of a commitment problem. It highlights the fact that this person can only have a relationship based on fantasy. The moment any commitment becomes real, the same problems will emerge.

It's a mistake to get caught up in the psychodrama of your ex-partner's new relationship. In our experience one of the following two patterns is likely to be taking place: Those with active conflicts behave the same way in all their relationships; or they find people with even greater conflicts and so much built-in distance that it never becomes genuinely intimate. Either way be thankful you got away. Now you can resolve your own issues and move on to the kind of relationship you want and deserve.

Protecting Yourself from Your Ex-partner's Anger

Your ex-partner seems so hostile and angry that someone might think you initiated the ending. The anger comes out in words and in actions. It comes out in behavior that is provocative and hurtful. It comes out in so many small, perverse ways that you can't even try to explain it to anyone else. This person's anger is so strange and so intense that it sometimes makes you feel that you must be at fault. Why is this person you love and care about so angry at you?

Keep in mind that your ex-partner knows better than you do what was promised and what was withheld, and is probably feeling guilty. One way of relieving this guilt is to shift the entire responsibility onto you whenever possible. If your ex-partner can believe that was all your fault, it's easier to sleep at night.

Your ex-partner's guilt can easily translate into additional hurt for you. He/she may be doing things to get your attention or to get your goat. Your ex-partner is acting as though it's your fault that it's over at the very time when you probably would do anything to still be together. He/she may even be flaunting a new relationship in a way that can't help but be extra hurtful.

Don't get fooled into feeling that you did something that caused this behavior. Protect yourself by maintaining as much distance as possible.

Making a Commitment to Yourself

As you are going through the recovery process, perhaps the best step you can take on the way to resolving your commitment conflicts is to learn how to make a commitment to yourself. That means promising yourself that you will spend more time looking at your own "stuff" than you will looking at what any of your partners are doing or not doing.

During this period you should be looking at your own fears, trying to establish why you have made the choices you've made and why you have allowed yourself to be so "committed" to an unstable situation. You have to ask yourself why you might sometimes feel that you are more committed to another human being than you are to yourself or any of the things you value or believe in. No partner or relationship should ever become that much more important than oneself or one's belief system. It's up to you to make certain it doesn't happen again.

Right now you should make a firm commitment: to start focusing your creative and psychic energies on building a life for yourself—a life that cannot be so totally disrupted by the breakup of a relationship, no matter how important that relationship may be.